55571714

Praise for
A Trader's First Book on Commodities,
First Edition

"This book provides the type of information every trader needs to know and the type of information too many traders had to learn the hard and expensive way. Carley offers practical need-to-know, real-world trading tips that are lacking in many books on futures. It will help not only the novice trader, but seasoned veterans as well. This book will serve as a must-have reference in every trader's library."

—**Phil Flynn**, Futures Account Executive at Price Futures Group,
and a Fox Business Network contributor

"Refreshing—It's nice to see a broker who has actually been exposed to the professional side of trading and who bridges that chasm between exchange floor trading and customer service. Carley takes the time to explain verbiage, not just throw buzz words around. A good educational read in my opinion."

—**Don Bright**, Director, Bright Trading, LLC

"This book has the perfect name, the perfect message, and the necessary information for any beginning trader. Take this book home!"

—**Glen Larson**, President, Genesis Financial Technologies, Inc.

"As a 35-year veteran of the CME/CBOT trading floor, I can tell you...those who think they can begin trading commodities without knowing the less talked about topics that Carley discusses in *A Trader's First Book on Commodities* are sadly mistaken. Anyone who trades their own account, or would like to, should read this book."

—**Danny Riley**, Mr.TopStep.com

A Trader's First Book on Commodities

A Trader's First Book on Commodities

An Introduction to the World's Fastest Growing Market, Second Edition

Carley Garner

Vice President, Publisher: Tim Moore
Associate Publisher and Director of Marketing: Amy Neidlinger
Executive Editor: Jim Boyd
Editorial Assistant: Pamela Boland
Operations Specialist: Jodi Kemper
Marketing Manager: Megan Graue
Cover Designer: Chuti Prasertsith
Managing Editor: Kristy Hart
Project Editor: Jovana San Nicolas-Shirley
Copy Editor: Krista Hansing Editorial Services, Inc.
Proofreader: Seth Kerney
Senior Indexer: Cheryl Lenser
Compositor: Nonie Ratcliff
Manufacturing Buyer: Dan Uhrig

This book is sold with the understanding that neither the author nor the publisher is engaged in rendering legal, accounting, or other professional services or advice by publishing this book. Each individual situation is unique. Thus, if legal or financial advice or other expert assistance is required in a specific situation, the services of a competent professional should be sought to ensure that the situation has been evaluated carefully and appropriately. The author and the publisher disclaim any liability, loss, or risk resulting directly or indirectly, from the use or application of any of the contents of this book.

There is substantial risk of loss in trading futures and options. It is not suitable for everyone.

FT Press offers excellent discounts on this book when ordered in quantity for bulk purchases or special sales. For more information, please contact U.S. Corporate and Government Sales, 1-800-382-3419, corpsales@pearsontechgroup.com. For sales outside the U.S., please contact International Sales at international@pearsoned.com.

Company and product names mentioned herein are the trademarks or registered trademarks of their respective owners.

Pearson Education LTD.
Pearson Education Australia PTY, Limited.
Pearson Education Singapore, Pte. Ltd.
Pearson Education Asia, Ltd.
Pearson Education Canada, Ltd.
Pearson Educación de Mexico, S.A. de C.V.
Pearson Education—Japan
Pearson Education Malaysia, Pte. Ltd.

The Library of Congress cataloging-in-publication data is on file.

*This book is dedicated to the resiliency of the futures industry,
the city of Chicago, whose capitalistic drive opens the door to success,
and loyal DeCarley Trading clients.*

Contents

Acknowledgments

I would like to thank Pearson and the FT Press production team for bringing this book together.

I am grateful for my friends and family, who have always been by my side and encouraged me to keep pushing.

Although difficult at the time, I appreciate the challenges that have been put before me. In the long run, I know these events and the lessons learned will pave the way to bigger and better things for myself and my brokerage clients.

About the Author

Carley Garner is a senior market strategist and an experienced commodity broker with DeCarley Trading, a division of Zaner Group, in Las Vegas, Nevada. She is a columnist for *Stocks & Commodities* and the author of *Commodity Options, A Trader's First Book on Commodities,* and *Currency Trading in the FOREX and Futures Markets.* Garner writes two widely distributed e-newsletters, *The Financial Futures Report* and *The DeCarley Perspective.* She is also a regular "Real Money" contributor at TheStreet.com.

Her work has been featured in multiple magazines, including *Stocks & Commodities, Futures, Active Trader, Option Trader, Currency Trader, Your Trading Edge, Equities,* and *PitNews.* She has been quoted in media ranging from Reuters to *Investor's Business Daily* and *The Wall Street Journal.*

Garner provides free trading education to investors at www.DeCarleyTrading.com.

The Boom and Bust Cycles of Commodities...and Now Brokerage Firms

Witnessing the grain complex shatter all-time-high price records and continue to climb during the now-infamous 2007–2008 commodity rally was nothing less than breathtaking. However, by late 2008, the party had ended. Many retail traders and fund managers watched in horror as the grains made their way relentlessly lower. The selling pressure and losses in the commodity markets were so profound that hedge fund managers experienced unprecedented numbers of redemption requests, adding fuel to the already raging fire.

"There is no tool to change human nature ... people are prone to recurring bouts of optimism and pessimism that manifest themselves from time to time in the buildup or cessation of speculative excesses."
—Alan Greenspan

Ironically, the same asset class that investors swarmed to for "diversification" from stocks played a role in the demise of equities during the 2008–2009 bear market. We now know that this boom-and-bust cycle was destined to be repeated, although in slightly less dramatic fashion. Perhaps feast-or-famine trade is the new reality: high margins, high risk, high reward, and even higher adrenaline rushes.

What Has Changed?

Several theories attempt to explain the historical volatility in the commodity markets near the turn of the decade. Valid contributors are likely ethanol demand and the government programs promoting it, the European debt crisis, sheer market exuberance in the absence of an attractive equity market, sidelined cash looking for a home, government stimulus, and, most of all, ease of market access for the average retail trader. One thing is certain: The commodity euphoria causes the agricultural, energy, and metals markets to overshoot equilibrium prices in both directions on a seemingly regular basis.

In the midst of the excitement, the lure of a swift commodity rally clouds the judgment of many. Looking back at boom-and-bust cycles, which are now relatively common, it is rather obvious that expecting market fundamentals to maintain such lofty prices is simply unrealistic. However, in the heat of the moment, nobody knows how high is "too high," and speculation runs rampant. Investors who enter the market "early" with bearish strategies likely pay dearly for their aggression. Yet when the tides finally turn, they do so in a vicious fashion, enabling well-timed bears to reap substantial rewards. After all, the stunning fall from grace is typically even steeper than the preceding rally.

In a speech delivered at the American Enterprise Institute in the late 1990s, then–Federal Reserve Board Chairman Alan Greenspan warned that the equity market might be overvalued through the use of "irrational exuberance." In my opinion, this is a good explanation of the illogical rallies and bear market sell-offs in the commodity markets. In an environment in which anyone with a computer (and a mouse) can buy or sell commodities with a single click, logic sometimes has little control over the outcome. Nevertheless, such cycles of excess and price contraction open the door for speculators to achieve abnormal profits, assuming that they are willing to manage and accept the corresponding risks.

Naturally, speculators aren't buying or selling commodities on a whim. They are holding on to some fundamental story that justifies the initial price move, but the bandwagon mentality often takes reality into fantasy. Here are a few of the primary factors driving the wave of commodity market volatility that began in 2007 and has continued to thrive.

Easy Market Access

Investors trading commodities in the 1990s knew that the only way to place a trade in the commodity markets was to pick up a phone and call a broker. Because brokerage firms relied on paper tickets and statements, they weren't necessarily able to keep close tabs on client trading accounts throughout the trading day. This posed large risks to traders and the firm. Accordingly, commodity trading was typically reserved for well-capitalized and sophisticated investors. That simply isn't true anymore. Anybody with at least a thousand dollars and an operable computer can buy or sell commodities online without ever picking up the phone.

Individually, such traders have little influence on the market, but collectively, this new breed of futures speculators can have a significant impact on price movements. If you don't believe me, look at the roller-coaster ride gold futures took following the S&P's credit downgrade of U.S. debt in Figure I.1. I speculate that much of the late-comer buying was done by inexperienced, yet convinced, retail traders who were unaware of the risks of having convenient online access to buy or sell commodities without being properly educated.

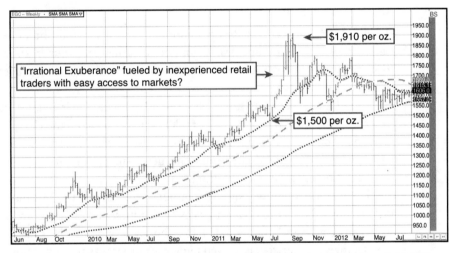

Figure I.1 It has been argued that the one-month gold rally that spanned $1,500 per ounce to $1,910 was largely fueled by small retail traders and a herd mentality. Once the last buyer was in, the market quickly retreated, to eliminate most of the gains, which equated to about $40,000 per contract. (Chart courtesy of QST.)

European Debt Crisis

The U.S. credit crunch eventually sent Europe into a tailspin. For years, the domestic financial and commodity markets have been hijacked by the possibility of a credit market collapse overseas, despite improvements in the homeland. Obviously, a healthy economy leads to healthy demand for commodities, but certainly other fundamental factors are at play. Nevertheless, there are times in which traders focus on European headlines and put individual commodity market fundamentals on the back burner.

Before the 2008 U.S. debt crisis and similar chaos to follow in Europe, financial market speculation only moderately influenced commodity prices. Yet in a post-credit crunch world, when the financial markets become enthralled with European headline risk, the commodity markets follow. As a result, commodities, currencies, and the U.S. stock market often become highly correlated. When all three asset classes begin moving in the same direction, it can be nearly impossible to stop the bleeding. This is because excessive moves in all three trigger margin calls galore in all three arenas, and the liquidation becomes a seemingly never-ending endeavor.

Quantitative Easing

In late 2008, the Federal Reserve announced that it would be undertaking a little-known practice known as quantitative easing. In summer 2012, the Fed declared it would continue to implement the quantitative easing program indefinitely.

Quantitative easing is now a household phrase, but it is most commonly referred to as QE. QE is a rather complex scheme in which the U.S. government essentially buys the Treasury bonds it issues. In layman's terms, the federal government is selling bonds to itself. The net result is a cash injection into the economy, or simply money printing.

The increase in money supply stemming from the Fed's QE campaign tends to put upward pressure on asset prices of all types, including commodities. This is because, all else being equal, more money is chasing the same number of goods; therefore, prices are driven higher. Another way to look at it is, the larger the money supply, the weaker the U.S. dollar. A discounted dollar tends to put upward pressure on asset prices because it results in more purchasing power for foreign buyers and, thus, higher demand.

Accordingly, much of the boom-and-bust pattern we've seen in commodities likely is exaggerated by artificial price inflation via QE and the subsequent correction from unrealistic levels.

Fear of a U.S. Financial System Collapse

Fearful savers have been known to store wealth in nonfiat currencies, namely gold and silver. The theory is that if the financial system as we know it fails, the "gold bugs" will manage to maintain their prosperity by exchanging precious metals holdings for goods and services. For example, in summer 2012, an older man in Nevada died in a humble Carson City home with about $200 in his bank account. As the home was being cleaned and prepared for resale, approximately $7 million in gold bullion was found hidden within secret compartments in the walls and in boxes in the garage. The metals hoard was said to be in response to the man's lack of faith in the current fiat money financial system. In my opinion, this type of thinking has had a profound impact on overzealous rallies in precious metals and might continue for quite some time. Figure I.2 depicts just how far fear of a failing domestic currency can drive precious metals prices beyond reason.

Figure I.2   Fear of a U.S. financial system collapse triggered an historic rally in silver prices that simply couldn't be sustained by fundamentals. (Chart courtesy of QST.)

The New Investment Fad

Swirling newscasts, financial newspaper editorials, never-ending infomercials, and social media buzz regarding the emerging opportunities in the commodity markets have successfully lured an enormous number of investors looking for opportunities other than traditional stocks and bonds.

For all intents and purposes, the U.S. equity markets made little or no progress throughout much of the 2000s, causing many investors to lose faith in the system. Frustrated by stocks, and with Treasury bond yields at record lows, savers found themselves intrigued by the commodity story. Accordingly, the general investment public is allotting substantial amounts of capital to self-directed or full-service commodity accounts, commodity hedge funds, commodity equity products such as electronic traded funds (ETFs), and Commodity Trading Advisors (CTAs). The newly discovered simplicity of participating in this alternative asset class has greatly benefited the industry but likely plays a part in the relentless boom-and-bust cycles. Unfortunately, in many cases, money is flowing into commodities from investors who have little experience in the futures markets and limited knowledge of the high levels of risk involved in participating.

Not only do I believe that too many speculative investors are relatively undereducated about the futures markets, but I also argue that numerous money managers might be as well. For instance, many of them fail to recognize a few things, such as the fact that the commodity markets aren't as deep as equity markets and are thus highly influenced by bandwagon trading. Naturally, this occurs in the equity markets as well—just look at social media shares such as LinkedIn, Facebook, and Zynga—but in the futures market, it takes arguably fewer dollars chasing assets to see a price reaction. In some of the smaller commodity markets, such as rough rice or even cotton futures, it is possible for prices to make substantial moves on the buying or selling of a moderate number of contracts. In other words, it isn't difficult for deep-pocketed speculators to temporarily alter the price of some commodities. With droves of cash making its way to the long side of commodities, it doesn't take long for things to get out of hand. This is why it is important to limit your trading activity to futures contracts with ample liquidity. Leave the exotic commodity markets to the "other guy."

Additionally, commodity prices normally trade in envelopes instead of ongoing inclines, as stocks tend to do. Yet commodity market newcomers sometimes behave as if this isn't the case, causing prices to increase sharply beyond what are feasibly sustainable levels. These simple concepts seem obvious, but fear of missing out on a rally, and the greed that prevents profit taking, sometimes overshadows the red flags and concerns of commodity veterans who "know" that the hysteria can't last.

At first it is easy to confuse a bull market with trading genius, but it can't last.

Of course, this is my personal perception, and it is in stark contrast to the opinions of some other analysts. In fact, well-respected and well-known market commentators believe that the original 2007 commodity boom was purely the result of tight supply and high demand. Although I agree 100% that this was the initial cause of the skyrocketing prices, I am not convinced that fundamentals alone blazed the trail for such unprecedented high pricing and volatility.

"If the models are telling you to sell, sell, sell, but only buyers are out there, don't be a jerk. Buy!"
—William Silber (NYU)

Unfortunately, markets and their participants are complex, and this often makes pinpointing the driving force behind any price move impossible.

The Speculator's Role in Volatility

Much debate centers on the speculator's role in commodity valuation. On more than one occasion, commodity market regulators testified to Congress and participated in interrogation hearings regarding the speculator's role in excessive market pricing. The popular view in Washington seems to be that most of the blame falls on traders. Ironically, the government's own QE program arguably plays a bigger role in higher commodity prices than speculators ever could. Nonetheless, for those of us with the luxury of being within the industry and understanding the nature of the marketplace, it is nothing short of scary to see our elected leaders making such uninformed assumptions and, eventually, decisions about what are intended to be free markets. The truth is, there is plenty of blame to go around, but there probably isn't a better alternative than capitalistic price discovery.

The commodity markets are built on speculation; without it, there would be no market. The futures markets were formed to facilitate the transfer of risk from producers and users to unrelated third parties hoping to profit from price changes; I cover this in detail in Chapter 1, "A Crash Course in Commodities."

Some evidence seems to suggest that speculation causes artificially inflated prices, at least temporarily. After all, commodities boom when anxious investors pour money into the alternative asset class in search of higher returns. Additionally, what was once an investment arena utilized only by the uber-rich and risk-hungry investors now sees money inflows from average retail investors and even pension funds. However, the door swings both ways; during waves of liquidation, as investors redeem funds from their commodity holdings, the market sometimes behaves as if someone is pulling the floor out from underneath it. Consequently, prices often fall much further and faster than they might have without speculative excess. In such a scenario, the economy enjoys commodities at highly *discounted* prices. Naturally, you will never hear complaints that speculators are driving gas prices too low!

In my opinion, speculators don't cause bubbles, or even pop them, but unfamiliar, inexperienced, or greedy speculators might share some of the blame for their magnitude. Without support from basic supply-and-demand fundamentals, a market cannot sustain pricing in the end. Thus, if and when

> *For every winner, there is a loser. Nonetheless, the winners get all the attention.*

speculation does move prices beyond what the equilibrium price might be, it eventually has to correct itself. The problem is that there is no telling how far and how long prices can remain distorted. Unfortunately, many traders are introduced to this the hard way.

It is critical to realize that, from a trading standpoint, it doesn't necessarily matter whether the market is driven by fundamentals, technicals, speculators, hedgers, or the Fed's QE efforts. What does matter is that prices move, and you want to be on the right side of it—or at least get out of its way. Markets are unforgiving; regardless of how strongly you feel that prices should behave in a particular way, they are sometimes driven by irrational speculation for much longer than you can financially and psychologically afford to be involved.

Excessive commodity market volatility and price excess creates unparalleled opportunities for futures, and options on futures, traders. With that in mind, it is imperative that traders approach the markets with the simple premise that anything is possible, and positions should be taken and risks managed with this in mind.

Commodity Volatility Leads to Fortunes Made and Lost

By nature, when we think of large price moves in leveraged markets, we assume that there are riches to be made. However, this isn't necessarily the case; traders must be on the right side of the trade to make money, and that is easier said than done. Even worse than missing a big price move is being caught on the wrong side of it. The media's (and politicians') arguments against "greedy" speculators seem to imply that a majority of traders make money and that it is somehow easy to do so. This couldn't be further from the truth; if it were, wouldn't they be doing it, too? Profitable trading is possible for those who are dedicated and capable of controlling their emotions, but it is far from being a sure-fire way for the "rich to get richer," as many assume.

Because of its profound impact on the economy and our daily lives, crude oil futures are often at the center of the debate. Believe me, not all speculators in the energy complex make money. Crude oil is one of the most challenging markets to trade successfully, regardless of whether you are a futures or options trader. The margin requirement is extremely high, and so are the volatility and risk. Figure I.3 portrays the magnitude of risk and reward energy traders might face.

Surprisingly, based on my experience and conversations with those within the futures and options industry, the 2007 commodity rally was paralyzing for many veteran traders but was a likely gold mine for investors who simply didn't know that wheat shouldn't trade in double digits, nor crude oil in mid-$150s. For investors who had been trading grains for many years, it was not only unimaginable, but in some cases, career ending.

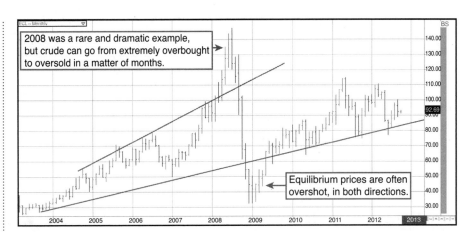

Figure I.3 **Crude oil traders have the potential for large gains, but the risk is of equal magnitude. Not many could have predicted that crude oil would rally to $150 per barrel, only to collapse to less than $40. Such a move represents more than $100,000 per contract. (Chart courtesy of QST.)**

Traders who spent the bulk of their adulthood speculating on grain and energy prices as they moved from high to low within their historical price envelopes quickly discovered that the markets no longer had boundaries. For example, before 2007, wheat was a commodity that was most comfortable trading between $2.00 and $4.00 per bushel, with a few brief stints in the $6.00 range. Looking at a long-term wheat chart, it is easy to see how a trader could unexpectedly get caught on the wrong side of a move that eventually got close to doubling the previous all-time high of the commodity. Those who did find themselves in such positions were in a state of denial and had a difficult time liquidating positions with large losses. As a result, the situation became worse as losses mounted, as did margin calls (see Figure I.4).

You might have heard about the rogue (unauthorized and reckless) wheat trader whose actions during the historic wheat rally resulted in a large loss at a major financial institution. Without permission from his brokerage firm, MF Global, the trader greatly exceeded his trading limits due to a loophole in the trading platforms. The culprit was a commodity broker located in Memphis, Tennessee, who reportedly put his account—and, ultimately, MF Global—in the hole more than $141 million. This is believed to be the largest unauthorized loss in the history of the agricultural markets. Ironically, MF Global survived the debacle despite its stock immediately losing nearly a third of its value but claimed bankruptcy a few years later due to large losses in trades authorized by its own CEO, Jon Corzine. We'll discuss this next.

Figure I.4 **Few could have predicted the magnitude of the 2007—2008 wheat rally that made a mockery of its previous all-time high. (Chart courtesy of QST.)**

Prior to the unauthorized wheat trade, the MF Global broker triggering the debacle had been a responsibly registered participant of the futures industry for more than 15 years; perhaps in this case, his experience worked against him, in that he was overly bearish in a market that simply wasn't "playing by the rules."

Keep in mind that, in the precommodity boom world, the margin to hold a wheat futures position overnight was less than $1,000. During its heyday, it was in the neighborhood of several thousand dollars. Therein lies much of the problem: As commodities become more volatile, they also become more expensive to hold. In such an environment, traders are forced to fold their hands due to a lack of margin or liquidity. The liquidation of short positions adds to the buying pressure of speculative long plays, and prices can quickly become astronomical.

Commodity Brokers Boom and Bust Too

In the late 2000s, the commodity markets made history, but in the early 2010s, it was commodity brokerage firms that were grabbing headlines. More specifically, the epic failure of two prominent players, MF Global and PFGBEST, showcased insolvency plagued by a lack of integrity. As Warren Buffett said, "Only when the tide goes out do you discover who has been swimming naked."

Brokerage Firm Business Models Break Down

For years, futures brokerage firms had operated within a business model in which revenues were generated by trading commission in conjunction with interest earned on the deposits made by clients to meet margin requirements. Simply put, if a client wires $10,000 to a futures broker to fund a trading account, the brokerage firm is free to invest that money in regulatory-approved interest-bearing securities such as Treasuries, bank deposits, and CDs. Historically, the interest generated from such investments accounted for a rather significant percentage of a brokerage firm's income. Yet federal programs forcing interest rates to near-zero levels eliminated the capability of firms to benefit from client deposits; accordingly, profitability was hindered and exclusive to the generation of commissions and fees.

Before the Federal Reserve's never-ending quest for near-zero interest rates, futures brokerage firms enjoyed returns on client deposits between 3% and 5%. Accordingly, as technology improved trading execution, many firms traveled the path of discounting commissions to attract client funds and, in turn, relied on earning somewhere near 4% interest on client deposits. They knew that carrying large profit margins on commission wasn't necessary if they could earn "the float," which is the industry term for interest earned on client money. However, this business plan didn't account for unfathomably low interest rates and eventually proved to be highly flawed.

Unfortunately, the practice of discounting commission to attract new clients is a slippery slope that eventually results in cannibalism of the industry. Firms went from competing on service, to competing on price; ultimately, profit margins shrank to levels at which brokers simply couldn't operate profitably in a low-interest-rate environment.

In addition to low interest rates and lower commissions, the financial collapse of 2008 tightened the purse strings of many speculators. This dealt another blow to the commodity brokerage industry causing many brokerage firms to fold their hands.

I entered the commodity industry in early 2004; during that time, I've witnessed the number of registered Futures Commission Merchants (also known as futures brokers) fall from about 90 firms to fewer than 50. Simply put, nearly half of all commodity brokerage firms in operation when I stepped into the business are no longer in operation. Regretfully, I worked as a broker for one failed firm and operated as an Introducing Broker for another. Chapter 5, "Choosing A Brokerage Firm," covers the definition of an Introducing Broker and a Futures Commission Merchant.

Through no fault of my own, or any of the other hard-working employees and brokers of these collapsed firms, I faced significant challenges in regrouping my life and business. Ensuring the most efficient transition to new brokerage arrangements possible for my firm and, more importantly, my clients was a difficult task. Part of the process involved establishing new relationships with the risk management departments of our new trade-clearing arrangements to make sure each of our clients had the opportunities and leeway they needed to better their odds of success. Additionally, we faced the burden of matching our clients with new trading platforms appropriate to their strategies, ensuring favorable margining and fee structures, and much more. On the bright side, the commodity industry is known as the "last bastion of capitalism"; therefore, survival of the fittest is in play. As difficult as it is for a broker and its clients to migrate to a new brokerage firm in the wake of the collapse of another, I can attest that the odds are in favor of an overall improvement in service and quality simply because only the strongest and most efficient survive.

Hard Times and Desperate Measures

The difficult futures brokerage environment led some to turn to highly question-able and illegal practices to stay afloat. Specifically, at least two firms violated long-standing, and previously concrete, safeguards of client funds by using customer margin deposits for business operations or, worse, personal embezzlement.

In fall 2011, MF Global, a mammoth commodity brokerage house, went down in dramatic fashion while misappropriating client funds to finance a "trade gone bad" on its proprietary desk in a fast and furious demise. Less than a year later, it was learned that the owner of PFGBEST, one of the ten largest privately held commodity brokerage firms, had been secretly pilfering funds from client accounts to finance operations, pay regulator fines, and fund a com-fortable lifestyle for himself. As you are probably aware, the top executive at PFGBEST was reporting false customer segregated funds figures to the oversee-ing bodies and using falsified bank statements to deter regulators from detecting the fraud. In a letter written before an attempted suicide, he pleaded, "I had no access to additional capital and I was forced into a difficult decision: Should I go out of business or cheat? I guess my ego was too big to admit failure. So I cheated, I falsified the very core of the financial documents of PFGBEST, the Bank Statements."

Prior to this dramatic confession and the sudden unraveling of PFGBEST, the brokerage firm was considered to be well-respected and among the most compliant in the commodity industry. Regrettably, for these reasons I chose to use PFGBEST as the exclusive brokerage firm to clear my clients' trades.

Customer Segregated Funds Violations

Before October 2011—more specifically, before the collapse of MF Global—few outside the futures industry were aware of the term *customer segregated funds*. In July 2012, the failure of PFGBEST to uphold the sanctity of customer segregated funds catapulted the phrase into daily usage in national media outlets, and maybe even the homes of many Americans.

Customer segregated funds are exactly what the name implies; they are monetary deposits made by clients that are segregated from the assets of the brokerage firm. Expressly, when a client wires funds to a brokerage account in his name, the money is sent to a bank account in the name of the broker but titled "Customer Segregated Fund." All funds held within this account are to be client monies and are not to be commingled with firm money.

The requirement that brokerage firms hold client funds in segregated accounts is a safeguard against brokerage firm bankruptcies. In theory, if the FCM (Futures Commission Merchant, a fancy word for brokerage firm) suffers financial trouble and files for bankruptcy, any client funds on deposit will be unaffected. In fact, in such a case, it is common practice for the funds and open positions to simply be transferred to an alternative brokerage firm, leaving the insolvent FCM to deal with its issues. Before MF Global and PFGBEST, commodity brokerage bankruptcies, mergers, and acquisitions were perhaps an inconvenience to traders, but no client had ever lost a dime in the process; that changed in 2011.

The failure of MF Global and PFGBEST to avoid the commingling of firm and client money crudely reminded us that segregated funds rules are only as good as their followers—and enforcers. Both FCMs displayed a flagrant disregard to compliance stipulations intended to protect the very customers who had enabled their long-standing success as brokerage firms. Deplorably, in both cases, industry regulators weren't able to detect the violations until after it was too late. Client funds had already been misappropriated and either spent or lost.

At the time this book was going to print, MF Global clients had recouped most of the money they had on deposit through liquidation of firm assets and other sources, but the process had taken approximately a year. PFGBEST clients hadn't fared so well; it took nearly four months after the firm's failure for the bankruptcy trustee to release 30% of the funds in what was a chaotic transfer of client assets to another brokerage firm. At the time of this writing, an uncertain amount of client funds would be recovered, but estimates ranged from 50 cents to about 80 cents on the dollar. Even with the most optimistic outcome, the burden of having funds unwillingly tied up and the emotional turmoil caused by the fiasco is substantial.

Collateral Damage

Brokerage clients are the obvious losers of the MF Global and PFGBEST breakdowns. However, other casualties are often overlooked, including the firm's employees, its brokers, third-party vendors (platforms, trading systems, and money managers), floor traders, market makers, and more. When MF Global and, later, PFGBEST went under, not only did they nearly take their clients with them, but the situation devastated the lives of many hard-working industry participants. The trading pits in Chicago saw an immediate and dramatic decline in participation, and several hundred back-office employees were suddenly out of work.

Painfully, my trading firm, DeCarley Trading, worked exclusively with PFGBEST until its demise in July 2012. I'll never forget July 9: A single email near the close of trading dashed all our hard work and dreams. Without any prior knowledge of troubles brewing at the firm, nor any reason to have suspected wrong doing, we were notified that PFGBEST's assets and client funds had been frozen pending an FBI investigation into the fraud of its president, Russell Wasendorf.

The commodity brokerage business is extremely demanding; few brokers achieve financial success, and those who do spend years building their business to get there. DeCarley Trading opened its door four years before the failure of PFGBEST and worked tirelessly around the clock to build clients' trust. Sadly, it was taken from us in the blink of an eye, through no culpability of our own. Fortunately, we were able to quickly recover by creating an even better trading environment for our brokerage clients; with some time and dedication, we are confident we will emerge as a "bigger and better" firm.

However, we were not alone in our hardship. Approximately 120 firms were engaging in a similar exclusive trade-clearing relationship with PFGBEST. As I was writing this, more than half of such firms had thrown in the towel and closed shop. After all, their ability to generate commission revenue stopped immediately; PFGBEST owed its brokers about a month and a half in commission, and the thought of starting from scratch to build a business in a nearly impossible environment for commodity brokers was a gut-wrenching task many weren't willing to attempt.

Each of us doing business with PFGBEST chose the firm with careful consideration and due diligence; nonetheless, each of us also learned that even doing your homework and confirming with the data reported by regulators isn't always enough. With that said, the industry and its regulatory bodies have gained insight and implemented practices that should successfully prevent a repeat of the PFGBEST and MF Global heartache.

How to Protect Yourself from Another MF Global or PFGBEST

The wounds left by MF Global and PFGBEST on the commodity industry were deep, but there have been positive developments in their aftermath such as the potential for deposit insurance and improvements in the way regulators audit futures brokerage houses. Similarly, futures traders should take the lessons learned by these events to safeguard themselves from potential hardships.

Follow the FCM Financial Data Report

The Commodity Futures Trading Commission (CFTC) requires that FCMs regularly report the status of their customer segregated funds account to regulators. With the data collected, the CFTC publishes a monthly report on the financial data of each FCM. Reports leading up to the PFGBEST debacle were a painful reminder that data portrayed on the CFTC's reports might not always be verified properly. However, this situation has largely changed. Government regulators now have *electronic* access to the customer segregated funds accounts of each commodity brokerage firm, for reliable and accurate real-time verification of funds.

The report includes information such as the total value of customer segregated deposits, whether the amount the brokerage firm has in the customer segregated funds account is enough to be compliant, and any excess or deficiency in the account. You might be wondering why an FCM would have more in its customer segregated funds account than its customers actually have on deposit. Cash inflows and outflows are constantly taking place as clients deposit and withdraw funds, buy and sell options and futures contracts, and pay brokerage fees. Plainly, the math isn't quite as easy as one might think; instead of being a black-and-white figure, there is quite a bit of gray. Nonetheless, the regulations in place that require brokerage firms to segregate customer funds from their own worked flawlessly to protect client funds for decades before MF Global and PFGBEST infamously pilfered customer segregated funds accounts and changed the way the industry operates.

Spread Funds Among Multiple Brokers

Clients trading substantial sums of money might consider using more than one brokerage firm to clear trades with the exchange. Traders choosing to work with an Independent Introducing Broker (defined in Chapter 5) enjoy the luxury of having one individual broker service their trading accounts at multiple brokerage firms. This cuts down on the additional hassles of maintaining multiple accounts while providing clients the advantage of diversifying risk of a brokerage firm failure in which client segregated funds are tampered with. Accordingly, my experience in the PFGBEST debacle lead me to conclude such an arrangement is necessary for probable success as a commodity broker. Not surprisingly, I am now operating under an Independent Introducing Brokerage arrangement and therefore offer my clients access to several brokerage houses while still dealing exclusively with my firm.

Although the odds of another incident similar to those with MF Global or PFGBEST occurring are slim, having peace of mind is important. After all, if the unthinkable happens again, it certainly won't occur at more than one firm at the same time.

What Regulators Are Doing to Protect Clients

As painful as back-to-back system failures were for clients, employees, and brokers of both MF Global and PFGBEST, some long-term good might come of it. For instance, as mentioned, in the aftermath of these events, the National Futures Association (NFA) has been provided electronic access to the bank accounts of FCMs, enabling frequent verification of customer segregated funds balances. A proposed insurance fund discussed within the CFTC also would provide deposit insurance to commodity traders on up to $250,000 of the account balance. This insurance fund would be similar to the banking system's FDIC deposit insurance and would eliminate the risk of unforeseen events such as bank insolvency or a brokerage failure to comply with segregation rules. As this book was going to print, deposit insurance for futures traders was a discussion rather than a reality, but I predict it will eventually be implemented.

Conclusion

Despite the recent hiccup in its track record, violation of customer segregated funds regulations is a rare and infrequent event. In fact, even without new regulatory safety nets in place to avoid another calamity of this sort, it likely would not happen again anytime soon. Nevertheless, those of us whose livelihood depends on a properly functioning marketplace in which we can all be confident, welcome positive changes in oversight with open arms.

Throughout this text, you find what I believe to be a realistic and candid view of the commodity markets. My intention isn't to deter you from trading commodities. After all, I am a broker who makes a living from commission, and I would love nothing more than to attract traders into what I believe to be some of the most exciting markets available to speculators. However, as a broker, it is also my job to make sure that you are aware of the potential hardships and, accordingly, that you will properly prepare yourself before putting your hard-earned money at risk.

If you walk away from this book with something, I hope it is the realization that anything is possible in the commodity markets. Never say "never"—if you do, you will eventually be proven wrong. Additionally, trading the markets is an art, not a science. Unfortunately, there are no black–and-white answers, nor are there fool-proof strategies—but that does not mean there aren't opportunities.

I am often asked what is the best technical tool or indicator to use when speculating in a market. My answer is always the same: No "best tool" exists, nor is there only a best way to use the tool. The paramount approach to any trading tool, whether technical, seasonal, or fundamental, is to use it—or, better yet, a combination of a few tools—to form an educated opinion in your expectations of market price. With their findings, traders should approach the market with a degree of humbleness and realistic expectations.

Remember, as a trader, you compete against the market—specifically, each participant in that particular market. Therefore, assuming that you can always beat the markets is assuming that you are somehow smarter and better informed than all other participants. Not only is this arrogant, but it also might be financial suicide. Instead, you should approach every trade with modesty and the understanding that you could be wrong. Having such an attitude might prevent you from sustaining large losses as the result of stubbornness.

With that in mind, in its simplest form, trading is a zero sum game. Aside from commissions paid to the brokerage firm and fees paid to the exchange, for every dollar lost in the market, someone else has gained a dollar. Becoming a consistently profitable trader isn't easy, but it isn't synonymous with chasing the proverbial end of the rainbow, either. With the proper background, hard work, and the experience that comes with inevitable tough lessons, long-term success is possible. I hope this book is the first step in your journey toward victory in the challenging, yet potentially rewarding, commodity markets.

chapter 1

A Crash Course in Commodities

How It All Began

Given the urban nature of the city of Chicago, we often forget that it is located in the agricultural heart of the Midwest. In the mid-1840s, the Windy City emerged as the agricultural market center for neighboring states. Chicago was the meeting place for farmers looking for buyers of their crops and grain mills looking to purchase product for their operations. However, despite the central location, timing and logistic issues created inefficient means of conducting business and thus inflated commodity prices.

At the time, grain elevators were sparse, so lack of storage made it critical that a farmer sell his crop upon harvest at the annual meeting in Chicago. Even those who did have a method of storing the grain faced frozen rivers and roadways that made travelling to Chicago nearly impossible during the winter months. Likewise, the springtime trails were often too muddy for wagon travel. Thus, during and immediately after harvest, grain supply was in such abundance that it was common for unsold grain to be dumped into Lake Michigan, for lack of means to transport and store unsold portions.

Commodity prices have always been a function of supply and demand, but before the futures markets, excess and shortages wreaked havoc on consumers and producers.

As you can imagine, as the year wore on, the grain supply dwindled, creating shortages. This annual cycle of extreme oversupply and subsequent undersupply created inefficient price discovery and led to hardships for both producers and consumers. The feast-or-famine cycle created circumstances in which farmers were forced to sell their goods at a large discount when supplies were high, but consumers were required to pay a large premium during times of tight supplies. Luckily, a few of the grain traders put their heads and resources together to develop a solution: an organized exchange now known as the Chicago Board of Trade (CBOT)—or, more accurately, what is now the CBOT division of the CME Group.

The Chicago Board of Trade

The Chicago Board of Trade was created by a handful of savvy grain traders to establish a central location for buyers and sellers to conduct business. The new formalized location and operation enticed wealthy investors to build storage silos to smooth the supply of grain throughout the year and, in turn, aid in price stability.

After spending the last decade and a half as one of the largest futures trading organizations in the world and a direct competitor to the Chicago Mercantile Exchange (CME), the CBOT and the CME merged July 12, 2007, to form the CME Group, creating the largest derivatives market ever.

The CBOT division of the CME Group is the home of the trading of agricultural products such as corn, soybeans, and wheat. However, the exchange has added several products over the years, to include Treasury bonds and notes and the Dow Jones Industrial Index. Since 1930, 141 West Jackson Boulevard. in downtown Chicago has been known as the Chicago Board of Trade Building. It is now designated as a National Historic Landmark.

The Chicago Mercantile Exchange

The success of the CBOT fueled investment dollars into exchanges that could facilitate the process of trading products other than grain. One of the offshoots of this new investment interest was the Chicago Mercantile Exchange. The CME was formed in 1874 under the operating name Chicago Produce Exchange; it also carried the title Chicago Butter and Egg Board before finally gaining its current name.

The contract that put this exchange on the map was frozen pork belly futures, or simply "bellies," as many insiders say. Hollywood and media portrayals of the futures industry often focus on the pork belly market. How could anyone forget the infamous scene in Trading Places in which Billy Ray Valentine plots his speculation of belly futures? Ironically, the CME Group delisted pork belly futures in July 2011 due to a "prolonged lack of trading volume."

According to New Yorkers, there is only one "Merc," and it isn't in Chicago.

The CME, a division of the CME Group, is responsible for trading in a vast variety of contracts, including cattle, hogs, stock index futures, currency futures, and short-term interest rates. The exchange also offers alternative trading vehicles such as weather and real-estate derivatives. At the time of this writing, and likely for some time to come, the CME has the largest open interest in options and futures contracts of any futures exchange in the world.

The New York Mercantile Exchange

Although the futures and options industry was born in Chicago, New York was quick to get in on the action. In the early 1880s, a crop of Manhattan dairy merchants created the Butter and Cheese Exchange of New York, which was later modified to the Butter, Cheese, and Egg Exchange and then, finally, the New York Mercantile Exchange (NYMEX).

The NYMEX division of the CME Group currently houses futures trading in the energy complex. Examples of NYMEX-listed futures contracts are crude oil, gasoline, and natural gas. A 1994 merger with the nearby Commodity Exchange (COMEX) exchange allowed the NYMEX to acquire the trading of precious metals futures such as gold and silver under what is referred to as its COMEX division.

In March 2008, NYMEX accepted a cash and stock offer from the CME Group that brought the New York futures exchange into the fold, along with the CBOT and the CME. On August 18, 2008, NYMEX seat-holders and share-holders accepted the proposal and the rest is history. The NYMEX division of the CME Group has been fully integrated with the CME and CBOT divisions of the exchange despite being located hundreds of miles away from downtown Chicago.

The CME Group

The CME Group consists of the three aforementioned divisions: the CBOT, CME, and NYMEX, which previously stood as independent exchanges. Accordingly, the CME is officially the world's largest derivatives exchange. As previously mentioned, on July 12, 2007, the merger of the CBOT and the CME created the CME Group, but NYMEX was acquired in 2008 to create a powerful and innovative entity.

Trade on the CME Group represents a majority of futures trading in the United States, but its largest competitor is the IntercontinentalExchange, known simply as ICE.

The CME Group currently serves the speculative and risk management needs of customers worldwide. Among the three divisions, the CME Group offers derivative products across nearly all imaginable asset classes.

Upon merging, the CBOT and the CME consolidated all floor-trading operations into a single location: the historic CBOT building on 141 West Jackson Boulevard in downtown Chicago. The actual move took place over three weekends, and no details were spared. The new combined trading floor spans 60,000 square feet.

IntercontinentalExchange

IntercontinentalExchange (ICE) is the newest player in U.S. futures trading. In stark contrast to the *original* models of the CBOT, the CME, and NYMEX, ICE primarily facilitates over-the-counter energy and commodity futures contracts. This simply means that there is no centralized location; nearly all trading takes place in cyberspace. However, ICE continues to operate floor-trading operations in some of its option markets. In addition, the CME Group has followed the lead of ICE and moved a majority of its futures contract execution to electronic means, as opposed to a trading pit with a physical location. We discuss the two types of execution in greater detail in Chapter 3, "The Organized Chaos of Open Outcry and the Advent of Electronic Trading."

ICE was established May 2000, with the mission of transforming OTC trading. By 2001, it had acquired a European energy futures exchange, but it didn't dig its claws deep into the heart of the U.S. futures industry until its acquisition of the New York Board of Trade (NYBOT) in 2007, along with the responsibility to facilitate trading in the softs complex. The term *soft* generally describes a commodity that is grown rather than mined; examples of contracts categorized as soft and traded on ICE in the United States include sugar, cocoa, coffee, and cotton. More recent additions are financial products including the Russell 2000 Index and the U.S. Dollar Index.

Evolution of the Forward Contract into a Futures Contract

The futures markets and the instruments traded there, as we know them today, have evolved from what began as private negotiations to buy and sell commodities between producers and users. The agreements that resulted from these negotiations are known as *forward contracts*. Fortunately, efficient-minded entrepreneurs discovered that standardized agreements can facilitate transactions in a much quicker manner than a privately negotiated forward contract. Thus, the futures contract was born. Next, we take a look at the advent of the forward contract and how the concept eventually bred the futures contract.

The Forward Contract

The ingenuity of agricultural trade didn't end with the creation of organized and centralized grain trade in the 1800s. Although this certainly worked toward price stabilization by leveling shortages and surpluses throughout the growing and harvest cycles, other factors worked against price efficiency. As a means of mitigating price risks, farmers and merchants began dealing in forward contracts.

A forward contract is a private negotiation developed to establish the price of a commodity to be delivered at a specific date in the future. For example, a farmer who has planted corn and expects it to be harvested and ready to sell in October might locate a party interested in purchasing the product in October. At that time, both parties might choose to enter an agreement for the transaction to take place at a specific date, price, and location. Such an agreement locks in the price for both the buyer and the seller of the commodity and, therefore, eliminates the risk of price fluctuation that both sides of the contract face without the benefit of a forward contract.

Along with a centralized grain trade, the forward contract was another big step toward price stability, but there was a problem. Forward contracts reduce price risk only if both parties to the arrangement live up to their end of the agreement. In other words, there is no protection against default. As you can imagine, a farmer who locks in a price to sell his crop in the spring through a forward contract and later discovers that he can sell the product for considerably more in the open market might choose to default on the forward contract.

In its simplest form, a futures contract is a standardized forward contract.

It is easy to see the lack of motivation for parties to a forward contract to uphold their end of the bargain. Even the most honest man would be tempted to default if it means a better life for his family.

To resolve the issue of merchants and farmers defaulting on forward contracts, the exchanges began requiring that each party of the transaction submit a good-faith deposit, or margin, with an unrelated third party. In the case of failure to comply with the contract, the party suffering the loss would receive the funds deposited in good faith to cover the inconvenience and at least part of the financial loss.

The Futures Contract

Exchange-traded forward contracts were extremely helpful in reducing the price risk that farmers and merchants normally were exposed to. Additionally, with the advent of exchange-traded forward contracts along with good-faith deposits, much of the default risk was eliminated. However, because forward contracts were negotiations between two individuals, it was a challenge to bring together buyers and sellers who shared the same needs in terms of quantity, timing, and so on. Also, forward contracts were subject to difficulties arising from uncontrollable circumstances such as drought. For example, a farmer obligated to deliver a certain amount of corn via a forward contract might not comply due to poor growing conditions, thus leaving the counterparty to the transaction in a dire predicament.

The exchanges' answer to problems arising from forward contracts was the standardized futures contract. In its simplest form, a futures contract is a forward contract that is standardized in terms of size, deliverable grade of the commodity, delivery date, and delivery location. The fact that each contract is identical to the next made the trading of futures much more convenient than attempting to negotiate a forward contract with an individual. The concept of standardization has allowed the futures markets to flourish into what they have become today.

According to the CME, the formal definition of a futures contract is as follows:

A legally binding, standardized agreement to buy or sell a standardized commodity, specifying quantity and quality at a set price on a future date.

In other words, the seller of a futures contract agrees to deliver the stated commodity on the stated delivery date. The buyer of a futures contract agrees to take delivery of the stated commodity at the stated delivery date. The only variable of a futures transaction is the price at which it is done, and buyers and sellers determine this in the marketplace.

> *A cash market transaction occurs in the present, but a futures market transaction is an agreement for an exchange of the underlying asset in the future.*

Although the futures contracts bought or sold represent an obligation to take or make delivery, according to the CME Group, approximately 97% of futures contracts never result in physical delivery of the underlying commodity. Instead, traders simply offset their holding prior to the expiration date. We discuss this in more detail later in the chapter.

In the evolution into the futures contract and away from the forward contract, exchanges also eliminated default risk associated with buying or selling futures contracts by guaranteeing the other side of the transaction. Thus, unlike a forward contract, or early versions of the futures contract, in which both parties are left to depend on the other to live up to their end of the contract, a futures contract is backed by the exchange. This exchange guarantee covers the entire value of the position, instead of being limited to the margin posted by participants.

Thanks to the standardization of each contract, the subsequent ease of buying or selling contracts, and a lack of default risk, futures trading has attracted price speculation. Participation is no longer limited to those who own, or would like to own, the underlying commodity. Instead, unrelated third parties can easily involve themselves in the markets in hopes of accurately predicting—and, therefore, profiting from—price fluctuations.

Cash Market Versus Futures Market

Currently, commodities are traded in two separate yet related markets: the cash market and the futures market. The cash market refers to the buying and selling of physical commodities. In a cash market transaction, the price and exchange of product occurs in the *present*. In contrast, the futures market deals with the buying or selling of *future* obligations to make or take delivery instead of the actual commodity.

Cost to Carry

Prices in the cash and futures market differ as a direct result of the disparity in the timing of delivery of the underlying product. After all, if a commodity is going to be delivered at some point in the future, it must be stored and insured in the meantime. The costs associated with holding the physical grain until the stated delivery date are referred to as the *costs to carry*.

Naturally, in normal market conditions, the cash price is cheaper than the futures price because of the expenses related to carrying the commodity until delivery. Likewise, the near-month futures price is generally cheaper than a distantly expiring futures contract. The progressive pricing is often referred to as a normal carrying charge market (see Figure 1.1). You might also hear this scenario described by the term *contango*.

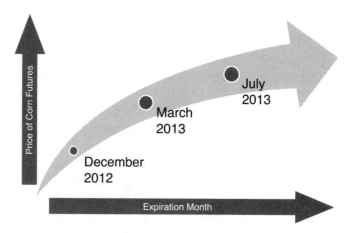

Figure 1.1   Normal carry charge market, or contango.

Normal carrying charge markets are possible only during times of ample supply, or inventory. If there is a shortage of the commodity in the near term, prices in the cash market increase to reflect market supply-and-demand fundamentals. The supply shortage can reduce the contango or, if severe enough, can actually reverse the contango if the spot price, and possibly the price of the nearby futures contract, exceeds the futures price in distant contracts, as shown in Figure 1.2.

It is important to understand that the contango shouldn't exceed the actual cost to carry the commodity. If it did, producers and consumers would have the opportunity for a "risk-free" profit through arbitrage.

"If you can take advantage of a situation in some way, it's your duty as an American to do it."
—C. Montgomery Burns
(from *The Simpsons*)

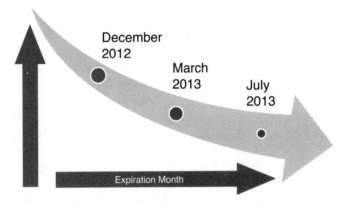

Figure 1.2 The opposite of contango is sometimes called backwardation and involves higher spot prices than futures prices.

Arbitrage

Arbitrage is the glue that holds the commodity markets together. Without arbitrage, there would be no incentive for prices in the futures market to correlate with prices in the cash market—and as I discuss in Chapter 2, "Hedging Versus Speculating," arbitrage enables efficient market pricing for hedgers and speculators. Specifically, if speculators notice that the price difference between the cash and futures prices of a commodity exceeds the cost to carry, they will buy the undervalued (cash market commodity) and sell the overvalued (futures contract written on underlying commodity). This is done until the spread between the prices in the two markets equals the cost to carry.

> Arbitrage is a "risk-free" profit, but for most of us, it might as well be a mirage. Markets are quick to eliminate such opportunities.

The true definition of *arbitrage* is a risk-free profit. Sounds great, doesn't it? Unfortunately, true arbitrage opportunities are uncommon, and those that do occur are opportunities for only the insanely quick. Chances are, you and I do not possess the speed, skill, and resources necessary to properly identify and react to most arbitrage opportunities in the marketplace.

For further clarification, an example of an arbitrage opportunity unrelated to cash market pricing is a scenario in which the e-mini S&P is trading at 1380.50 and the full-size version of the contract is trading at 1380.70. In theory, if you noticed this discrepancy in a timely fashion, it would be possible to buy five mini contracts and sell one big S&P. The mini contract is exactly one-fifth the size of the original and is fungible; this means that trading five mini contracts is identical to trading one big contract. Consequently, a trader who can execute each side of the trade at the noted prices can request that the positions offset each other to lock in a profit of 20 cents, or $50 before transactions costs. It doesn't sound like much, but if it truly is an arbitrage opportunity, a $50 risk-free profit isn't such a bad deal.

Contract Expiration

By definition, futures contracts are expiring agreements for buyers and sellers of those contracts to exchange the underlying physical commodity. Most market participants choose to avoid dealing with the underlying assets by offsetting their obligation at some point before the futures contract expires or, in some cases, prior to first notice day. I cover the process of offsetting positions later in the chapter.

First Notice Day

First notice day occurs before the corresponding futures contract expires. The official definition of *first notice day* is the day on which the buyer of a futures contract can be called upon by the exchange to take delivery of the underlying commodity. On this day, the exchange estimates the number of traders who are expected to make delivery of the commodity (those short futures contracts) and distributes delivery notices to those long futures on a first-in basis. Simply put, traders who hold long positions into the first notice day run the *risk* of being delivered upon but might not *actually* be delivered upon, depending on the amount of time the position has been open. For instance, a trader who has been long a futures contract for several weeks will receive a delivery notice before a trader who has established a position the day before first notice day. Note that the danger of receiving a delivery notice applies to those long the market only. Short traders don't have to worry about delivery until expiration day—yet they should be out of the market well before expiration because market volume and liquidity dry up immediately preceding and beyond the first notice day.

After a delivery notice is distributed, a trader isn't forced to accept it, so panicking is unnecessary. Instead, he can instruct his brokerage firm to "retender" the notice, which equates to selling the obligation in an open market to an interested party. Although the trader avoids being forced to find a home for 5,000 bushels of corn, or whatever the commodity might be, he faces substantial processing fees. All speculators should diligently avoid being part of the delivery process.

Not all futures contracts have a first notice day; some stipulate a cash settlement process instead of delivery of the underlying product. Cash settlement works just as it sounds and is explained next.

Futures Expiration

Expiration is the time and day that a particular delivery month of a futures contract ceases trading and the final settlement price is determined. The actual delivery process begins at expiration of the futures contract for markets that involve a physical commodity exchange. Conversely, a select number of futures contracts are cash settled. If this is the case, investors who hold positions into expiration agree to allow the exchange to determine a final valuation for the futures contract at hand and adjust the value of individual trading accounts accordingly. In my opinion, it is generally a bad idea to hold positions into expiration in cash-settled markets because it leaves the fate of profit and losses in the hands of a relatively arbitrary exchange-derived contract value. Likewise, unless you are willing to make, or take, delivery of the underlying commodity, you shouldn't have an open position in a deliverable commodity contract into expiration.

The Mechanics of Futures Contracts

So far, we have learned that futures contracts are standardized and are guaranteed by the exchange. However, there is a lot more to be learned, and you must fully understand the basics before you can expect to be a successful futures trader.

Futures traders don't have to own or borrow assets before they can sell.

The Long and Short of It

Commodity trading is a world full of insider lingo; it is almost as if the industry created a language of its own. If you want to be a participant, you must become familiar with commonly used terms and phrases. Doing so avoids miscommunication between yourself and your broker.

I cover several commonly used phrases and terms in a later chapter; however, the two most critical terms to be aware of are *long* and *short*. In essence, the term *long* is synonymous with *buy*, and the term *short* is synonymous with *sell*. This is the case whether the instrument in question is a futures contract or an option. Specifically, if a trader buys a futures or option contract, he is going

In futures market slang, long and short describe a speculative position.

long. If a trader sells a futures or option contract, he is going short.

It is important to realize that you will sometimes hear industry insiders say that they are *long the market* with options, futures spreads, and such. Although in strict context of the phrase *long* implies that something has been purchased, in loosely used lingo, being *long a market* might simply mean having a bullish stance. This can mean long futures, long call options, short put options, bullish option or futures spreads, or any other speculative play that profits from an increase in the price of the underlying asset. Consequently, you might hear a trader mention that she is *short the market;* this might mean that she is short futures, short call options, long puts, or engaged in a bearish option or futures spread. Despite the alternative uses, however, beginning traders should first be comfortable using *long* in the context of buying and *short* in the context of selling.

Buy or Sell in Any Order

One of the most difficult concepts for beginning commodity traders to grasp is the fact that a futures contract can be bought and sold in any order. The

Trading futures and options is as simple as buying low and selling high—but simple doesn't mean it is easy.

common thinking is that you can't possibly sell something before you own it, and even if you could, some interest likely would be charged for borrowing the asset that you intend to sell. Although that might be true in stock trading, that logic doesn't apply to the futures markets. Let's take a look at why this is the case.

Unlike stocks, futures contracts are not assets; they are liabilities. The purchase of a futures contract does not represent ownership of the underlying commodity; instead, it represents an obligation to take delivery of the underlying commodity at a specified date. Likewise, the seller of a futures contract isn't selling an asset; he is simply agreeing to make delivery of the stated asset on the appropriate date.

Because there is no ownership or exchange of the asset at the time the futures trade is made, it isn't necessary to own the underlying commodity or even be prepared to take ownership. Thus, buying or selling in any order isn't an issue for futures traders.

Offsetting and Rolling Over Trades

As mentioned, most investors who participate in the futures markets are simply attempting to profit from variations in price movement and are not interested in taking or making delivery of the underlying commodity. Again, to avoid the delivery process, it is necessary to offset holdings prior to expiration—or, more specifically, the first notice day.

The notion of offsetting is simple: To offset a trade, it is necessary to execute a position opposite the one that you originally entered the market with. To illustrate, if you bought a December corn futures, you would need to sell a December corn futures to get out of the position. When you are out of the market, you are said to be *flat*. This means that you do not have any open trades and are no longer exposed to price risk or margin. Of course, being flat the market doesn't necessarily mean that the risk of emotional turmoil is eliminated. Unfortunately, many beginning traders have incorrectly looked at missed opportunities as monetary losses. We look at the psychological impact of such emotions in Chapter 11, "The Only Magic in Trading—Emotional Stability."

When a trade is offset, the trader is said to be flat *the market. This means that all positions are closed and there is no exposure to price risk, aside from a potential "missed trade."*

The concept of offsetting can be best explained by an example. In September 2012, the corn futures contract expiring in December 2012 experienced a minor correction and seemed to be approaching trend line support. A trader who believed that prices would appreciate might purchase a futures contract in hopes of a rally. At that point, the trader has an open long position with the exchange and continues to have an open position until it is offset. As mentioned, the only way to offset an open position is to execute a transaction opposite the one used to enter the market. Looking at Figure 1.3, you can see that the trader purchased a December 2012 corn futures contract at $7.34. In Chapter 8, "Making Cents of Commodity Quotes," I explain the details in quoting and calculating grain futures.

To get out of the market, the trader must sell a December 2012 corn futures contract, hopefully at a higher price. Naturally, if a trader can buy low and sell high, regardless of the order, he will be profitable (see Figure 1.4). As simple as this premise is, execution can be challenging. In fact, a majority of speculators walk away from the game with less money than they started with merely because they couldn't find a way to consistently buy low and sell high.

The same concept would be true for someone who sold a December corn futures contract to enter the position rather than bought one. Aside from holding the futures into expiration and actually making delivery of the underlying asset, the only way to get out of a short December futures trade would be to buy a December futures contract to offset the position.

Figure 1.3 Futures traders can buy and sell in any order but must take the opposite action to exit. This trader is going long December corn and will later have to sell it to offset the position. (Chart courtesy of QST.)

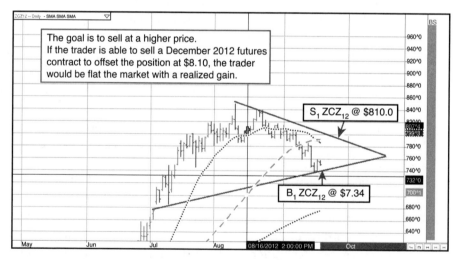

Figure 1.4 When a trader no longer has an open position, he is said to be "flat" the market. This trader is hoping to sell his contract, and his obligation with the exchange, near $8.10. (Chart courtesy of QST.)

The term *rolling,* or *rolling over,* is commonly used to describe the practice of offsetting a trade in a contract that is facing expiration and entering a similar position in a contract with a distant expiration date. Rolling over is simply offsetting one position and getting into another. Many beginning traders make the mistake of assuming that rolling into a new contract somehow avoids exiting the original position and simply changes the contract month. Perhaps it is wishful thinking for those who would prefer not to lock in a loss on an open position; unfortunately, in doing so is a necessary evil if the goal is to move into an alternative contract month.

To illustrate, a trader who is long a June T-note futures contract with the first notice day quickly approaching might choose to roll into the September contract to avoid delivery while still maintaining a bullish speculative position in the market. In this case, rolling would include selling the June contract and buying September.

Bid/Ask Spread

The notion of a bid/ask spread can be confusing. This is especially true given the differing perspectives of written literature available for beginning traders. Some articles and books seem to insist on explaining the bid/ask spread from both a market maker's point of view and a retail trader's perspective. However, in my opinion, providing details of both sides of the story simply creates more confusion than is necessary to get a good grasp of what a bid/ask spread is and how to cope with it as a trader.

The easiest way to understand the spread between the bid and the ask is to come to peace with the fact that there are essentially two market prices at any given time. There is a price at which you can buy the contract (the ask) and a price at which you can sell it (the bid). As a retail trader, you will always be paying the higher price and selling the lower price. It takes money to make money, and if you want to participate in a market, you must pay the bid/ask spread. For instance, a corn trader might buy corn at $6.21 and sell corn at $6.21[1/2]. The difference of a half a cent is the bid/ask spread, and it translates into a component of the transaction cost associated with executing a trade in this market.

Nothing is free. Paying spreads are a part of trading costs. Don't get mad; get savvy.

Keep in mind that the bid/ask spread is how floor brokers, or market makers, are compensated for executing your trade and providing liquidity to the markets. Just as you pay a commission to the retail broker who took your order, the executing broker or market maker, must be paid in the form of the bid/ask spread. Think about it: If as a retail trader you are always paying the ask and buying the bid, you are a net loser even if the price of the futures contract remains unchanged. The beneficiary of the difference between the bid and the ask is the executing broker or market maker making fluidity of trade possible.

The spread between the bid and the ask isn't something that investors should resent—in liquid markets, anyway. After all, the executing broker must be compensated for accepting the risk involved with taking the other side of your trade. In general, he wants to offset his position and risk as soon as possible; his intention is to "make a market" and profit from the difference in the bid/ask spread, not to speculate on price movement. In highly liquid markets, there are often no market makers but there is still a natural bid/ask spread of a tick.

As a trader, it is important to be aware of the bid/ask spread and the implications that its size will have on your trading results. A couple prominent factors that affect the size of the spread are market liquidity and volatility. As market liquidity decreases, the size of the bid/ask spread widens, and thus the costs associated with participating in such a market increases. This makes sense. If the executing broker is anticipating a lack of volume and the corresponding difficulty offsetting his trade, he will require more compensation for taking the other side of your trade.

Likewise, if volatility is high, the executing broker faces more price risk during the time in which he takes the other side of your trade and can subsequently offset the position. Thus, he requires higher compensation for his efforts, which creates a relatively wide bid/ask spread.

One of the biggest mistakes I have witnessed beginning traders make is to ignore the repercussions of large bid/ask spreads. Most futures contracts are fluidly traded enough for this to be a nonissue. However, in the option trading arena, this is a big concern. It is extremely important that you understand that bid/ask spreads are a part of doing business and know how to adjust your trading strategy accordingly.

Bid/ask spreads hinder a trader's ability to make money; the wider the spreads, the more difficult it is to be profitable. In fact, certain markets have bid/ask spreads so wide that I believe investors have no incentive to trade them. This avoidance stems from the idea that excessively wide spreads create a scenario in which the trader must not only be right in the direction of the market, but must also be extremely right to overcome the hefty transaction cost. Imagine trading copper options that often have bid/ask spreads in excess of 1 cent in premium, or $250. Immediately after initiating the trade, it is a loser in the amount of $250, regardless of movement in the futures price. As you can see, this can make trading even more challenging.

Round Turns and Transaction Costs

Unlike the world of stocks, in which transaction costs are often quoted on a per-side basis and in the form of a *ticket charge,* commodity trades are typically charged on a round-turn basis. However, as the nature of the industry shifts from broker-assisted trading to discount online, futures brokers are beginning to quote commissions per side in an effort to make the transaction costs seem cheaper than they actually are. A single round turn consists of the purchase and sale of the same futures or option contract. Simply put, it is getting in and getting out of a market.

Many beginning traders mistakenly assume that the commission and fees charged to them depend on the number of order tickets rather than the number of contracts, but this is not the case. If a trader buys 10 e-mini crude oil contracts at $91.00 and later sells all 10 at $92.00, he has executed 10 round-turns and will be charged 10 commissions. This is true regardless of whether the 10 contracts were purchased and sold on single tickets or whether there were 10 separate orders to buy 1 contract at $91.00 and then 10 separate orders to sell 1 contract at $92.00.

Of course, not all traders are day-trading, and it is common for positions to be entered on one day and exited at some date in the future. In this case, a futures trader is charged a half of a round-turn commission on the day the trade is initiated and is then charged the other half the day that the trade is offset. Notice that I specifically noted *futures* traders; option traders normally are charged the entire round-turn commission when they enter the trade. Therefore, a trader who buys a soybean $12.00 put would be charged a commission to enter the position but would be able to exit the trade without being charged.

Keep in mind that I have been referring strictly to commissions, which your brokerage firm charges. Each round-turn is accompanied by exchange fees, minimal National Futures Association (NFA) fees, and possible transaction fees charged by the clearing firm. Transaction fees are charged on a per-side basis, regardless of whether the instrument being traded is an option or a futures contract.

When negotiating a commission rate with your brokerage firm, be sure to confirm that the quoted rates are per round-turn. You should also be aware of whether they include the additional fees. Because exchange fees vary from product to product, most firms state commission rates on a round-turn-plus-fees basis. This means that you have to account for any exchange, NFA, and clearing fees in addition to the commission. Some firms, typically deep discount brokerages, quote rates as "all inclusive," which already account for incremental fees. Many of these firms also quote rates on a per-side basis simply because it "sounds" cheaper and can be an effective marketing tool.

Price Speculation

As easy as it is to have the freedom to buy or sell in any order, sticking to the overall goal of buying low and selling high can be challenging. The price of a given asset, whether it be grains, metals, energies, or Treasury bonds, depends on a seemingly unlimited number of factors. Even as a market is making a large price move, it is nearly impossible to determine the driving force behind the change in valuation and whether it will last.

Not only are prices the result of supply and demand fundamentals, but they can also be swayed by logistical issues such as light volume, option expiration, and excessive margin calls. A primary catalyst for some of the largest commodity plunges in history was the sweeping number of forced liquidations due to insufficient margin in speculative trading accounts.

In addition, a seemingly unlimited number of intermarket relationships can be used as a guide but not a guarantee. For instance, a strong dollar often works against commodity prices, but that doesn't mean that if the dollar is down, commodities will *always* rally. Another example is the negative correlation between Treasuries and stocks. In theory, investors have two major asset classes to choose from, stocks and bonds. If money is flowing into one, it is likely flowing out of the other. This is a useful but simplistic bit of information. Although this relationship tends to exist over time, in many cases, both markets travel together, and stubbornly trading according to the historical relationship could lead to large losses.

This discussion isn't intended to discourage you from attempting to speculate on the price of commodities or to insinuate that it can't be done; it can. However, I want you to recognize that analyses should be done with an open mind and a willingness to adapt to changes in what you consider to be the norm.

Futures Spreads

The practice of buying one futures contract and selling another that is similar in nature is known as *spread trading*—specifically, *futures spread trading*. The goal of a futures spread is to profit from the change in the price difference between the two related futures contracts involved. Simply, a futures spread trader isn't necessarily concerned with the direction of the underlying market. Instead, the trader is speculating on the relationship (spread) between the prices of the two contracts in question. Two basic futures spreads exist: the intracommodity spread and the intercommodity spread.

Exchange-recognized futures spreads involve discounted margin requirements; before trading spreads be sure that you are properly capitalized.

● **Intracommodity spread.** In reference to a futures spread, there are a plethora of interpretations or meanings. However, the most commonly used spread strategy is the *intracommodity spread,* which is often referred to as a *calendar spread.* Specifically, this entails simultaneously holding a long position in one contract month of a specific commodity and a short position in another contract month of the same commodity.

For example, a grain trader might buy a July corn futures contract and sell a December corn futures contract. Whether the position is a winner or a loser doesn't depend on whether corn prices go up or down; instead, it depends on how much more July corn increases relative to the December contract or how much less it decreases. Specifically, it is concerned with whether the spread widens or narrows.

● **Intercommodity spread.** Don't get *intracommodity* and *intercommodity* spreads confused. The prefix *intra* denotes that the spread is with the same commodity; the prefix *inter* indicates that the spread is between two different but related commodities. As you can imagine, due to less obvious correlation between the components of an intercommodity spread relative to those in an intracommodity spread, intercommodity spreads tend to be much more volatile and expose traders to more risk.

An intercommodity spread consists of purchasing a futures contract in a given delivery month and simultaneously holding a short position in a related commodity market but the same delivery month. An example of popular intercommodity spreads include the *crack spread* (spreading crude oil against unleaded gasoline and heating oil) and the *crush spread* (spreading soybeans against soybean oil and soybean meal).

Similar to an option spread that can have its own quote, a futures spread can also be referenced in terms of a package. Consequently, spreads are traded in a separate trading pit located near the pit in which outright futures are traded, or electronically through designated networks and market

The term spread typically implies hedge. In theory, one or some of the components of the spread will hedge the risk of others.

makers. This enables traders to name the spread price and place the order to execute both sides of the position on a single ticket.

For example, if July corn futures are trading at $6.00 and December corn is trading at $7.10, the bid/ask spread on this particular intracommodity spread might be $1.10/$1.12. Thus, a spread trader could buy the spread for $1.12 or sell the spread for $1.10, or choose to work a limit order at an alternative price. Alternatively, a spread trader could choose to execute each leg of the spread separately, as opposed to a package, by executing two order tickets—one for the July corn futures and one for December.

A Brief Introduction to Commodity Options

The theory and practice of option trading is diverse and sometimes complicated. Accordingly, it is impossible to do the topic justice in such a brief mention. The purpose of this section is to merely introduce the subject.

Options can be purchased outright, in conjunction with futures contracts, or even as a package with both short and long options of various types. There are no limits to the versatility of option trading. Commodity options provide a flexible and effective way to trade in the futures markets with various amounts of potential risk and reward. For example, through the combination of long and short calls and puts, investors can design a strategy that fits their needs and expectations; such an arrangement is referred to as an *option spread*.

The method and strategy should be determined by personality, risk capital, time horizon, market sentiment, and risk aversion. Plainly, if you aren't an aggressive individual with a high tolerance for pain, you probably shouldn't be employing a trading strategy that involves elevated risk. Doing so often results in panicked liquidation of trades at inopportune times and other unsound emotional decisions.

What Is an Option?

Before it is possible to understand how options can be used, it is important to know what they are and how they work. The buyer of an option pays a premium (payment) to the seller of an option for the right, not the obligation, to take delivery of the underlying futures contract (exercise). This financial value is treated as an asset, although eroding, to the option buyer and a liability to the seller. There are two types of options, a *call* option and a *put* option.

- **Call options.** Give the buyer the right, but not the obligation, to buy the underlying at the stated strike price within a specific period of time. Conversely, the seller of a call option is obligated to deliver a long position in the underlying futures contract from the strike price if the buyer opts to exercise the option. Essentially, this means that the seller is forced to take a short position in the market when the option is exercised.

- **Put options.** Give the buyer the right, but not the obligation, to sell the underlying at the stated strike price within a specific period of time. The seller of a put option is obligated to deliver a short position from the strike price if the buyer chooses to exercise the option. Keep in mind that delivering a short futures contract simply means being long from the strike price.

Similar to futures contracts, there are two sides to every option trade: a buyer and a seller. Option buyers are paying for the underlying right, whereas sellers are selling that right. The most important point to remember is that option *buyers* are exposed to risk limited to the amount of premium paid, whereas option *sellers* face theoretically unlimited risk. Conversely, option *buyers* have the possibility of potentially unlimited gains, whereas the profit potential for *sellers* is limited to the amount of premium collected (see Table 1.1).

Table 1.1   Relationship Between Calls and Puts

	Call	Put	
Buy	🐂	🐻	Limited risk
Sell	🐻	🐂	Unlimited risk

Traders who are willing to accept considerable amounts of risk can write (or sell) options, collecting the premium and taking advantage of the well-known belief that more options than not expire worthless. The premium collected by a seller is seen as a liability until either the option is offset (by buying it back) or it expires.

Option Spreads

The majority of beginning option traders prefer trading outright options (buying or selling calls or puts), due to their simplicity. However, there are definite advantages to becoming familiar with the flexibility of risk and reward when using option spreads.

An option spread is the combination of two different option types or strike prices to attain a common goal. The term *option spread* can be used to refer to an unlimited number of possibilities. For example, an option spread can involve the purchase of both a call and a put with the same strike prices, or it can be the purchase and sale of two calls with different strike prices. The sheer number of possibilities makes this topic beyond the scope of this book, but if you are interested in learning more on option spreads, you might want to pick up a copy of *Commodity Options,* which I authored and was published by FT Press.

To add to the confusion surrounding commodity vocabulary, an *option spread* has its own bid/ask spread. Just as a single call or put would have a price that you can buy it for and a price you can sell it for, a spread is priced as a package and has both a bid and an ask that represent the purchase or sales price for the combination of options.

Fortunately, when dealing with a spread on a spread, most insiders identify the bid/ask spread by its full name and also refer to the option spread by its specific name. For example, if a broker calls the trading floor to get a quote for an option spread, she might say something like this to the clerk who answers the phone: "Will you get me the bid/ask on the 900/950 call spread?" Similarly, when accessing an option spread quote via an electronic trading platform, a trader inputs the appropriate strike prices and designates the query as a "vertical call spread," or some other type of recognized spread structure.

It is important to realize that, when getting a quote for an option spread, it isn't necessary to decipher whether you will be buying or selling the spread. This is because the broker or trading platform gives you the quote for doing each. Therefore the bid/ask spread—the spread can be bought at the ask and sold at the bid.

Once again, option spreads are too complex to discuss in any detail within this text. However, you need to realize that, when it comes to option spreads, if the price of the long option of the spread is higher than the price of the short options, the trader is buying the spread. If it is possible to collect more premium for the short legs than is paid for the long legs, the trader is selling the spread.

The increasing popularity of electronic trading platforms, and the resulting transparent option pricing, has encouraged many traders to place separate order tickets on various legs of their spreads instead of entering a single ticket to enter the trade as a package. For instance, an option spread between a long and a short call option could be entered using a spread order in which both legs are executed simultaneously. Alternatively, a trader could simply place an order to buy the desired call option, and then another to sell the other call option to complete the spread.

For margin purposes, option spreads are treated the same whether they are entered on one ticket or multiple tickets. However, some brokers with strict order entry risk policies might prefer traders to enter spreads on a single order ticket so that they know the trader's intention before approving and executing the order. In other words, overactive risk-management desks might reject certain orders intended to be a part of a spread due to misunderstood risk and margin consequences.

In conclusion, traders are doing themselves a disservice by ignoring the potential benefits of incorporating option trading into speculation. Although option trading can seem complex on the surface, you owe it to yourself to be familiar with all the tools available to you as a trader. After all, taking the "easy road" in life often fails to be beneficial in the end, and this may be no different.

chapter 2

Hedging Versus Speculating

As discussed in Chapter 1, "A Crash Course in Commodities," the futures markets were created to facilitate commodity transactions and give producers and end users the means to hedge price risk. In its simplest form, *hedging* is the basic practice of shifting price risk to a party that is willing to accept it, the spec-

> The futures markets were created for hedgers but are made possible by speculators.

ulator. I don't cover hedging concepts in detail simply because a large majority of market participants are speculators. Therefore, being aware of the overall concept and its implications in the marketplace should provide a sufficient background for beginning traders.

Commodity Hedgers

Now more than ever, businesses are looking to the futures markets for an efficient means of mitigating the price risk associated with their operations. However, the opportunity to hedge isn't without costs or even inconveniences. Nonetheless, the excessive volatility in commodity prices has created an environment in which the burden of hedging can easily be justified by the potential detriment of assuming the price risk outright.

Why Hedge?

Producers and users of commodities are constantly faced with price and production risk due to an unlimited number of unpredictable factors, including weather, currency exchange rates, and economic cycles. As volatility in the agricultural and energy markets has increased, so has the risk exposure to those involved in cash transactions of affected commodities. For instance, during the 2008 energy boom, many major airlines were facing bankruptcy at the direct hand of unhedged exposure to the price of crude oil, which rallied from $50 per barrel to $150 in a year and a half. On the contrary, Southwest Airlines notoriously hedged its price risk and managed to avoid the financial hardship that its competitors endured. Not only was it rewarded by the commodity markets, but its hedge of energy price risk made it possible for the company to keep fees and fares at a minimum to increase its market share.

Firms that choose not to hedge their risk are essentially speculators. Many insiders refer to them as "cash market speculators" because they behave as if they are predicting favorable price changes by not taking action to counteract the risk of unfavorable market moves. For instance, many unhedged farmers missed out on several hundred thousand dollars, or more, as the prices of corn and wheat plummeted from their all-time highs in the late 2000s. By choosing not to participate in a hedging strategy, they were indirectly betting on higher prices at which they could sell their crops. Unfortunately, in this case, many farmers lost their wagers.

> *Hedging is similar to buying insurance; it is nice to have when you need it, but costly if you don't.*

Nothing in Life Is Free

The concept of hedging is based on the same premise insurance companies use. Similar to the purchase of car insurance to protect yourself from the unknown damage that you or others might cause to your vehicle, commodity producers and users find solace in knowing that they have a security blanket when it comes to changes in price and market volatility. Likewise, just as the benefits of car insurance come with strings attached, such as premiums and deductibles, users and producers face expenditures to hedging price risk.

It is quite possible that the position taken with the intent to hedge price risk will become a burden. For example, if market prices move favorably (higher) for a producer subsequent to execution of price hedge, the potential cash markets gains are forfeited along with any transactional costs incurred. On the contrary, if a producer undergoes adverse (lower) market prices *while being hedged,* he will likely be thankful. To clarify, a commodity producer benefits from higher market prices because he can realize a larger profit when the goods are sold in the cash market. Therefore, producers might prefer to hedge their risk of price decline by selling futures contracts to avoid the detriment caused to the cash market sale. I go over this concept in detail in the next section, "Using Futures to Hedge Price Risk."

As you can see, the purpose of a price hedge isn't to profit, but to eliminate the price uncertainty that can contribute to potential operating losses. When price uncertainty is removed, it is easy for commodity consumers and producers to properly manage their business affairs to ensure that they are not working for free or even losing money in the process. Simply put, without price risk, it is possible to budget operations and make decisions accordingly.

Using Futures to Hedge Price Risk

The futures market is arguably the most efficient means of hedging commodity price risk. This is due to the trading of standardized contracts on organized and regulated exchanges, and thanks to the market liquidity brought by speculators. Additionally, prices in the futures and cash market tend to be highly correlated, meaning that they move up and down together. For that reason, investors exposed to price risk in the cash market have the capability to take on an equal and opposite position in the futures market to shift the price risk to speculators.

Businesses can choose three basic situations to mitigate price risk through hedging: storage, production, and future purchases. In each of these instances, the same course of action can be employed; take a position in the futures market opposite of that being held in the cash market to reduce price risk. Simply put, for those long the cash market (holding the physical commodity), price risk can be largely offset by selling an equal value in the futures markets. Any gains in the cash market will be nearly, completely, or slightly excessively offset by losses in the futures and vice versa. Again, it is important to note that a price hedge is an insurance and, therefore, entails an opportunity cost, in that any potential cash market gains are forfeited.

Grain elevators, or those in the business of storing commodities for future use or sale, run the risk of the value of their inventory declining while it is being stored. In other words, if between the time that the grain is acquired and then subsequently sold, the price of the commodity in question decreases significantly, a grain elevator might lose money on the transaction. Had the grain elevator operator in this situation opted to reduce price exposure by selling a futures contract when the commodity storage began, the profit on the futures position would have offset all or most of the loss in the cash market. This is because of the tendency of cash and futures prices to move up and down in tandem.

Similarly, a corn farmer faces a considerable amount of price risk throughout the planting, growing, and harvesting cycle. If a farmer plants his crop in the spring with the intention of harvesting in the fall and selling the proceeds of his efforts in October, a proper hedge could be created by selling a December corn futures contract for each 5,000 bushels of expected crop yield. Doing so eliminates the price uncertainty involved with the cash market transaction and allows the farmer to accurately budget his expenses to ensure an acceptable profit.

Example

Again, I don't feel as though it is critical that you be able to calculate profit and loss of a hedge, but you should understand the concept. Let's take a look at a simple example that gives you a broad-based view of the premise behind using the futures market for the price protection of cash market assets and transactions.

A soybean farmer completes the planting in his field in late April, with the intention of harvesting and selling the beans in late September. Based on planted acreage and projected conditions, he expects to yield 50,000 bushels of soybeans. At the time of planting, the farmer considers the market price for the grain to determine his budget and profit margin. Without a price hedge, he stands to benefit from any market price appreciation, but he might suffer considerable financial losses if the price of soybeans falls. Naturally, as a businessperson, it is a luxury to know that, on the day of reckoning, barring any unpredictable adversity, there will be a nearly guaranteed profit. The price of having such comfort is the opportunity cost of giving up any potential price appreciation in the commodity.

It is important to realize that, for a farmer expecting to yield 50,000 bushels of soybeans, each penny in price change affects the overall revenue of the sale by $500. In a market that can sometimes move $1.00 in a short period of time (equivalent to $50,000 in this example), you can see that the stakes are high. Although farmers might have an insider's look at the industry and might believe that they are capable of predicting price movements, they are in the business of producing the product, not speculating in its price. Therefore, in many cases, it is preferential for them to remove the uncertainty involved in their eventual cash market transaction by hedging their price risk.

The farmer in this example has the ability to shift his cash market price risk to futures market speculators by selling an equal position in futures that he holds in the cash commodity. Note that because the farmer owns the soybeans, he is said to be long the cash market and would look to sell futures contracts to hedge his price risk. In this example, the expected 50,000 yield is equivalent to 10 CBOT soybean futures contracts, with a standardized size of 5,000 bushels (50,000 ÷ 5,000 = 10).

At the time of planting and execution of the hedge, September soybean futures are trading at $12.95, and the cash price of the commodity in the farmer's area is $12.70. Before you get excited that the farmer is already locking in a gain of 25 cents, remember that commodities with distant maturity dates trade at a premium to closer-dated futures contracts and the cash market, due to the cost to carry, also known as the contango.

If the price of soybeans declines between the time the hedge is executed and the futures position is offset, and the cash crop is liquidated, the farmer will be profitable in his short futures position but worse off in terms of his cash market sale. For example, assuming that the farmer can sell ten September futures contracts (equal to a crop yield of 50,000 bushels) at $12.95, if the futures price is $12.20 and the cash market is $11.95 at the time the farmer unwinds his hedge and sells his crop, he will have completely offset his price risk. Ignoring transaction costs, the futures hedge will have been profitable by exactly 75 cents, while he would have given up exactly 75 cents on the price at which he can sell his crop in the cash market (see Table 2.1). By taking an equal and opposite position in the futures market as is held in the cash market, it is possible to reduce, or even eliminate, the risk of price fluctuation in the cash market.

Table 2.1 Futures Hedge

Timeline	Cash Market	Futures Market
At planting	$12.70 (long)	$12.95 (Short)
At crop sale	$11.95 (short)	12.20 (Long)
Results	Minus proceeds in cash market	Profit in futures transaction
	−75 cents × 50,000 = −$37,500	+75 cents × 50,000 × 10 = +$37,500

Keep in mind that this example leaves out consideration of the basis, which is the difference between the local cash market price and the futures price. Yes, various prices are available in the cash market, depending on the locale. In addition, farmers typically don't hedge their entire expected production because there are no certainties that they will yield what is anticipated in terms of crop size. Hedges aren't always this clean cut, but this should help you grasp the overall goal of removing price risk from business operations and shifting it to speculators who are ready and willing to accept the risk in hopes of large profits.

Long Hedge Versus Short Hedge

The previous example depicts a *short hedge* because the farmer sold futures to alleviate his cash market price risk. However, it is also possible to buy futures to place a hedge against adverse price movement. Doing so is referred to as a *long hedge*. You might wonder how farmers determine whether they buy or sell futures to protect themselves; taking a step back and looking at the big picture, the concept is relatively elementary. In a nutshell, commodity *users* are long hedgers, and commodity producers are short hedgers.

Speculators create the liquidity necessary for hedgers to shift price risk in hopes of earning a monetary reward.

Long hedgers, those who need to *buy futures* to shift price risk, plan to buy a commodity at some point in the future and are therefore *short the cash market* (because they need it but don't have it yet). Some examples of long hedgers are a homebuilder who needs to buy lumber, a meat packer who must purchase pork, a portfolio manager who must buy stock with future allocations, and a flour mill owner who must purchase wheat.

Short hedgers, those who must *sell futures* contracts to offset their price risk, plan to sell a commodity at some point in the future and are, therefore, *long the cash market* (because they own it and would eventually like to sell it). Some examples of short hedgers are a lumber mill owner who needs to sell lumber, a hog farmer who would like to sell his livestock, a wheat farmer who wants to sell his crop, and a pension fund manager who must sell holdings for retirement redemptions in the future.

Leverage gives speculators the potential for abnormal profits and gives hedgers the ability to reduce price risk with relatively little capital tied up.

It is certainly possible for the same firm to be long hedgers in one instance and short hedgers in another. For instance, a farmer wanting to reduce price exposure of his crop would sell futures to accomplish his goal (because he is long the cash market). The same farmer might be interested in hedging the price risk of gasoline if his expected consumption is material enough to justify the burden. This action requires a long hedge because fuel costs typically are incurred in the future. Simply put, he is short the cash market because he needs fuel to operate his machinery, but he has not yet purchased it or locked in the price. As you can see, the label of a long or short hedge is applied to the action itself instead of the parties making the transactions.

Commodity Speculators

If you are reading this book, you most likely fall into the speculator category. Speculators make up the lion's share of the daily trading volume in most commodity futures contracts. They enter the market in hopes of lavish profits—or, at least, hopes of coming out ahead. In return for the profit potential that comes with commodity trading, speculators must be willing to accept a great deal of risk of loss. This is in stark contrast to the intentions of the hedger who comes to the futures markets to manage risk.

Despite arguments against speculation and its place in the commodity markets that shape our economy—and, therefore, our lives—without it, producers and users of commodities would have a difficult time facilitating transactions. Thanks to speculators, there is always a buyer for every seller and a seller for every buyer. Without them and the liquidity they provide, hedgers would likely be forced to endure much larger bid/ask spreads and, in theory, price volatility. Consumers would also suffer in the absence of speculators simply because producers would be forced to pass on their increased costs to allow for favorable profit margins.

Unfortunately for us, speculators are not provided crystal balls. Instead, they are left to rely on technical, seasonal, and fundamental market analysis along with their best guess of what might occur next. Consequently, most speculators fail to make money in the markets, but don't forget that some flourish.

Unlike some hedgers, speculators have no intention of making or taking delivery of the traded commodity; they will most likely never see or touch the commodity they are trading. Additionally, some speculators, focused on technical analysis, might not have a clue of the harvest cycle, production figures, or supply-and-demand picture involved in the market they are trading. This is because many speculators believe it is possible to be accurate in price prediction without much knowledge of the commodity being traded. Conversely, by nature of their business, hedgers are extremely familiar with the underlying fundamentals of the markets in which they are shifting price risk. Simply being a speculator doesn't require knowledge or skill; the only requirement is the acceptance of risk.

Leverage in Hedging and Speculating

It is likely clear by now that speculators in the futures markets enjoy, or perhaps suffer from, a considerable amount of leverage. The source of the leverage stems from low margin requirements set by the exchange to buy or sell futures contracts relative to the actual value of the commodity that is traded. For instance, a Eurodollar trader experiences profits or losses based on the value of $1,000,000 of the underlying asset for as little as $1,000 deposited into a futures trading account. In essence, if the trader is correct in price assumptions, he stands to be wildly profitable if the market conditions support such success. However, inaccurate predictions can be just as painful as the winners are triumphant.

What might not be so obvious is the reality that the exchange provides hedgers even *more* leverage. Assuming that an account can prove to the FCM (Futures Commission Merchant) that the investor is a bona fide hedger, the trader is granted discounted margin requirements. A bona fide hedge is one in which the account holder actually owns the underlying commodity and takes a position in the futures market opposite of the cash market position. With that said, hedgers are subject to margin calls if they lose money on their futures position. Naturally, if this is the case, they are also gaining the difference in their cash market holdings. Nonetheless, the cash proceeds from the sale of the commodity don't come to realization until the sale takes place. In the meantime, the hedger needs to come up with the margin to continue holding the price hedge. As you can imagine, this isn't always an easy task. Thus, leverage can work for and against a hedger, just as it can a speculator.

chapter 3

The Organized Chaos of Open Outcry and the Advent of Electronic Trading

The futures markets are the birthplace of a method of communication between trading professionals known as *open outcry.* Open outcry is an exciting form of trade execution in which shouting and hand signals transfer the details of intent to buy or sell a commodity and in what quantity. You might also hear this method of execution referred to as *pit trading,* for reasons discussed later in the chapter.

The language of trading floor hand signals is referred to as Arb, short for arbitrage.

You have likely been exposed to open outcry via the media and in movies such as *Trading Places.* After all, the energy projected from the trading pits is thrilling and can make for good television. Those who have had the opportunity to experience the trading floor will tell you that it is even more electrifying in person.

In recent decades, technological advances have greatly altered the way open outcry business is conducted. For example, electronic quote boards, handheld computers, computerized order entry, and electronic fill reporting are now an integral part of the process. Each of these features has improved the efficiency and effectiveness of the practice.

Ironically, although improved technology has contributed to the efficiency of open outcry, it has also played a role in reducing the number of contracts traded in a pit environment. A large majority of futures trading now takes place in Over the Counter (OTC) markets in which execution is electronic and, thus, there is no physical trading location.

It is important to realize that the difference between open outcry and electronically traded futures and options is based on the location of execution, not the method of order placement. For example, it is possible to use a computerized order entry platform to submit an order that will be executed in the open outcry pit. Conversely, it is less common but possible that your broker might call his contacts on the trading floor to execute an options or futures order for a contract that is executed electronically.

Although most futures contracts are now traded electronically, some options, option spreads, and futures spreads are still executed in an open outcry environment. Nevertheless, even if open outcry trading was completely abolished, it is important to know where the industry has been and how commodity trading has evolved with technology.

Don't Judge a Book by Its Cover

The exchange floor might appear to be unorganized, but it is far from it. Everything is meticulously designed to reduce confusion and propel a proficient trading arena. For example, exchanges require that exchange members, employees, clerks, and brokerage firm employees wear color-coded jackets to assist in role identification. Also, electronic date and time boards often are displayed in the corners of the room, and in some cases, a letter or symbol is displayed so that traders can distinguish 15-minute time brackets. In essence, filled tickets are denoted with the appropriate mark to narrow the time of execution to a 15-minute span. Exchanges, traders, and brokers face excessive liabilities regarding timely and efficient order execution. Thus, the ability to pinpoint events chronologically is critical to resolving any issues as they occur; this makes an extremely organized operation a must.

The Pit

Open outcry trading takes place in what has been dubbed a trading *pit*. The name likely stems from the shape of the execution venue, which are typically tiered areas, similar to bleachers. Trading pits vary in size but are traditionally in the shape of an octagon. Within this tiered arena, you see traders violently shouting and signaling trades with their hands. As mentioned, this process is known as open outcry or pit trading. You might hear your broker say, "I will take this order to the floor." This simply means that she will be calling the exchange floor and placing your trade verbally with a broker to be executed in a trading pit rather than sending the order electronically via an electronic execution platform.

In general, each pit represents a different commodity; therefore, traders wouldn't be buying or selling corn and soybeans in the same marked area. Trading in a specific commodity takes place only within the designated pit on the trading floor. Although corn, wheat, and soybean trading pits are close to each other, trading them is exclusive to their designated pits. Also, futures and options transactions between exchange members are authorized only within the trading pits. Two members may not facilitate a trade between each other at the water cooler.

Traders within the pits have the luxury of keeping an eye on other futures contracts and stocks around the world. Electronic tickers and display boards line the walls of the exchanges and are viewable from the trading floor. Other electronic displays provide appropriate information such as spot market prices and exchange news. As you can imagine, the vibrant colors and timely information create an exhilarating and addicting atmosphere for traders.

To facilitate ease of execution, the corresponding option pits are typically adjacent to the futures trading pits. For example, S&P 500 *options* are executed in a pit close to the S&P 500 *futures* pit. With that said, most futures volume is now electronically executed; as a result, the arrangement is less imperative than it once was.

Surrounding the trading pits are workstations simply known as *desks* in which orders are received. Orders arrive at the desk by phone or by printed trade ticket from both individual retail traders and large institutions worldwide. After acknowledged by a desk clerk, the orders are carried to the pit by a *runner* or are flashed to the appropriate recipients via hand signals. Thanks to technological advances, in some cases, the orders are transmitted via handheld computers. From there, the order is said to be *working* as the executing floor broker attempts to fill it according to the type and price specified. In the case of a market order, it is filled immediately.

When the order is filled, a runner takes the information back to the order desk to be reported by either making a phone call to the appropriate party or, most likely, entering the fill price into a computer. Obviously, the process can be somewhat challenged in regard to time. Nonetheless, in most cases, this process has been considerably shortened by the use of handheld terminals that eliminate much of the human transmission of information.

As we discuss in Chapter 4, "Account Access, Trading Platforms, and Quote Vendors," due to the cumbersome nature of open outcry trade execution, subscribing to real-time data in these markets can be costly. On the other hand, we also find that the advent of electronic trade-matching environments has greatly reduced the burden of obtaining live market data for retail futures and options traders. In fact, paying for costly open outcry data is no longer necessary for most traders. Instead, traders have the opportunity to access live real-time quotes from the electronically executed versions of the contract at little or no cost. Some commodity brokers provide clients with real-time electronic market data for free within their trading platforms.

Electronically Traded Markets

Once again, domestic futures exchanges have spent the last decade gradually moving away from open outcry execution and into electronic trade matching. In recent years, the volume on electronically traded futures has surpassed that of open outcry on U.S. exchanges. Electronic trading volume continues to gain ground as traders enjoy the newfound transparency along with instant order execution and fill reporting made possible by advances in technology.

To reiterate, unlike its predecessor, open outcry, electronic trade matching technology gives traders from all over the world inexpensive access to accurate bid/ask pricing, real-time volume data, and price ladders that display the market depth. *Market depth* is simply the capability to see the number of orders working at the available bids and offers; you might also hear price ladders referred to as DOM panels (*DOM* stands for *depth of market*). Some traders feel as though visual access to the potential trading volume at each price and any possible overweighting on the buy or sell side can provide an edge in speculation. Perhaps this is true in some regard, but the reality is that, in the current environment, all traders have access to the same information. Consequently, it is imperative to realize that, as with technical analysis, there are no guarantees—only educated guesses.

Side by Side

Electronic trade-matching platforms began as a way to facilitate trading overnight in key contracts during times when the trading pits were closed but the world was still turning and events were unfolding that could impact the price of various commodities. The result was a venue in which traders could manage positions and risk in some of the most heavily traded commodity markets while they should be fast asleep. Eventually, the overnight electronic sessions extended into the day session and became the norm rather than the exception. Electronic trading is now offered nearly 24 hours per day in most futures markets.

Futures and options traders have the luxury of choosing their preferred method of execution. Most U.S. futures exchanges offer *side-by-side* trading in both futures and options. This simply means that traders have the choice to execute their orders either through the electronic trade-matching platform or through the open outcry pit. It is even possible to buy in one venue and sell in the other because both methods facilitate transactions on the same underlying futures contract; the only difference is the manner of execution.

Therefore, a trader can choose to buy NYMEX light sweet crude oil electronically in overnight trading following the announcement of an overseas event that is believed to be bullish for the energy complex. The same trader might discover that the impact of the event wasn't exactly what he had in mind and can opt to place an order to offset the position in the open outcry trading pit when the day session opens for trade, or he

Why choose? Many products have identical electronic and open outcry versions. This offers traders two choices of venue for one product.

can exit at any time via electronic execution. Keep in mind that although many futures contracts trade side by side, some contracts are available only electronically; included are the e-mini S&P 500, the e-mini NASDAQ, and the e-mini Dow (formerly known as the mini-size Dow). However, some contracts trade electronically overnight but trade only in an open outcry environment during the day. An example of this is the full-size S&P 500 futures and the original-size Dow.

It is safe to say that most futures traders prefer the efficiency of using electronic trade matching as their execution method; however, there are certain benefits of using an open outcry. Case in point: Retail brokers who have good relationships with floor brokers can place specialized or contingent orders that might not be accepted in the electronic market. An example of this is an MIT (Market if Touched) order or an FOK (Fill or Kill). Thus, the level of service and flexibility in terms of accepted order types can be increased. With that said, these types of privileges are afforded only to investors who provide enough business to the retail and floor brokers. After all, they make their living through commission, and like you and me, they don't work for free.

Electronic trade matching is believed to have leveled the playing field for market participants in that it gives retail traders admission to the same information, market access, and fill quality that anybody else might have. Specifically, in the case of the e-mini S&P and a handful of other markets, there are no market makers. In theory, this provides an arena in which traders of all sizes are treated equally in terms of fills; this is true whether they are trading 1 or 100 contracts at a time.

The markets don't sleep, and neither will your positions.

Also, there are no membership requirements to trading electronically executed futures and options. Anybody who has an account with a futures brokerage firm is free to submit orders directly to the exchange for execution. On the contrary, having an open and funded trading account doesn't give you the authority to enter the exchange, walk into the pit, and execute trades in the same environment that a floor trader can. Instead, you would need to place an order with a broker or through a brokerage firm's trading platform to execute a trade in the open outcry arena.

Electronic Symbols

Contracts that trade side by side or trade electronically in an overnight session and on the trading floor during the day must have different symbols to distinguish them from each other. For example, the symbol for corn futures executed on the trading floor is C, but the electronically traded version of the contract is ZC. Corn is a CBOT division product, and in most cases, the symbol for the electronic version of CBOT contracts begins with a Z. Likewise, electronic COMEX products are denoted by an E before the traditional open outcry symbol. To illustrate, although the symbol for gold traded in the open outcry is GC, the symbol for the electronically executed contract is EGC.

Because most futures contracts are traded electronically, traders have grown accustomed to the electronic symbols and have nearly forgotten about their open outcry counterpart. If you ask a new trader the symbol for any given futures market, she'll likely give you the electronic version.

Note that some brokerage firms or trading platforms offer access to only electronic execution. Therefore, they often use the original open outcry symbol for order entry and quote monitoring. Other brokerages and platforms offer both open outcry and electronic execution for certain markets, but not all of them do. For example, it is possible that a trading platform would use GC as the only offered gold product, and orders placed on this contract would likely be directed to electronic execution, despite the fact that the symbol is that of the original open outcry execution. It is a good idea to confirm with your broker where the trade will be routed for various trading symbols.

Knowing which contracts are traded in which venue and learning the appropriate symbols can be overwhelming for beginning traders, but not being familiar with these market characteristics can also be costly. Fully understanding which alternatives are available to you in terms of method and timing of execution has a profound impact on the effectiveness of your orders. This is especially true when it comes to placing stop-loss orders.

For example, if you go long January soybeans through open outcry and place your sell stop-loss order using the open outcry symbol as well, the stop order will be defending your position only during the day session. You are subject to gains and losses in the electronic overnight trading session without the benefit of a stop-loss order. Even worse, if the open outcry session opens below your stop price, you will be liquidated at the market, and that price might be well below the price of your original stop-loss order. That said, some traders prefer their stop-loss orders to not work during the overnight session. The argument for this is that light trading volume during the night session can sometimes result in exaggerated price moves and possibly unnecessarily elected stop orders. However, I believe that the overnight volume in many of the futures markets has picked up to a level at which I recommend that any traders who want to use stop-loss orders ensure that they are working 24 hours per day, which requires traders place stop orders in the electronic market.

Don't be fooled into assuming that because you are trading the open outcry contract, your position isn't gaining or losing value throughout the night session. If you go long corn using the pit for execution and the market trades down ten cents in the electronic overnight session, chances are, when the day session opens, your position will be losing about ten cents in value based on the previous pit session close. Remember, money never sleeps. The futures markets trade virtually around the clock, and your positions will be changing value accordingly.

Also, it is important that you understand the differences between the electronic and open outcry versions of each contract, to ensure that you can communicate effectively with your broker. A good broker assumes that you prefer electronic execution for futures because of fill efficiency and determines where the best quality execution for option trades is likely, but it is never a good idea to rely on someone else to keep you out of trouble. You are responsible for your own actions and orders, regardless of whether you have properly prepared yourself.

chapter 4

Account Access, Trading Platforms, and Quote Vendors

The commodity markets are volatile and often unforgiving. Thus, it is imperative that traders receive accurate information regarding their trading accounts and ample market access. After all, I believe that the largest component to trading success is psychological, and it is hard to be calm, cool, and collected if you are essentially blind when it comes to market price, account positions, and balances.

With that said, the phrase "ample market access" can have wildly different meanings among various traders. For instance, a professional trader likely needs real-time quotes and charts, point-and-click trading capabilities, and immediate access to current account balances. On the contrary, average retail traders with day jobs might well be happy with intraday access to their account information, slightly delayed quotes, and a broker available to place trades for them.

You might be asking yourself why anyone would opt to work with delayed information. The answer is, quite simply, cost or convenience. Unlike the equity markets, in which real-time quotes and charts are readily available, real-time commodity quotes can be accessed only through a live trading account or from a quote vendor that sells futures exchange data. In this chapter, we discuss the possible costs related to such information. In the past, these costs were surprisingly high, but with the advent of electronic trade execution, this information is now virtually free to any active account holder.

Additionally, we take a detailed look at the process involved in gaining access to real-time futures and options quotes and the necessity of doing so. From there, we discuss the different types of trading platforms, their capabilities, and their potential costs.

Commodity Quotes Can Be Costly, But They Don't Have to Be

Although electronic execution has made it possible for exchanges to extend free or cheap market data, the software used to display it and eventually trade it might not be as affordable. For newcomers, the amount of money that can be spent subscribing to high-end charting applications and order entry software can be shocking. Fortunately, for retail futures and option traders, the growing popularity and availability of electronically traded futures contracts has greatly increased the capabilities of many of the free trading platforms brokerage firms offer. Likewise, the upgraded software packages are now more reasonably priced simply because the burden of paying for data has been lifted in some circumstances. Before electronic trading, traders looking for fancy setups were forced to pay for both software and market data separately; this can quickly add up to hundreds of dollars per month.

Trading is a business. Sometimes it takes money to make money. You can't put a price on information.

Open Outcry Quote Reporting and Access

Accessing live price data in open outcry contracts, as opposed to data in electronically executed contracts, can be costly, but in today's environment, this is a relatively obsolete practice anyway. The expense stems from the method in which pit-traded futures and options contracts are executed, the way price data is collected, and the corresponding challenges in distributing timely information.

Along with traders, open outcry pits have market reporters, trained professionals responsible for reporting price changes in their assigned markets. Through a walkie-talkie or a PDA-type handheld console, market reporters communicate changes in price. After price changes are entered into a computer terminal, either through the handheld device of the market reporter or by someone receiving the information verbally, they are transmitted to quote boards within the exchange and to quotation systems used by brokers and traders around the world. Although the process seems tedious, it is surprisingly quick and effective. Open outcry trading volume is dying, along with this method of quote reporting.

As you can see, the exchanges go to great lengths to transmit accurate pit pricing data. Nevertheless, they are compensated well for their efforts. Futures exchanges charge a monthly data fee of approximately $30 to $50 for access to their real-time open outcry quote feed. The fee must be paid to *each* exchange—or, more accurately—each division of the CME Group, in which the subscriber would like real-time data for nonelectronically traded markets. As you can imagine, the costs can be extensive for a trader seeking timely open outcry data on NYMEX contracts as well as CBOT and CME products. In my opinion, paying for open outcry data is a poor allocation of resources for most traders.

Understanding Option Quotes

Option market liquidity is far less than that of the underlying futures contracts. The typical order flow of each individual option can be spotty, at best, compared to the constant flow of incoming trades seen in most futures markets. Accordingly, video monitors in many option pits keep traders informed of

Traders shouldn't assume that the last trade of an option contract is its current value.

the current market quote or bid/ask spread instead of the last trade. Similarly, electronic trading platforms provided to traders, or option quoting software, prominently display the spread between the current bid and ask prices, along with the last trade. This is important because it is relatively common for an option with a specific strike price in a particular commodity to go several hours without being traded. If this is the case, the last traded price might not be indicative of the current value.

Because the option markets don't have as many participants as most futures contracts, the bid/ask quote typically represents the price a market maker is willing to execute rather than the working orders of other retail traders similar to yourself. Option market makers literally "make a market" by offering to take the other side of a retail transaction at the quoted price. This is absolutely necessary to create a viable option trading arena. On the contrary, most liquid futures contracts experience trading action nearly constantly around the clock, so market makers are not needed in such an environment. Without market makers in the option markets, we would be forced to rely on the orders of other traders to provide price discovery and the ability to execute. However, take it from me that, in such a scenario, option trading would be extremely inefficient and likely an impossible money pit for anybody who dared to venture in.

Nearly 24-hour electronic trading in most futures markets has also led to 24-hour option markets. Nonetheless, the market being open doesn't guarantee that you will be able to trade options at prices you will be happy with. Each market has different liquidity and execution quality in overnight trade. For instance, the Treasury options have great market makers with fairly priced spreads. In such a market, traders are likely comfortable executing trades around the clock, although there will still be far better fill quality during the official day session. Some of the grain options—namely corn and soybeans—often have competitive market makers throughout the night. Although it is best to try to execute during the day session, in some instances, it makes sense to place trades before the morning open.

On the other hand, some of the option markets traded in New York, such as gold and crude oil, rarely have market makers available during off hours. Accordingly, pulling up a quote on a particular option in either market during the night session would likely reveal a shockingly wide bid/ask spread, or perhaps no spread at all. These markets should not be traded outside the official day session, despite the fact that they are technically "open." By the way, the unmanageable quotes seen during the night session in gold and crude oil are what most option markets might look like without market makers—even during the day session.

For example, if a December corn $6.00 call option last traded three hours ago at 25 cents and corn futures have since rallied 20 cents, the value of the $6.00 call option would likely be much higher. A buyer shouldn't expect to purchase the option at 25 cents because that price doesn't reflect the recent 20 cent rally that would have increased the value of the $6.00 call.

With so many option contracts available (various strike prices and months), it would be nearly impossible for traders and brokers to keep tabs on each of them. Thus, access to live bid/ask spreads is imperative; ironically, knowing the last trade is rather useless. Even if you were provided a time stamp along with the last trade price, determining an estimated current fair value would take some time. With that said, despite having live bid and ask access, during fast-moving futures markets, determining the true market value of a particular option can sometimes be extremely difficult. This scenario occurs as the spread between the bid and the ask balloon, leading to uncertain values and, thus, wide price ranges in each option. Adding to the potential chaos is the tendency for a great influx of option orders during or after a large move in the futures price.

Those attempting to trade electronic options in the e-mini S&P 500 or Treasury futures on May 6, 2010, the now infamous Flash Crash, can testify to this. On this day, seeing options quoted with thousands of dollars between the bid and the ask was not uncommon. For instance, e-mini S&P options were being quoted as 15.00 bid, at 45.00. Each point in the e-mini equates to $50, so traders could have sold this option for $750 ($50 × 15.00) or bought it for $2,250 ($50 × 45.00). Likewise, some Treasury options were quoted 1'15 bid at 3'20. The math is complicated, so I spare the details here, but this equates to a difference of more than $2,000 between the price a trader could buy at and the price he could sell at. To put this into perspective, a more typical spread is less than $50. As this example portrays, despite conventional wisdom, highly chaotic pricing is possible *even* in an electronic trading environment.

Dramatic option price changes are possible, or even likely, if a period of low volume and volatility is followed by a sudden burst of sizable volume and high volatility. In such a case, the quote monitors are no match for the disarray in option pricing.

A good example of this phenomenon in open outcry trading was the precious metals "crash" in April 2006. At this time, electronic options were newly available, but open outcry execution was still preferable and far more liquid. In a matter of minutes, silver and gold violently sold off, causing astronomical losses for long futures traders, and even more so for option traders who couldn't "see" the value of their holdings and, in some cases, were forced to blindly enter market orders to liquidate. Based on my observations, the execution prices of metals options on that particular day were less than agreeable by most but difficult to argue, given the circumstances.

Specifically, traders covering short puts in the midst of the pandemonium might have received fill prices in excess of $2,000 worse than they were expecting, based on estimated theoretical values. The price of silver dropped $2 ($10,000 per futures contract) that day, so losses due to actual changes in market price combined with excessive "slippage" as a result of frenzied conditions led to large losses for many. Such an event is rare, but traders should be aware of the fierce potential of market behavior at all times.

It is important to realize that some option markets see higher trading volume than others. Likewise, within option markets, some months and strike prices have more liquidity. In general, options with strike prices that are closer-to-the-money will have more players, and months with less time to expiration will also attract more trading interest.

The quality of the quotes available in any particular option market or strike price is highly dependent on trading volume. This is true even for traders who are paying for open outcry data. Bluntly, if you are paying for real-time pit quotes but no quotes (trades) are reported and no one is willing to trade the option at that time, you still will be left with uncertainty regarding option pricing. Many brokers, on the other hand, have direct access to the floors where they can, under normal circumstances, get accurate option values from market makers even if there is otherwise no "market" at all. However, if the market maker is truly "making a market" just for you, the prices will likely be unattractive.

My intention isn't to deter you from trading options; in fact, I prefer option trading over futures in many cases. Nonetheless, I do feel as though it is my responsibility to warn you of option market characteristics so that you are better prepared and know what to expect in terms of pricing and execution. Keep in mind that I used dramatic examples of inefficient option pricing in this section, but day-to-day trading in "normal" circumstances provides commodity option traders with liquid, viable, and attractive opportunities for speculation.

Electronic Quote Transmission

To recap, unlike the open outcry quote reporting that is a cumbersome process and, thus, expensive for end users to access, real-time quotes on electronically executed futures contracts are easy to compile and distribute. As a result, retail traders have access to relatively affordable and accurate streaming futures quotes. The new availability of quotes and charts for retail traders has likely been a major catalyst for larger volumes on the major futures exchanges.

Most brokerage firms now also offer trading platforms that provide real-time bid/ask spreads on electronically traded options. A good brokerage firm will even provide clients access to live option chains. If you are unfamiliar with option chains, they are simply grids that include all the listed options available for any given underlying contract with the corresponding price and volume data.

In recent years, exchanges and programmers have worked together to make it possible for traders to execute option spreads via electronic means, to avoid the hassles of the open outcry pit execution. Although it is a work in progress, it is possible to execute some strategies such as the iron condor, vertical spreads, and ratio spreads through the electronic option market.

Subscribing to Quotes

Once again, to gain access to real-time quotes and charts, a trader must either subscribe to a quote vending service or utilize a live trading platform that offers a data feed from a broker. Alternatively, it is also possible to subscribe to data feeds from quote vendors to be run through a trading platform such as Ninja-Trader. Some traders do this because they believe the vendor can provide more accurate, or perhaps faster, data than they would otherwise have access to, or they prefer a dataless platform. Such vendors often charge on a per-trade basis, ranging from 10 cents to 50 cents; others charge a flat monthly fee. Examples of fee-based vendors are Zen-Fire and TT; monthly data providers include Barchart.com and Kinetick.

In the case of a quote subscription (outside a trading platform), the trader must pay for the exchange fees in addition to the quote vendor's monthly software fee. For example, a quote vendor might charge $50 per month simply for access to its quote and chart software. From there, the trader would need to pay the exchange fees, plus any additional charges levied by the vendor. If a trader opts to subscribe to open outcry or option data for both the CME and the CBOT divisions of the CME Group, the ICE, and NYMEX, the tab could easily run more than $250 per month—and, in most instances, costs would be much higher. Keep in mind that this cost does not include trade execution or any other relative fees your brokerage firm charges.

As I have highlighted, most exchanges provide electronic futures data to *traders* on a complimentary basis, with the idea that doing so provides revenue in the form of exchange fees charged on every transaction. They have incentive to do so because volume-based exchange fees can dramatically exceed the flat monthly data feed subscription for many active traders. Not surprisingly, exchange data feed fees are typically waived *only* within trading platforms or quote boards that can double as a trading platform. This shift in data distribution by exchanges has led services such as eSignal, which previously offered software to display, organize, and chart data, to move into trade execution. Most brokerage firms have arranged to allow clients to access and trade accounts through eSignal. In other words, what was once just a quote board is now doubling as a trading platform. You've probably guessed that using eSignal as a trading platform results in some of the electronic data fees being waived. Another popular quote and chart application is Barchart.

> "Those who cannot remember the past are condemned to repeat it."
> —George Santayana

Believe it or not, even though all quote vendors offer essentially the same information as a free live trading platform, there can be significant differences in each. If you feel it is worth footing the bill for such a service, I encourage you to run demos on multiple platforms and quote software vendors to determine which is most convenient and useful to you.

Quote providers and most trading platforms enable customization in terms of markets covered, news services such as Dow Jones or Reuters, and many other options, all of which could incur additional charges. As you can imagine, the bill can add up quickly. I recommend starting with a minimal package and upgrading as you discover what you lack.

Charting

For many position traders, access to a premium trading application simply isn't worth the subscription costs or hassles. However, the charting capabilities offered within some free applications can be subpar when it comes to customizing a chart, and this seems to be a bigger burden than not having real-time data. The majority of free charting services via the Internet or a brokerage firm trading platform often fail to provide traders with extensive drawing capabilities such as a Fibonacci Ruler, Gann Fans, trend lines, and so forth. Nonetheless, a handful of free trading platforms offer very capable charting, and others provide high-end charting features to an otherwise challenged package for an incremental monthly fee.

I am not a fan of Gann theory, but plenty of traders consider the tool to be a necessity for proper chart analysis. Accordingly, it might be worth the effort or price tag to seek out access to software that provides the luxury of deluxe charting capabilities such as the Gann Fan. Trading platform offerings, software competence, and price change frequently, but I've worked hard to give my brokerage clients access to nearly all available futures trading platforms. You will find a list with price and function specifications at www.DeCarleyTrading.com.

On the other hand, position traders might find that they can reduce unnecessary costs in accessing premium charts and analytics by opting for an end-of-the-day data subscription package. Obviously, day traders won't find much use for it, but if you base your decisions on extensive chart work conducted at the end of the day, this could be a viable alternative. I know of some end-of-day charting services, such as NinjaTrader, that offer free and unlimited access to top-of-the-line technical analysis tools. (See www.DeCarleyTrading.com for a free trial offer.)

Don't trip over dollars chasing pennies; if your trading strategy requires an upgraded platform, it is worth the money.

Free Trading Platforms and Market Access

Brokerage firms are in the business of trade execution. Therefore, it is in their best interest to ensure that clients have a convenient and reliable means of placing orders on behalf of their trading accounts. For many traders, this simply means having someone at the other end of a telephone line, email address, or text message to execute a trade; others rely on computerized trading platforms. The method of trade placement that works best for you depends on your trading style and your personality.

Most brokerage firms offer a complimentary order entry platform, and they typically have several upgraded options, most of which involve a monthly fee, a transaction fee, or both.

Free platforms characteristically offer marked-to-market data on open positions and orders, but as mentioned, they might or might not have free real-time streaming quotes and adequate charts. Therefore, traders must be well aware of the platform offerings and their needs before making a decision on a brokerage firm or means of order entry.

Thanks to technology and competition, most retail commodity traders, whether futures or options, find that their needs are sufficiently met with their brokers' free trading platforms. Aside from some of the charting challenges discussed, most free platforms are sufficient in delivering timely price data and efficient trade execution. These are critical when dealing with leveraged contracts that stand to create large profits and losses in a short period of time.

Paid Trading Platforms

Paid platforms give traders access to streaming real-time quotes with deluxe charting and point-and-click order entry capabilities. Although many of the free platforms provide similar functions, paid platforms advertise low-latency execution, more convenient order entry features, more capable user-friendly charting, the capability to automate strategies, and the potential to possibly even develop your own technical indicators.

For instance, these types of platforms enable traders to enter multiple entry prices when trading more than one contract; once filled, they can instruct the platform to place multiple exit orders at various prices and even trail stop-loss orders higher to protect open profits. Traders might also program the platform to enter a trade if particular events occur, such as specific prices being hit or technical oscillators behaving in a certain way.

> "You must automate, emigrate, or evaporate."
> —James A. Baker, GE

These types of orders are known as contingency orders because they are contingent on a specific event occurring. With that in mind, traders should be aware of whether such orders are held server-side or on the trader's computer. We discuss OCO orders in detail in Chapter 7, "Order Types and How to Use Them," but for now, all you need to know is that contingent orders rely on software to execute or cancel an order, based on another event occurring. Therefore, if you will be utilizing them, it is a good idea to choose a platform/broker that is capable of holding the accompanying execution instructions on an offsite server, not on your computer. This is because, in a server-side arrangement, your orders will still be working and executed even if your personal computer loses connection or crashes.

Several premium trading platforms are available to futures and options traders, but not all platforms are compatible with all brokerage firms. If you have your heart set on a particular platform, I recommend confirming that your prospective brokerage firm offers it before you open an account. On the contrary, if you believe that you have found the perfect brokerage firm for you but it doesn't offer a particular trading platform, it likely still can meet your platform needs because many of the popular trading platforms are similar in nature. Remember, commodity brokers make money only if you trade. Therefore, they do everything within their power to ensure that doing business with them is as easy as possible.

Also don't let the word *paid* discourage you; this is no time to pinch pennies. If an upgraded platform has any positive impact on your trading results, it will cover the cost of the application, plus some. In fact, in recent years, the costs associated with platform upgrades have come down considerably; you might be pleasantly surprised. In many cases, I recommend using an upgraded platform or choosing a brokerage that offers a nicely equipped free platform. Even if you place orders through a broker, a capable-free platform is helpful to gain access to real-time quotes and charts without the hefty exchange fees and quote vendor fees that you could otherwise face. Accordingly, I strive to ensure that all of my clients have access to a fully equipped free trading platform, along with multiple affordable upgrade options.

Per-Side Transaction Costs Versus a Flat Monthly Fee

Many upgraded platforms charge a usage fee on a per-side basis. This simply means that a set fee is charged to the trading account each time a trade is executed. I have witnessed fees ranging from as high as $1.50 per side to as low as 15 cents per side. More often than not, the brokerage firm subsidizes platform costs that fall on the lower end of the spectrum.

Active traders should avoid platforms that are charged on a volume basis.

Remember that a trade consists of two sides, referred to as a round-turn; therefore, a trader being charged a per-side platform fee is charged when entering the market and again when exiting.

I have found that the functionality difference between a platform charging a fee on the high end of the price range relative to one on the low end is somewhat minimal. The higher-priced platforms tend to offer automated system trading and development to justify higher fees. Yet others charge higher transaction fees and claim to offer faster server communication with the exchange. For those who aren't developing and implementing proprietary systems, or scalping small intraday price moves, less costly platforms are often recommended.

Keep in mind that traders who intend to do a considerable amount of volume will likely be better off choosing a trading platform that offers flat monthly fees instead of transaction-based fees. On the other hand, lower-volume traders have the comfort of knowing that they will pay only for what they use. Fifteen cents per side doesn't seem like a lot of money, but it equates to 30 cents per round-turn and $300 for those trading 1,000 round-turns per month. Some flat monthly subscription-based platforms fall into this price range, but most of them go for far less, with chart capabilities and order entry features to meet the needs of most traders.

Conversely, those looking for advanced platform features for high-volume trading are likely better off choosing a platform that levies a flat monthly fee. Doing so helps prevent traders from overpaying for market access. A typical monthly fee ranges anywhere from $50 to $350 per month.

Keep in mind that platform vendors might have pricing structures that incorporate both a monthly fee and a transaction fee. Before choosing one of these platforms, do your research to ensure that the costs will support your overall goal of making money instead of acting as an obstacle to your success.

Auto Approval Versus Manual Approval

A commonly overlooked function of a firm's trading platform is its capability to approve or reject entered orders based on margin requirements and account funding. Some firms and some platforms approve and reject incoming orders on an automatic basis, whereas others require human intervention. In other words, some platforms deem you able to trade a market according to account funding and the appropriate margin requirement, whereas others rely on a brokerage staff member for the credit approval process.

Each approach has obvious advantages and disadvantages, and you need to understand their possible implications on your trading.

To my knowledge, all the premium platforms and the majority of the free platforms available to futures traders involve automatic approval or denial of placed orders. By "premium," I simply mean those other than the free platform the Futures Commission Merchant (FCM) provides. Nevertheless, these trading options might reveal that order approval isn't automatic at all.

Intraday trading, often referred to simply as day trading, is the practice of entering and exiting positions within a single trading session. Day traders tend to avoid having open positions at the close of trade and, therefore, are never levied the overnight margin rate established by the exchange. Within an auto approval environment, it is possible for brokerage firms to set and freely adjust *intraday* margins levied by the platform. In Chapter 10, "Coping with Margin Calls," I discuss the key differences between a margin charged within a trading session and a margin charged when a position is held into the close of trade.

In the meantime, you need to understand that platforms with auto approval capabilities allow for instant credit approval and execution along with discounted day trading margins. This is in contrast to a platform that involves manual approval, which can involve a considerable amount of time between order entry and authorization. Obviously, this can have a significant impact on the speed and efficiency of the order placement and execution process.

Some firms still rely on human order approval in certain scenarios, but most often for option traders. Each brokerage firm varies widely in policy, and you must be aware of the circumstances. Human intervention offers definite benefits when it comes to credit approval. For example, a human is capable of assessing the overall risk of the account by assessing open positions before accepting or rejecting an order.

An automated process cannot "think" and will often erroneously reject orders in accounts that are trading option strategies or futures spreads. For example, if a trader wants to buy July corn and sell September corn, an automatic credit approval system might reject the order because it is assuming margin on both sides of the trade. In reality, a spread between two corn futures is exchange recognized and is provided discounted margin. Similarly, an account that lacks the required margin by a few

> "Knowing others is intelligence; knowing yourself is true wisdom. Mastering others is strength; mastering yourself is true power."
> —Lau Tzu

dollars would experience order rejections with an automatic system due to a mere technicality. With human intervention, such a scenario is recognized and incorporated into the order approval process. However, this luxury comes with the opportunity cost of time.

Multiple Order-Entry Methods

Electronic order-entry platforms come in all shapes, sizes, and abilities. Most of them accept order entry in more than one way. For instance, many platforms offer traders access to a price ladder, often called a price DOM (depth of market), in which orders can be placed with a single click. A DOM panel displays the prices and quantities of other traders' orders alongside a progression of prices. Traders simply click their mouse on either the buy side or the sell side of the ladder to enter an order. In such an arrangement, stop and limit orders are displayed in the corresponding columns and can be modified by simply dragging them higher or lower to change the price.

Similarly, most premium platforms—and even some free platforms—offer traders the opportunity to enter orders directly from a price chart. This enables traders to simultaneously chart price and enter orders. As with a DOM, those trading from a price chart can simply drag orders higher or lower to change price without the burden of typing numbers or even scrolling.

Traders who are uncomfortable with quick-click trading should look for a platform that allows them to enter orders in a more cumbersome but perhaps less error-prone manner. Most platforms have such a capability in the form of an order ticket screen with drop-down menus.

Popular Premium Trading Platforms

The "free-to-use" trading platforms brokerage firms provide clients are often developed in-house and, therefore, are available only at the particular firm offering it. However, premium platforms are developed by third parties whose sole purpose is to generate revenue via platform subscriptions, sales, and fees. Accordingly, these third-party vendors do not benefit from commission charged, or any other fees you might pay to your brokerage firm.

Some of the most popular "pay-to-use" trading platforms are QST (Quick Screen Trading), NinjaTrader, Cunningham Trading System's T4, and Rithmic's R-Trader. Each of these platforms has significant capabilities with various strengths; consequently, I've arranged to offer all of them to my brokerage clients, along with several "free" platforms. A brief description cannot do any of these platforms justice, but here's a fleeting synopsis.

- **QST:** In my opinion, this is the best all-around trading platform available to those trading both futures and options. QST offers a robust charting package with nearly unlimited choices of indicators, drawing tools, and the capability to create your own indicators. It also enables traders to trade directly from a price chart, enter option orders from an advanced option chain, and provides some option analytics. The only potential downside to using this platform might be the cost. At the time of this writing, the base package started at $50 per month, plus 50 cents per trade, but for those looking for the Cadillac version, the price goes up to $300 per month.

- **NinjaTrader:** This platform does not offer option trading, but it does offer futures traders an extremely capable means of charting and order entry at a reasonable cost. Users enjoy multiple methods of quick order entry, convenient strategy placement in which traders can instruct the platform to automatically enter, and exit positions based on predetermined parameters. In addition, several automated strategy vendors have programmed systems that can be purchased and easily executed via NinjaTrader. NinjaTrader can be purchased outright or can be leased for as little as $60 per month for live trading, but traders must arrange for a data feed. Data can be purchased on a monthly or per-trade basis. A good broker will be able to point you in the right direction based on your needs. Keep in mind that using NinjaTrader for end-of-day charting (no intraday data) is free.

- **Cunningham's T4:** The T4 is a no-nonsense platform for both options and futures traders. It excels in its capability to execute option and futures spread orders and its extremely quick futures order DOM. Some might consider the fact that it offers only one method of order entry, the DOM panel, a negative. Perhaps the most compelling argument for using this platform is ease of account access. The T4 offers traders three ways to log into their trading account to monitor positions or enter new orders: via the traditional desktop version (downloaded software), through a web browser quickly accessible from any computer with Internet without the hassles of downloading a program application, or on a mobile smartphone. The cost of the T4 varies by package, but traders can access the base version (which would likely meet the needs of most traders) for a cost of 50 cents per trade, with a $25 monthly minimum.

- **Rithmic's R-Trader:** The highlight of this platform is its simplicity without sacrificing function. It offers a clean user interface with friendly controls. Traders can execute both options and futures with this platform but must upgrade to the pro version to access charting. However, even with the cost of integrated charts at $20 per month, this platform is affordable, at 50 cents per trade.

Order Desk ("The Desk")

Most brokerage firms offer traders a 24-hour live order desk in which clients are free to phone in their orders and verbally place them with a desk clerk in the absence of their full-service broker or in the case of a malfunctioning trading platform. Depending on the brokerage firm you deal with, such a service might have additional fees. I've found that the days of free order desks are largely gone.

Because of dramatic reductions in the average commission rate charged to clients for trade execution, brokerage firms can no longer afford to offer the luxury of a complimentary order desk. As a result, most firms charge clients about $2 per contract for orders called into a trade desk; this fee does not apply to orders called into a full-service broker. Be sure you know exactly what you will be charged to use an order desk for trade placement. Some deep discount brokers charge outrageous fees to use this service.

An order desk is provided as a courtesy to the client. For self-directed online traders, the desk is available in case complications arise, such as platform issues, Internet or power outage, or any other events that would prevent clients from entering the trade on their own into an online trading environment. However, the trade desk is not intended to be used as a free source for market quotes or a regular method of order entry for accounts paying deeply discounted commission. In fact, if you open a trading account at a discounted commission and subsequently use the order desk for a majority of your trading execution, you will likely find the firm looking to adjust your commission rate higher or reduce your privileges.

An order desk is just that; don't expect to call an order desk and get free quotes or advice on a regular basis. That's what your broker is for.

This often upsets beginning traders, but you need to realize that providing an order desk is a costly venture for a brokerage firm because the risk of order placement error shifts from the client to the brokerage firm. Therefore, the FCM accepting such risk must be compensated to justify the service. Those expecting to pay the bare minimum and receive top-notch service are unrealistic. To be fair to the broker, discount online traders should make it a point to conduct their business via online trading platforms unless circumstances prevent it.

Many brokerage firms that cater to the deep discount traders offer limited access to a live trading desk or even live customer support. Most of their business is conducted via Internet outlets such as email. Many have also been known to charge $25 per contract or more for phone access to an order desk and other support features. If you opt for one of these types of brokerage firms, you need to be confident in your market knowledge and ability to execute properly because you probably won't have anyone to lean on when times get rough.

On the contrary, clients paying full-service or broker-assisted commission rates are welcome to place trades with their brokers or the order desk at their discretion. After all, they pay for the luxury of doing so. With that said, full-service and broker-assisted clients should opt to use the desk only in their broker's absence or during his out-of-office hours.

Is It Worth Paying Platform Fees or Subscribing to Quotes?

Each trader has different needs and desires; therefore, there isn't a simple answer to this question. The decision should be made after considering factors such as the chosen trading strategy, psychological factors, and informational needs.

To illustrate, a long option position trader might not consider real-time intraday data as a necessity, whereas a day-trading scalper likely couldn't function without it. Likewise, a trader strictly trading futures probably wouldn't find any value in subscribing to open outcry option quote data or using a front-end platform that offers such at an increased rate.

Another commonly overlooked aspect of choosing whether to use an upgraded platform or subscribe to a quote vendor is the mental turmoil that live market access might cause. Some traders simply aren't capable of remaining objective and patient, with the excitement of the markets flashing in front of their eyes. Some are better off doing their research, placing their orders, and walking away from what might happen next. Access to real-time data often prevents traders from accepting their fate and could lead to panicked decision making as they watch each price tick pass.

If you don't know yourself, the markets will be an expensive way to learn.

In many cases, I recommend that traders use an affordable platform upgrade if the free platforms provided by their brokerage firm lack in terms of real-time quotes. This is because using a trading platform as a means of market data can be much more affordable than subscribing via a quote vendor, simply because the CME Group often waives monthly data fees for electronic products in most trading platforms. The exchange had incentive to do this due to the assumption that the data will promote trading and ultimately increase the exchange revenue collected via transaction fees. Likewise, having access to a superior charting application might be important to technical traders; using an upgraded platform is an economical way to gain access to such functionality.

Don't forget, with per-side charged platforms, market data can be costly for high-volume traders, and neither the brokerage firm nor the trading platform vendor will allow you to have access to a platform if it is not regularly used. Those trying to "beat the system" might be disappointed; most per-side-based platform fees are charged regardless of the actual platform used. Thus, if you place a trade with your broker who is using an alternative platform, it is assumed that you are using the upgraded platform for market data and will be charged accordingly.

Again, when it comes to gaining access to the proper market information to fit your needs, being "cheap" isn't a good idea. You should be willing to open your pocketbook if it is necessary for your situation. On the flip side, don't be foolish; if you can get away with a Civic, there's no need to buy the Cadillac.

chapter 5

Choosing a Brokerage Firm

Deciding on a brokerage firm is often taken lightly, but I argue that this decision can have a large impact on the bottom line of your trading. You probably have already spent, or intend to spend, a massive amount of time studying market theory and strategy. Apply the same intensity to choosing the firm that will be responsible for executing and clearing your trades and handling the incoming and outgoing funds from your account. Most importantly, choose a firm that you trust will follow appropriate regulations set forth to safeguard client funds. The PFGBEST and MF Global failures taught us that the rules regulators make are only as good as those following them and enforcing them. Furthermore, the brokerage firm you trade with should display healthy financial standing and a relatively clear regulatory record; after all, hard times provide incentive for firms to misappropriate funds.

If you think commission is expensive, try getting what you paid for.

Before committing to a brokerage firm, it is essential that you conduct the proper research into its services. This includes experience, trading platforms, margin policies, and commission structure. Perhaps more important, determine whether your trading style and personality are compatible with the services the firm provides. For example, beginning traders shouldn't look to a deep discount online brokerage firm—they likely won't get the guidance they need as a novice. In this case, saving a bit of money in commission can mean costly errors in judgment and order placement. Similarly, a seasoned trader wouldn't want to choose a firm that focuses on high-end service with a hefty price tag because there is no reason to pay for services that aren't needed. In this case, commission is "baggage" and could have a slightly negative impact on overall performance. However, it is important to realize that the real differences between success and failure generally lie in the trading itself, not the transaction costs. Ideally, most traders are best off working with a firm that offers services on both sides of the gamut. This makes it easy for full-service traders to migrate to online trading while staying with the same broker. Also, discount online traders might want to employ strategies developed by a full-service broker within the same trading account to diversify risk.

Introducing Brokers, Futures Commission Merchants, and Broker/Dealers

A lot of talk among retail traders centers on the differences between trading with an Introducing Broker (IB) and a Futures Commission Merchant (FCM).

The primary difference between an FCM and an IB is the FCM's ability to accept customer funds.

Likewise, there seems to be a lot of misconception surrounding the topic. Hopefully, I can set the record straight and aid you in choosing the type of firm that best fits your needs as a trader and gives you the most "bang for your buck."

What Is an FCM?

The CME defines an FCM as an individual, association, partnership, corporation, or trust that solicits or accepts orders for the execution of a commodity transaction pursuant to the rules of a futures contract market and that accepts payment from or extends credit to customers. To the average trader, that means this: The primary function of an FCM is to represent the trading interests of individuals or firms who do not hold membership in the exchanges. Simply, an FCM is a futures brokerage firm.

Briefly, FCMs accept money for deposit in a segregated account that clients can use toward the margin and capital required to buy or sell futures and options. As the world learned by the dramatic collapse of two prominent FCMs in 2011 and 2012, requirements to keep client money separate from brokerage firm money in a segregated account aren't guaranteed to be honored. However, following these events, the Commodity Futures Trading Commission (CFTC) and the National Futures Association (NFA) scrambled to improve the protection of customer money and institute auditing procedures to ensure proper execution of the regulations. I believe the actions taken by regulatory bodies were effective in mitigating the risk of another breach of the broker's fiduciary obligation and the client's trust when it comes to money management. Unfortunately, for the victims of these two events, it felt like too little, too late.

FCMs are also responsible for executing trades on behalf of their customers; clearing those trades with the exchange; and then communicating fills, statements, and margin requirements to customers. Some peripheral services that a good FCM provides include trader education, market research, and strategy guidance.

You might have also heard an FCM referred to as a wire house, brokerage house, and, my favorite, commission house. Some FCMs conduct business strictly in options and futures; others are involved in all types of financial investment transactions, including but not limited to stocks, bonds, and FOREX. Naturally, trading products and markets might play a role in the firm you choose. Firms offering stocks and bonds are known as broker/dealers and are subject to additional registration, licensing, and regulation requirements. We discuss these types of firms later in the chapter, but I'm compelled to mention that the convenience of a "one-stop shop" is not necessarily the most efficient arrangement. In fact, I believe traders are likely better off working with firms that specialize in the particular asset they are trading, whether it be stocks, bonds, futures, or FOREX.

FCMs are required to become "registered member firms" of the futures exchanges and registered members of the NFA before handling or trading accounts in the corresponding markets. Most exchanges allow only individual memberships instead of firm membership. This usually means corporate officers or the like registering on behalf of their stated firms. As a means of achieving accountability, the named individual is responsible for the actions of the firm and its employees in terms of exchange regulation.

What Is an IB?

The textbook definition of an IB is a firm or person engaged in soliciting or accepting orders for the purchase or sale of futures contracts. In today's high tech world, this often means providing access to an appropriate futures trading platform and ensuring everything runs smoothly for the trader. IBs are subject to the rules of a futures exchange and regulatory bodies,

Introducing Brokers are often thought of as being small firms, but some have grown to be much larger than some FCMs.

but they do not accept money or securities to margin trades or contracts—that is the distinguishing factor between an IB and an FCM. The IB is associated with at least one correspondent Futures Commission Merchant and must be licensed by the CFTC; likewise, the IB must be a registered member of the NFA.

The relationship between an IB and an FCM can most easily be described in terms of a subcontractor. An IB is, in essence, a miniature brokerage firm that is in business for the sole purpose of soliciting accounts for an FCM. The IB is then paid as a subcontractor and issued a Form 1099 at the end of the year. This is in contrast to a broker working directly for the FCM and paid commission; at the end of the year, the broker is issued a W-2. Not all IBs are small, though—some are very large, and many have even surpassed the size of some registered FCMs.

Simply put, an IB brings clients to an FCM, and the FCM holds client funds for margin and executes and clears trades ordered by the IB or its clients. As briefly mentioned, an IB doesn't accept client money in its own name. Those trading with an IB are asked to make checks payable to the FCM or to wire funds directly to a segregated customer fund account in the name of the FCM. This requirement is a measure taken to prevent "rogue" IBs from accepting client money without actually delivering trading services and execution.

Despite what your account statement suggests, if you trade with an Introducing Broker, your account is with the IB; the FCM clears your trades and holds your margin funds.

An IB often relies on the FCM for back-office operations such as customer service and technical support. This includes handling requests for outgoing funds, end-of-year tax form preparation for each trading account, execution solutions (trading platforms), fill reporting, and so on.

Because customer statements and end-of-year tax reporting (1099s) are issued directly from the FCM, retail traders are often confused about who their broker actually is and where to go for help if an issue arises. A quality IB can efficiently assist you in many of the day-to-day activities, so make it a rule to refer to your broker (IB) first and your brokerage firm (FCM) second. Only after you are unsatisfied with the response or resolution of your IB should you escalate your concerns to the FCM.

Without fully understanding the relationship between an IB and FCM, brokerage statements can be especially confusing for those trading with an IB. A client account statement always includes the name, and likely the logo, of the FCM handling the account. The only reference to the IB is normally in relatively small text labeled with "Business Introduced By."

Justifiably so, beginning traders or those simply not familiar with the futures industry assume that they have an account with the FCM, when, in reality, they have an account with an IB in which margin funds are held at the FCM. In turn, the IB clears trades through that particular FCM. Keep in mind that your introducing broker is free to change the FCMs in which client trades are cleared and statements are issued, with only moderate hassles. If your IB decides to switch clearing firms, your account travels to the new firm in what insiders refer to as a *bulk transfer*. Unless you specifically object, your account stays with your broker and begins clearing trades through the new FCM. Simply put, you are the client of the IB and not the FCM, unless, of course, you want to change brokers.

If you are part of a bulk transfer, aside from having a different logo on your statement and being provided with new contact information for customer service and tech support, you might not notice much of a difference in how your account is handled.

In some cases, it is actually possible for your IB to clear trades through more than one FCM. This type of IB is known as an Independent Introducing Broker (IIB) and is a much more popular arrangement in the aftermath of the demise of PFGBEST and MF Global because it offers IBs a way to diversify their business and enables clients to diversify their funds on deposit while working with an individual broker. Simply put, if a brokerage firm has clients dispersed among various FCMs, in the unlikely event of a brokerage failure to uphold segregation rules of customer funds, the impact on the IB and the clients will be less significant than it would be if the broker were an IB dealing with a single FCM. Accordingly, traders with larger accounts might find it comforting to spread their funds among different brokerage firms as a means of spreading risk against the unthinkable (a repeat of MF Global or PFGBEST).

Clients of an IIB also tend to have a much larger selection of trading platforms, relative to those of an IB exclusive to a single FCM. This is because each FCM typically has a suite of software for electronic trade execution, so simply having access to multiple FCMs opens the door to a nearly endless list of options. Similarly, most FCMs have some sort of specialty offering or areas in which they excel. A good IIB can guide clients to the appropriate brokerage firm based on platform access and margining needs. In other words, using an IIB saves the client the hassle of doing the footwork and research required to find the best fit.

I can personally vouch for the difficulty and frustration of determining the optimal FCM for each type of trader. Following our forced departure from being an IB of PFGBEST, we opted to join an already established IIB operation. This was a great way to give our clients flexibility and options, but we also learned that there is no such thing as a perfect FCM for all trading strategies. Instead, it took a considerable amount of research and bargaining with risk managers at each FCM to find a suitable home for various clients. I suspect that the average retail trader would have a difficult time determining the best arrangement and negotiating the terms in his favor. This is a good example of why it typically is *not* advantageous to open an account directly with the FCM. Despite conventional wisdom that suggests cutting out the middle man will reduce costs and simplify your experience, an IIB has more negotiating power than an individual trader. This isn't unlike the ability for employers to get better insurance rates in a group plan than individuals can get on their own.

In most instances, the convenience of using an IIB to shorten the learning curve in shopping for an FCM can be done without incurring higher fees or commission. So why not utilize such a service?

Going forward, we'll use the term "IB" to refer to both types of IBs.

What Is a Broker/Dealer?

By definition, a broker/dealer is an organization that trades securities such as stocks and bonds for itself or on behalf of its clients. When the firm is executing trades on its own behalf, it is said to be acting as a dealer; when it buys or sells securities for its clients, it is said to be acting as a broker. Although the primary business of such firms is dealing with traditional investment and trading vehicles, many have begun offering a limited array of futures and options on futures. Therefore, unlike IBs and FCMs, broker/dealers are also regulated by the Securities and Exchange Commission.

I have found that some broker/dealers offering futures products are limited to a handful of electronically traded contracts. In other words, clients do not have access to open outcry option or futures execution at all. Additionally, they typically don't offer products outside the mainstream offerings, such as the e-mini S&P, the Euro, and crude oil. You might find trading agricultural futures and options either difficult or impossible. Similarly, if you are interested in selling options on futures, a broker/dealer likely will require a substantial amount of funding above and beyond the margin requirement. After all, commodities aren't their primary business, and for all intents and purposes, futures are offered to complement their bread and butter. Accordingly, in my opinion, most serious commodity traders are better off trading with a capable firm that is highly familiar with the futures and options trading arena. With that said, broker/dealers are popular for offering a convenient way to trade commodities alongside stocks. If you strongly feel that you are prepared to trade on your own, you won't be trading options, and you intend to trade the most commonly traded futures contracts, this might be a viable alternative.

Fill Quality

Despite what you might have heard or read regarding the disadvantages of trading with an IB instead of an FCM, I believe that the quality of service lies in the individual broker that you deal with rather than the compensation arrangement that your broker has with the clearing firm.

As long as you are trading liquid contracts through a reputable brokerage, market success and failure will be determined by client speculation, not a possible split-second difference in fill quality.

All else being equal, aside from the talent and disposition of the individual broker you deal with, as a retail trader, you shouldn't see a significant difference in terms of service between working with a broker employed by an FCM or an IB. Again, the primary distinction between the two is as simple as the difference between a W-2 employee and a 1099 subcontractor.

It seems relatively common for brokers who work directly for FCMs to insinuate that because they are clearing members of the exchange, they can somehow provide clients with more efficient fills. Conceivably, this might have been the case several years ago when phone orders were common; however, I argue that the advent of online trade execution has interfered with the validity of such implications. Electronic trade execution has done wonders for fill efficiency, and the benefits aren't rooted from the FCM; all traders enjoy them, regardless of their brokerage arrangement. After all, clients with an IB are placing orders on the same platform and via the same data server that a client trading directly with the FCM would.

Hypothetically, if you placed a market order to purchase an e-mini S&P futures contract at the market through the trading platform of an IB and simultaneously placed the same trade through an FCM, chances are, you wouldn't see a significant difference in the execution price. Any discrepancy in price would likely be better explained by your inability to pull the trigger at exactly the same time than by which brokerage firm services your account. However, significant differences in trading platforms might arise due to margin approval issues, as discussed in Chapter 4, "Account Access, Trading Platforms, and Quote Vendors."

Behind the Scenes of Transaction Costs

A common assumption is that an IB isn't capable of offering commission rates competitive with those of an FCM. This is often argued by the logic that an IB is essentially a "middle man" between the client and the FCM. Conventional wisdom suggests that more hands in the cookie jar will translate into higher costs to the consumer. On the surface, this seems to be a reliable argument; after all, brokers and brokerage firms are in business to make money, not donate services. If there are more mouths to feed, chances are, costs will be higher. However, this argument overlooks the fact that there might be more internal parties to be paid

Scratching beneath the surface, it becomes clear that brokers employed at an FCM often have incentive to charge higher fees than those of an IB.

in an FCM, leaving a far smaller cut for the broker. Accordingly, FCM brokers might have an incentive to charge higher rates to clients relative to a broker working for an IB.

As a retail broker who has worked under both arrangements, I argue that IBs might have the ability to offer lower transaction costs than many FCMs, or more specifically, brokers employed at FCMs. I believe this to be the result of the common business practice of FCMs giving brokers the ability to set their commission schedules within preapproved boundaries, combined with the premise that FCM brokers are, in my opinion, often provided inferior commission payouts relative to an IB.

The payout of a broker working directly for an FCM is typically predetermined and often involves a percentage structure in which the higher the rate charged, the more income for both the broker and the brokerage firm. In theory, the increased exposure and name recognition of being employed by an FCM should outweigh the difference in payout, but that argument is well beyond the scope of this chapter.

On the contrary, an individual who opts to become an IB is required to pay the clearing firm a predetermined flat fee for every transaction executed but isn't required to pay a percentage to the house, as an FCM broker is likely to do. In other words, for every commission charged to the client, the FCM receives an agreed-upon clearing fee, and the IB is paid a rebate in the amount of commission charged above and beyond the clearing fee paid to the FCM. This type of structure paves the way for more competitive commission rates for IB customers than FCM brokers would be able to offer.

I have found that IBs with multiple members have payout structures similar to that of an FCM but seem to be more broker-friendly. Keep in mind that this is simply an observation and is open for debate. With that said, a broker who receives a higher commission payout might be willing to negotiate more competitive rates without giving up his income potential. Accordingly, you might find that many IBs are very competitive in terms of transaction costs.

In my opinion, there are no benefits to trading with an IB over an FCM or vice versa. The true value is in finding an individual broker who meets your needs; handle your account efficiently; and is capable of offering quality strategy reports, news feeds, and market analysis. Whether they realize it or not, even clients entering orders online have a broker assigned to their account. If you are an online trader and do not know who your individual broker is, he might not be earning his keep.

Discount Brokerage or Full-Service Specialization

Not all brokerage firms are created equal. There are those that are in the business of providing clients with a blended array of services, to be a one-stop shop for futures and options traders. Yet others are dedicated to being extremely efficient at meeting the needs of one specific type of trader. Perhaps the most common focus of specialized firms is the distinction between full-service and deep discount brokerage services.

To avoid the costly mistake of choosing a firm that isn't capable of providing the desired service, it is imperative that traders be honest with themselves. This requires a subjective look at skill level, market knowledge, and the necessities based on trading style. Being candid with yourself is sometimes difficult, but it is a must. How can you possibly choose what services are best for you if you are making the decision on something other than reality?

> *Knowledge is the most valuable commodity.*

After you determine what you are looking for, you need to keep a few things in mind. Based on my observations and assumptions, I have found that as you move down the commission scale (from high rates to low rates), the adage "you get what you pay for" becomes more appropriate.

In other words, paying $100 per round-turn doesn't necessarily mean that you will receive extraordinary service or trading results. Conversely, if you are paying 99 cents per side, you will likely get what you pay for, which is very little. Paying next to nothing and receiving a level of service appropriate with the costs isn't always a negative. Experienced traders with adequate market knowledge, familiarity with trading platforms, a reliable Internet connection, and no day job, might be comfortable without having someone to lean on. If this is the case, there is no reason to pay for service that you won't use. If you do not fit this description, I strongly recommend that you seek services that might be a little more expensive in terms of commission but potentially much cheaper in regard to trading mishaps or a lack of helpful strategy guidance and research. In essence, saving a miniscule amount of money on a round-turn commission doesn't compare to losing the hundreds or thousands of dollars at stake if you make an error in judgment or trade placement.

Being correct in market speculation is only half the battle. The commodity markets are full of intricacies that create landmines for inexperienced traders. For example, imagine inadvertently entering a highly illiquid market and experiencing trouble offsetting your trade. Exchanges will reject market orders if there isn't anyone to take the other side of your trade; it can be helpful to have a broker to get you out of a jam by calling the exchange floor and locating someone to make a market for you and offset your mistake. Unfortunately, I have seen this scenario play out on several occasions. A common trap that beginners fall into is placing a trade in one of the NYMEX soft contracts instead of the much more popularly traded ICE versions, or entering the wrong contract month or year. Just one false click of the mouse or stroke of a key can mean disaster for your trading account.

A deep discount brokerage is often staffed with less than experienced brokers who might not have the knowledge or exchange contacts to help you through your predicament. However, history suggests that this can be a painful lesson and, in many cases, can be avoided by simply using a full-service broker until you're properly acquainted with the markets, or at least trading online with a firm that is capable of backing you up in dire predicaments.

Along with servicing client accounts, brokers are compensated in the form of commission for accepting the brokerage firm's risk of carrying that account.

Similarly, Internet connection failures can and do happen. Envision yourself without Internet access. After calling your deep discount brokerage firm, you find yourself on hold waiting for a representative. Meanwhile, your open positions are quickly eating away at your trading account. Finally, after the clerk on duty offsets your trades, you discover a desk fee of $25 per contract for placing a phone order. This is a rather extreme circumstance, but it is important to realize that it is a realistic scenario. Depending on your needs, it might be worth paying slightly more in commission in an attempt to avoid "paying" far more in market losses.

You need to be aware that your broker earns a living through commission. During times of high volume, volatility, and stress, brokers are sometimes forced to consciously choose which issues to conquer first. It is irrational and naive to believe that a broker will approach the situation with anything else but the intention to take care of those that "take care of him" in the form of commission. Accordingly, you should be prepared to pay a reasonable rate based on the level of service that will be required to give you the best probability of success—nothing more and nothing less.

What You Should Know About Commission Structure: Blanket or Variable Rates?

A concept that many beginning retail traders overlook is the burden of risk that a brokerage firm and even an individual broker faces simply by opening a client trading account. Aside from the normal business risks such as litigation or economic drawdowns, a futures and options brokerage firm faces risk of client default. The risk primarily stems from the fact that, in the world of commodities, it is possible for clients to lose more money than is on deposit in their account.

Before you can effectively determine what is and isn't a fair commission rate based on your personal characteristics and service needs, you need to understand a side of the business that you likely haven't taken the time to consider. Little, if any, written resources cover this aspect of commodity trading, but as an industry insider, I feel that understanding what goes on behind the scenes is crucial.

Clients Are Risky

Like a majority of brokers in this industry, I have gotten to experience the anguish of a client account going negative (losing more than is on deposit). The experience might be psychologically devastating to a trader but is equally stressful to a brokerage firm and the broker personally responsible for the debit account balance, at least until the client refunds. Broker liability is the dark side of the industry that most are unaware of. Before you make the decision to trade beyond your means, think twice about the damage that you could potentially do to innocent parties, along with the pain and suffering that you might cause yourself.

The brokerage firm is expected to cover any negative balance with the exchange immediately, and this often translates into commission withholding from the individual broker in the amount of the negative balance. As you can imagine, large debit balances can mean several months without pay to a broker. In essence, brokers are potentially responsible for the trading decisions that their clients make, regardless of whether they played a role in the demise of the account. It isn't necessarily fair, but we all know that nothing in life is fair. With this known, it is easy to see that any commission charged is partly attributable to the risk of a negative account that the firm is facing by taking you as a client.

After the client refunds the account to bring it to a positive balance, the brokerage firm typically releases the withheld commission. In extreme cases, such as those in which the client cannot pay the monies owed, the broker might find that the sins of her client were permanently paid by her commissions. This liability remains even though the broker wouldn't have shared in the profits had the outcome been different. Simply put, the ultimate risk is put on the party that doesn't stand to share in the glory if it occurs.

Naturally, the broker and the brokerage firm will do everything within their power to prevent a client account from suffering a negative balance. This is simply because, when an account loses more money than is on deposit, the client is essentially trading with money "borrowed" without permission from the brokerage firm. Likewise, when an account loses more money than it was funded with, a client that refuses to pay the balance to bring the account into good standing with the exchange should expect legal ramifications from the brokerage firm.

Commission Should Be Based on Client Risk and Not a Predetermined Flat Rate

With the risks posed on the brokerage firm and individual broker, commission charged to clients should depend on the deemed level of risk that an account poses. As with any other industry, risk and reward are highly correlated. Along with this premise, reckless and undercapitalized traders are charged a relatively higher commission rate. Although a brokerage firm's primary business is executing trades and the firm welcomes business and traders of all types, it must also think like an insurance company.

Flat-rate commission structures enable low-risk traders to subsidize the transaction costs of high-risk traders.

To prevent low-risk policy holders from subsidizing high-risk policy holders, insurance companies collect the personal data and characteristics of each applicant to determine an appropriate premium according to the perceived risk. In short, this practice creates an environment in which each policy holder is paying for the coverage rendered, nothing more or nothing less.

In the absence of risk profiling, blanket premiums would create a socialistic system in which all participants carry the same costs, regardless of their potential claims. To illustrate, if this were the case, a devoted smoker would be paying an identical amount of money for an identical health insurance policy provided to an avid jogger. The smoker would be getting a great deal and would be paying less than his policy was worth, based on the inherent risks to the insurer. The jogger, on the other hand, would be overpaying the actual worth of the policy to compensate the insurer for the risk of others. I believe that resourceful brokerage firms, whether an IB or an FCM, should create a similar model in determining the commission schedule of a firm. Rewarding negative behavior is an inefficient business plan for futures brokers and, in the long run, will have a negative impact on the firm and the firm's clients.

Unfortunately, the characteristics of a trader aren't always black-and-white; they most often come down to verbal claims instead of concrete evidence.

However, brokers should casually collect certain pieces of information before determining what they believe to be an appropriate commission rate.

Account size is often a large contributor in determining an appropriate commission rate. All else being equal, a trader with a large account poses less risk and is more valuable than a trader with a relatively small account. Therefore, in most circumstances, a trader with a larger account deserves a lower commission rate than one with a smaller account. However, this isn't a clear-cut rule. I have witnessed traders with large accounts trade in a manner that poses a great deal of risk to the broker and the brokerage firm. Again, highly aggressive traders should face higher transaction costs due to danger they present to the firm.

Trading style is another component often used to determine commission structure. This is often something that might be determined after the account has been open and trading. For instance, a trader who has a well-funded account and typically uses approximately half of the available margin on a given day is a relatively low-risk client. On the other hand, a trader, who is constantly pushing the limits in terms of margin, exposes the trading firm to a substantial amount of risk. Similarly, long-option-only traders are exposed to limited risk, and so are their brokers; they should be provided a discount commission accordingly.

Understanding these basic concepts of commission and how brokerage firms assess risk, it should be obvious that, in most cases, trading with a firm that offers a flexible rather than fixed commission structure is preferable. Fixed commission structures lead to inefficient policy in which some clients subsidize the risk of others, and vice versa.

Market Access

The options and futures markets move quickly, making it imperative that traders have efficient logistics in trade execution. What exactly this means is dependent on the time horizon and strategy of the trader, but traders should think about it long before it comes time to begin speculation.

Online Account Access and Trading Platforms

If you are a position trader using options or futures, fancy trading platforms shouldn't be a high priority, but online account access should be. For position traders, simply having the means to easily place trades and/or monitor the account is sufficient. There is no need to complicate things unnecessarily.

On the contrary, as discussed in Chapter 4, if you are scalping or doing any other form of day trading, the front-end platform that you use to enter trades becomes important. Not only must the platform be quick and easy to use and understand, but it also can't be so quick and easy that mistakes are highly probable. Day traders are most likely following, and intending to trade, electronically executed contracts. If this is the case, most platforms are offered in live demo versions in which you can practice order entry and trade monitoring to determine which is more suited to your needs before you commit real money.

Exchange Presence and Clearing Arrangement

Insiders often refer to clearing FCMs as having *floor presence*. This means that they own a seat on the exchange and have the ability to clear their own trades. The common perception is that, because they are privy to the action, they provide clients with better execution and timelier fill reports. However, I haven't found this to be necessarily true. In fact, throughout my career, I have found that the best service comes from independent third-party execution brokers. They are generally referred to as *give-up brokers*. This is because they are in the business of executing trades for customers and then giving the trades up to the clearing firms of their customers. Give-up brokers are not exchange members, but they are located on the exchange floor.

> *In option trading, the use of give-up brokers can significantly increase the quality of execution and communication of the fill.*

If you're trading open outcry options or option spreads, I recommend using an experienced full-service broker who has access to give-up brokers. A broker who handles a lot of option business will have reliable contacts with give-up brokers on the trading floor. These give-up operations will be happy to execute trades for a small fee, normally between $1 and $4. However, the fill quality is worth far more than the incremental cost. If using a give-up broker saves you a mere one tick in the full size S&P, that is equivalent to $25. As you can see, it isn't difficult to recoup any give-up fees paid. This is the perfect example of not tripping over dollars trying to save pennies. If you intend to do a significant amount of open outcry option business (spreads, or those contracts traded only in pits), I strongly recommend working with a broker who is capable of executing your order through a give-up firm.

I believe that trading through give-up brokers eliminates any benefit that an exchange member trading firm can offer. Simply put, your execution might rely on the individual broker servicing your account rather than the brokerage firm he works for. We look into this in more detail in Chapter 6, "Finding a Broker That Fits and Choosing a Service Level."

Electronic Contract Execution

As Chapter 3, "The Organized Chaos of Open Outcry and the Advent of Electronic Trading," discussed, electronic futures contracts are described as such based on the method of execution, not trade placement. Thus, it is entirely possible to enter a trade on an electronic trading platform that will be executed in an open outcry pit (usually using a specific contract symbol that denotes the order to be routed to the open outcry pit). Conversely, you can call your broker and place a trade to be executed electronically. When describing how a trade was placed, a broker might use the term *online* to reference an order entered via an electronic trading platform. If it were entered by calling an executing broker, it is said to have been placed *on paper*.

The term electronic describes the method of execution, not how the order is placed.

When it comes to the execution of electronic contracts, the time and efficiency of your trade execution will not likely differ substantially from firm to firm. Many firms market their belief that technology shaves split seconds off the execution of their clients' trades (and even charge a premium transaction fee for it), but in my opinion, this shouldn't be a decisive factor. Regardless of whether you are trading with a firm that is a member of an exchange or a so-called superior data connection, the execution of electronically traded contracts shouldn't have a positive or negative impact on your bottom line because fills are instant.

Shaving one-tenth of a second off a market order will work in your favor at times and against you at times, making the speed of electronic execution an irrelevant selling point. Don't allow your opinion to be swayed by brokers who claim otherwise.

Beyond Your Broker

Having nontrading issues with your account can be frustrating. After all, trading itself is a high-stress endeavor; the last thing you need to worry about is a mishap with your wire, your statement, or your trading platform. Your brokerage firm's ability to minimize unnecessary problems and quickly alleviate those that do occur can make a difference in your bottom line.

Customer Service and Back-Office Operations

We all know that fear and greed are the two biggest emotions in trading, but another one is often overlooked: frustration. Expecting to be unaffected psychologically by an unorganized, inefficient, or simply incompetent customer service department is unrealistic. Unfortunately, difficulty in handling the behind-the-scenes aspects of your account can easily have an adverse impact on your ability to focus on trading and, ultimately, the results of your efforts.

A well-functioning customer service department enables you to focus on trading simply by being well informed and capable of meeting your needs in a timely manner. The trick is to determine whether a customer service department is efficient before your account has been open long enough to experience its capabilities or shortcomings.

It is a good idea to browse Internet forums and message boards in search of ratings and comments on a prospective brokerage firm. Those looking to trade with an IB should be looking for information on the quality of customer service provided by the FCM *and* the IB. As the client of an IB, you will primarily be dealing directly with your broker, but the FCM must be able to deliver when called upon.

You wouldn't commit to purchasing a car without taking it for a spin. Similarly, consider "test-driving" the support staff. Simply call and/or email with general questions about services. A great way to do this is through a simulated trading account. As you work your way through the trading demo, you probably will find yourself wanting to ask questions, and this is the perfect time to do just that. Doing so can give you a good idea of the extent of the staff's knowledge, the promptness of their replies, and their ability to problem-solve.

Technical Support

In a day and age of electronic everything, it is absolutely crucial that traders have access to a properly staffed and knowledgeable tech support staff. Without the ability to resolve technical issues in a timely and effective manner, you can find yourself in an extremely frustrating situation.

Put yourself in the shoes of a trader who, minutes after entering a market, experiences a frozen (inoperable) trading platform. Most firms offer 24-hour trade desks, making it possible for you to simply make a phone call to exit the trade; if you are with a firm that doesn't offer this service, or does but implements an unreasonable fee to use it, I strongly recommend that you reconsider. However, upon exiting your trade, you would want immediate resolution to your issue; without it, you might be missing opportunities in the markets, and

Time is money, especially when you are on hold.

this can be both financially and psychologically devastating. Trading is difficult enough; the last obstacle that you want in your way is an ineffectual technical support staff.

As with customer service, determining the quality of a tech support staff is a challenge without having an open trading account to experience the service in real time. However, you might want to go as far as to ask your prospective firm approximately how many people make up its tech support department.

You might be taken aback by the answer. I have known sizable firms to have small technical support departments. One- or two-member staffs might be adequate for smaller firms, but this is likely not enough to meet the needs of a considerably large firm.

I recommend opening a simulated trading account with a firm to access its technical support department and experience what it has to offer.

A common symptom of a small technical support staff is long hold times while trying to reach a representative by phone. Delayed responses to email inquiries also might be a red flag.

Margin Policy

Many traders fail to realize that although the exchange sets minimum margin requirements, individual firms and brokers have the right to ask clients for additional funds to be on deposit. As mentioned previously, brokerage firms and brokers are subject to a considerable amount of risk for each client they accept. This liability can sometimes be incentive to increase margin requirements above and beyond what the exchange specifies.

Margin is something that you want if you need it. However, just because you have it doesn't mean that you should use it.

With that said, futures and options traders are attracted to this arena by the availability of leverage without the costs of borrowing securities or funds as you would need to do in a stock trading account. Therefore, retail traders should be concerned with finding a brokerage firm that can margin their account based on exchange minimums. Even traders who use the leverage granted conservatively can find themselves in an adverse market move; various levels of margin required can mean the difference between receiving a margin call and squeaking by without one. In Chapter 10, "Coping with Margin Calls," we revisit the concept of margin and leverage in greater detail. Nevertheless, I'm compelled to mention two areas concerning margin in which the brokerage firm you choose will make an immense difference in your trading results.

Day Trading Margin

In Chapter 10, we discuss the fact that traders who offset their positions before the close of trade each day face lower margin requirements than those who hold positions overnight (beyond the close). Most traders assume that trading with a brokerage firm that is willing to offer lower day trading margins makes sense. After all, they are giving you the freedom of more leverage without additional costs. However, this is flawed logic simply because things are not always as they seem on the surface.

Beware of firms that advertise ultra-low day trading margin rates; smoke-and-mirror tactics often are in play. For instance, some deep discount brokers focused on attracting high-volume day traders advertise $300 to $500 margin rates on some products. However, the same firms often shave client positions as they see fit if the firm's risk management team gets "uncomfortable" or, worse, outright liquidate the entire account at their discretion. Some brokerage firms go as far as to blindly liquidate their clients' accounts, regardless of the trader's wishes, at the close of each trading session to avoid any overnight risk.

These types of firms might also have a knockout policy. A knockout occurs if a client loses a stipulated percentage of the trading account in a single session. For example, if the knockout is 60%, a client who started the day with $10,000 and draws down to $4,000, would be automatically liquidated and locked out of the account. This might not be such a bad thing, but it shifts control away from the trader and to the brokerage firm, and that is always undesirable.

In essence, the risk-management tactics used by firms that advertise highly discounted margins completely mitigate any potential benefit the lower requirements offer. To sum it up, ultra-low margin rates are simply a ploy for brokerage firms to increase trader volume; in the end, the increased brokerage commission revenue is at the expense of the trader. When choosing a brokerage firm, margin discounts for day traders should not be on the top of the list of priorities.

Short Option Trading Margin

Short option margin policies can be highly complex, making it unfeasible to discuss details. Nonetheless, if you plan on trading options at all, the first question you should ask prospective brokers is whether they have any restrictions for short option traders beyond the exchange minimum margin requirements. For instance, several commodity brokerage firms have developed strict—and, in some cases, unreasonable—margin policies to deter clients from participating in a short option strategy. Other firms outright forbid the practice.

In my opinion, such firms are foolish. I believe that option selling has the potential to provide traders with the highest probability of success while facing far less overall risk than most other strategies. Accordingly, it is in your best interest to choose a brokerage firm that will allow you to sell options at your discretion, as long as you are obeying exchange margin requirements. Even those who do not intend to sell options early in their trading careers should ensure that they have the freedom to do so simply because markets are dynamic, and your trading approach should be also.

Conclusion

Choosing the right brokerage firm is a big step toward success and should be treated as such. However, whether you are an online trader or full-service client, your ultimate experience might be largely influenced by the individual broker that handles your account. An experienced broker can deliver efficient execution, recommend proper trading platforms, and provide excellent service regardless of whether she works for an IB or FCM. With that said, don't forget that IBs, specifically IIBs, generally offer clients more platform, clearing, and margin choices. Although it isn't as fulfilling, you should be researching brokerage firms and prospective brokers nearly as much as you research the markets. In Chapter 6, we talk about some of the most important factors in determining which broker best fits your trading needs.

Finding a Broker That Fits and Choosing a Service Level

Too many beginning commodity traders focus on trading platforms, margins, and commission when it comes to choosing brokers to service their accounts. Unfortunately, the quality of information provided, such as newsletters and educational material, comes in at a distant third. Worse yet, most traders never even consider inquiring about the hours their broker is available to answer questions, place trades, or provide quotes; further, their ability to do so efficiently and effectively. Believe it or not, these aspects are critical even for those who enter their orders online without the help of a full-service broker.

The broker you choose could have a profound impact on your trading results.

Leaps and bounds of progress forged in trading technology, combined with an improved flow of information, have many in the trading community overlooking the benefits of a full-service broker. As a result, most new trading accounts opened seem to be opting for self-directed online service. In other words, many traders prefer to bypass the broker and enter their orders directly through an online trading platform. However, I argue that an experienced and competent broker can make a profoundly positive influence on the trading experience of beginning traders and should be considered for those who simply aren't comfortable with placing trades on their own, prefer to have someone to offer a second opinion, or simply aren't adequately familiar with contract symbols and market characteristics.

Despite what you might have been led to believe, full-service brokers are not obsolete and won't be anytime soon. The differences in point values, exchange procedures, trading hours, and such among the various commodity contracts surround the markets with a cloud of mystery that can be best unraveled with the help of an experienced broker.

Likewise, those who choose to open a self-directed online trading account can likely benefit from having a proficient broker available in emergencies as a backup plan, an occasional opinion on strategy, margin help, or for quick and easy support. Many traders assume that if they trade online, they don't have a broker. In most cases, this is untrue. The brokerage business is a commission-based industry; accordingly, even online traders were brought to the firm by a broker in some capacity. That person is likely earning commission every time a trade is executed. Under normal circumstances, the person who originally introduced your account to the brokerage and is being compensated for commission earned is responsible for meeting the needs, wants, and desires of a trading account (within reason, of course). Naturally, the better equipped this person is, the better the experience will be for the client.

With this said, traders of all types and desired service levels want to make sure that they have a knowledgeable broker to rely on, not necessarily one who is willing to agree to the lowest commission rate. Choosing a broker is a good example of "you get what you pay for," and sometimes saving money now might mean paying more down the road in the form of trading mishaps or improperly handled tech support and customer service issues.

Lower commission and online trading access hasn't improved the odds of success that retail traders face.

Supporting my claim that less service at a cheaper rate isn't always better is the fact that the retail trader hasn't managed to improve his odds of success over the years. Based on my research and assumptions, I have found that the average retail trader has consistently been a net loser in the world of options and futures trading. Unfortunately, lower commissions and self-directed trading haven't improved the success rate.

Whether you open a full-service or discount-trading account, it is necessary to take the research one step beyond commissions, margins, and trading platforms. As mentioned in Chapter 5, "Choosing a Brokerage Firm," traders must chose a brokerage firm that can meet their needs based on the parameters discussed; however, the decision-making process doesn't end there. It is even more critical that an individual broker be chosen based on the feasibility of efficient communication, the trader's comfort with the experience of the proposed broker, and, most of all, faith in the broker's ability to help the trader on his journey to being successful.

Once again, choosing the person you will be relying on for properly executing your trades, acting as the backup for your online order entry, and handling your account isn't a decision to be taken lightly. Several key points, including the background of the individual and execution ability, are critical in the decision-making process. Here is a closer look.

Understand Your Broker's Business

The media often paints a different picture, but believe it or not, being a futures and options broker has few perks...unless, of course, you are at the top of your game. Because the brokerage industry is commission based, no limitations constrain how much or how little a broker can make. Those willing to put forth the effort can make a respectable living; those who aren't would likely fare better on unemployment benefits.

> Be sure that your broker works for you, not just for the commission.

For many brokers in the commodity industry, the hours are long, but it is easy to see how people can become addicted to the excitement of the markets. Being a successful broker entails an open mind, a constant yearning for information, and a commitment to provide unparalleled service. Additionally, networking with floor brokers, research providers, margin departments, and other industry insiders to ensure proper execution, flow of information, and leeway on margin calls for clients is imperative to success in this field.

A big concern facing the industry is that brokers are provided incentives in the form of commission. Those who are short-sighted and fail to employ a long-term business plan are tempted to churn commission paid by clients by encouraging them to overtrade their accounts, without always holding to the best interest of the client. Naturally, you are venturing into futures and options in hopes of your own success, not your broker's. It is my goal to provide you with the knowledge you need to avoid the frustrating and costly mistake of hiring a broker with ulterior motives. On a side note, many of the most egregious examples of churning I've witnessed have been self-inflicted by online traders and have nothing to do with the broker on the account.

> "Goodness is the only investment that never fails."
> —Henry David Thoreau

The 80/20 Rule

In the world of commodities, and perhaps most incentive-based industries, roughly 20% of the brokers make 80% of the money, and vice versa. This is an opinion, not a proven fact, but I can tell you that I haven't seen any evidence to prove otherwise. It is my guess, and hope, that the 20% of the brokers who do enjoy success are doing so by providing their clients with the service they deserve at a reasonable price.

Ironically, I have found that many of the brokers who approach their clients aggressively in terms of promoting high volume or implementing a high commission rate in an attempt to generate excessive revenue fall into the 80% of brokers who struggle to survive. You can take a few steps to evaluate whether your broker fits your needs as a trader and is qualified to earn your business.

What It Takes to Be a Commodity Broker

You might be disappointed to discover that the only requirement to becoming a commodity broker is a passing score on a proficiency exam administered by the Financial Industry Regulatory Authority (FINRA) and written by the National Futures Association (NFA). The exam is known as the Series 3. Don't get me wrong; the test is somewhat challenging and does require some market and regulation knowledge, but the hurdle seems to be low, considering the responsibilities that come with passing the test.

With the bar set so low, many new commodity brokers have made their way to the industry from completely unrelated career paths and backgrounds. For example, I have witnessed people ranging from chiropractors to window washers enter the commodity brokerage business with no formal training.

Granted, coming from unrelated fields doesn't mean that they aren't capable of brokering in options and futures. In fact, some of the most honest and hard-working brokers that I have known started out as inexperienced in finance and trading. However, it does mean that you should pay attention to their background and judge their ability to service your needs accordingly.

Lack of knowledge breeds risk.

I am not providing this information to trigger doubt in the system, but as a potential commodity trader, I feel that this is an important realization. After all, you have likely seen the movie *Trading Places;* the film paints a much different picture.

Get to Know Your Futures Broker

You probably wouldn't choose a business partner if you haven't established the potential for efficient communication, don't have confidence in that person's ability to bring something positive to the relationship, and, most of all, don't have mutual trust. Why would you think of choosing a broker without considering these things? Even online traders should be asking themselves this question. Trust me, if you ever need to bypass the platform and go to your broker for execution, guidance, or margin help, you will be glad you did your homework. Fast-moving markets are merciless; time is money and each second counts!

Becoming familiar with your broker before you ever begin trading is a significant step in the right direction. The vital areas of concern are educational background, experience in the industry, and, most important, general market knowledge. A college degree in finance isn't necessarily a reason to open an account with someone, nor is the fact that a broker has been in the business for 20 years. Considering these factors in conjunction with a well-rounded grasp of market characteristics and proper lines of communication is key. For instance, I provide clients with access to me via phone, email, instant message, and SMS text message 15 or more hours per day during the week and, in most cases, on the weekend. The markets don't sleep, so having access to proficient support personnel is key to mitigating collateral damage caused by technical issues or an inability to understand market specifications. The ability to email a broker to quickly confirm the positions and working orders in your account is immeasurable.

You should be able to determine whether a broker fits your needs and personality with a 20–30-minute conversation. During this time, don't be shy. If the broker wants to do business with you, she must answer your questions, assuming they are sensible.

Use Available Resources

After you identify a possible candidate for a brokerage firm and individual broker, I encourage you to visit www.NFA.Futures.org to research your choice. The NFA is a regulatory body of the futures and options industry and offers investors complimentary background information on brokers and firms. Unfortunately, many traders are simply unaware of this valuable resource.

> "If a man empties his purse into his head, no man can take it away from him. An investment in knowledge always pays the best interest."
> —Benjamin Franklin

The NFA's website offers access to a database known as BASIC (Background Affiliation Status Information Center). BASIC contains CFTC (Commodity Futures Trading Commission) registration and NFA membership information, such as the length of a broker's time in the business as a registered member of the regulatory bodies and a list of any regulatory actions. Listed actions include NFA arbitration awards and CFTC reparation cases involving the broker. The same information exists for a brokerage firm.

It is important to realize that listed CFTC reparations do not infer guilt. A displayed claim might have been settled, dismissed, or withdrawn but will be on the BASIC record of the broker for as long as the database is available. As you can imagine, although the intent is to protect investors, it can sometimes result in false assumptions about the ethics of some industry insiders.

I recommend that you confront your broker to discuss any possible infringements of regulation or ethics. After all, it is your money, and you deserve to fully understand the caliber of person that you will be hiring to help you find your way around the futures and options markets.

The NFA's online BASIC database also provides traders with information on any NFA arbitrations. Unlike the previously discussed CFTC reparations that involve a possible infraction of regulation, NFA arbitration is a dispute resolution forum. Naturally, you want to know whether your broker might have been party to questionable practices in the past. However, again, it is only fair that you get your broker's side of the story; simply being part of an arbitration hearing might not translate into any wrongdoing.

Work Ethic

Having convenient access to your broker is an important step toward successful trading. Even if you are an online trader, if something goes wrong, you don't want to go through the stress of being unable to reach a knowledgeable party to straighten out the situation.

As a prospective client, you want to test the broker by simply communicating via telephone, email, instant message, and maybe even SMS text. If she is hard to get a hold of or slow to return your inquires, consider shopping around for another broker. Many brokers consider themselves off duty when the closing bell rings and they leave the office. However, this doesn't make themselves available for their clients. In my opinion, traders paying anything other than bottom-basement commission rates deserve better. I'm not picking on traders who opt to do business with deep discount brokerage houses, but the reality is, if the broker is making a nickel or a dime each time you trade, he cannot afford to answer your questions; he will be too busy trying to bring in other clients.

Work Experience

When shopping for a broker, I believe that it's a good idea to put yourself in the role of an employer. To fully trust the person you will be working with, you can't have any looming uncertainty. If you were managing a restaurant, one of the first things you would require applicants to provide is a list of prior employers. Why wouldn't you extend the same scrutiny to the person you will be hiring to aid you in trading your hard-earned money? I believe that judging the quality of a broker's skill is difficult without also knowing his employment background.

Naturally, you don't want to be irrational in your quest for information. A general idea of work experience is enough to properly evaluate the service you will be paying for. Remember, the only requirement to being a commodity broker is passing the Series 3 exam. Again, although the proficiency exam is challenging, the standard isn't set incredibly high. I am not trying to discourage you from having faith in the industry; I simply want you to keep your eyes open to the realities and encourage you to know who you are dealing with.

Trading Background

Don't be afraid to ask prospective brokers how long they have been involved in trading.

Don't assume that your prospective broker's experience is equivalent to the NFA registration data displayed on the NFA's BASIC database. It is highly possible that a broker has been involved in the markets before registration and is relatively distant to the markets while being registered.

Don't be immediately turned off if your prospective broker isn't currently trading a personal account; many currently registered brokers are forbidden to trade accounts in their own name and maybe even for friends and family. For obvious reasons, a personal trading account is seen as a conflict of interest. As a result, brokers often have to take a back seat in their trading. It is also important to realize that your broker is often left slightly behind the curve when it comes to trading. For example, preferable fill allocation on a bulk ticket (a single order with multiple contracts to be allocated into multiple accounts) always goes to the client, leaving the least favorable fill to the broker. Similarly, brokers not entering trades on a bulk ticket must always execute client orders before their own. Clearly, this rule is in place to protect the client, and I don't think that anyone could argue that the intention is flawed. Nonetheless, these and other rules and regulations act as deterrents for brokers to trade. Further, a broker's income is in many ways tied to his ability to provide clients with successful trading ideas and guidance. Accordingly, in an indirect way, a broker's income is always at risk and, therefore, similar to a large and never-ending "trade."

I think that you will agree that a broker who is paying attention to client accounts instead of profits and losses in his personal trading account is capable of better and more objective service. Furthermore, although the most basic function of a broker is to execute trades, if you plan to place orders online but use your broker for backup, trading guidance, or strategy newsletters, you likely wouldn't want to do so with somebody who has never traded or has real money on the line.

Trade Execution

Open outcry option traders should strongly consider using a full-service broker for execution. Fills that are more efficient will likely offset higher transaction costs.

Speculation is a difficult venture, and many obstacles to success are beyond your control. Yet increasing your odds of proper trade execution is one aspect that you can dictate if you do the proper research when choosing a broker. Ideally, you want to choose a broker who offers execution through multiple methods, including a capable trading platform and an experienced order taker, who preferably accepts orders by phone and electronically (text message, instant message, email).

Recognize that, with electronically traded contracts such as the e-mini S&P or Globex currency futures, very little, if any, difference exists in fill quality between firms—assuming that the platform used to enter the trades is reliable, of course. As a reminder, an electronically traded contract isn't one in which the order is entered online, although it can be. An electronically traded contract is one in which the actual execution takes place in a cyber environment instead of a physical trading pit.

If paid to the right broker with the right motives, commission is an investment rather than an expense.

However, when it comes to fill quality between brokers in open outcry execution, the distinction can be tremendous. This applies only to option traders; futures traders should almost always opt for electronic execution. An experienced retail broker has contacts located on the trading floor that can provide accurate bid/ask spreads from the pit; she can then compare prices with the electronic market to determine which venue will provide the most efficient and effective fills. In regard to pit execution, the executing brokers are often *give-up brokers*. As discussed in Chapter 5, give-up brokers are not clearing members of the exchange. They are simply in the business of executing trades and then "giving them up" to the clearing firm for allocation to customer accounts. Regardless of whether the broker determines the electronic option market or the pit as offering favorable prices, the counterparty to the trade (the person on the other side of execution) will likely be a market maker (someone who adds liquidity to the market in hopes of profiting from the bid/ask spread.

Help in Choosing a Platform

The greatest part about technology is that it gets cheaper, faster, and better with each day that passes. As a result, the futures and options on futures industry has bred a seemingly endless array of execution platforms for traders. Unfortunately, with choice and features comes confusion. Most trading platforms have a specialty, in that they cater to specific types of traders, whether day traders or option traders; other platforms are sufficient for all traders but don't necessarily excel in any particular area. Adding to the anxiety, each trading platform is backed by an FCM (the brokerage firm that handles your money, levies margin policy, and issues statements), or, in some cases, a platform is compatible with several FCMs and the client chooses which arrangement is appropriate.

Most beginning traders might not be capable of choosing the platform and clearing arrangements. Even those who think they've done their research and know what they want will likely discover unintended consequences of their decision. For instance, a day trader choosing a platform because of fancy features, low margin rates, and low commissions might discover the brokerage firm "shaving" contracts off their position size at their discretion, or flattening the trading account at 3:00 p.m. sharp, with no regard for price or the trader's opinion.

Having access to an experienced broker, as opposed to a salesman or clerk, when it comes to choosing a platform can do wonders for reducing frustration and improving the bottom-line results.

Market Research

Collecting and analyzing market fundamentals, seasonal tendencies and technical factors can be a time-consuming and overwhelming process. I've found that traders might be better off letting their broker do the legwork for them. For instance, several brokers and brokerage firms publish daily market commentary and trading strategy reports. This type of convenient research can cut the workload of traders considerably while simultaneously exposing them to market news and trading ideas. Although these types of informational sources are highly beneficial for traders, it is important to be an objective reader. Even the best trading newsletters can be wrong in price predictions at times. Similarly, access to all the fundamental statistics available doesn't guarantee success; the market doesn't always comply with common sense.

Consider the Future

The commodity industry is known for its transient nature. Make sure your prospective broker is in it for the long haul before you invest too much time in the relationship. Unfortunately, the opportunities in the futures and options markets attract attention from individuals with a get-rich-quick mentality. Those privy to the industry understand that this perception is the furthest possible from reality. Nonetheless, traders, system vendors, and even brokers often insist on learning the hard way. Accordingly, many commodity brokerage careers are cut short by the harsh realities of the business.

If your broker leaves the firm or the business, your account will be assigned to another executive. You might or might not have a choice in the matter. Thus, you want to be sure that you choose an established broker who intends to remain in business for quite some time.

Full-Service Broker or Self-Directed Online?

The decision to trade either online or through a full-service broker will undoubtedly make a large impact on your bottom line. However, the impact might or might not be what you had in mind. If you aren't ready to begin placing your orders online on your own, despite saving money on commission, it could be the most costly mistake you ever make.

Although commission is baggage, paying a slightly higher rate might be worth every penny, assuming that your broker is truly giving you what you are paying for: reliable and efficient execution, along with quality guidance in strategy and analyses.

Hopefully this section opens your eyes to the realities of transaction costs. Although experienced traders should look for reasonable rates with quality service, novice traders can benefit greatly from the hand-holding of a good broker. In this case, commission paid can be thought of as an investment rather than an expense.

If a broker guarantees that you will make money trading with him, I recommend that you hang up the phone. There are no guarantees in options and futures trading, yet an ethical broker will provide exceptional service at an equitable price to ensure that you are provided the best opportunities and odds of success. Additionally, in many circumstances, the amount of commission paid, or not paid, doesn't normally have an impact on whether you are profitable in the long run.

Sometimes Less Actually Is More

If you are an experienced trader, there is no reason for you to pay hefty commissions for a service that you don't necessarily need. Placing self-directed trades online is economical and efficient, and if you're ready, you should take advantage of every opportunity to do so. With that said, when it comes to open outcry option trading, your best bet is to work with a broker who has direct access to the trading floor; this is true even for experienced option traders. Placing such trades online is arguably much more expensive in terms of fill quality than paying a broker could ever be.

Clearly, sometimes you are away from your computer or are experiencing technical difficulties and need assistance in placing your trade. A quality brokerage firm will enable you to place your trade through a broker or trade desk during such times with little or no financial consequences. Deep discount brokers deter clients from placing phone orders by charging excessive "desk fees." In some cases, a trader could easily spend more on desk fees during the infrequent times he needs assistance than he saves by opting for a "cheap" commission rate in the first place.

Trade online, but do it with competent backup!

Although most brokerage firms specialize in either full-service or discount online accounts, several well-rounded firms enable traders to enter trades via an electronic platform and also allow them to contact a broker if they need trading, margin, or strategy advice from time to time. This type of hybrid arrangement is essentially the best of all worlds: It provides traders economical and efficient execution without making them give up the benefits of a full-service broker. With that said, firms that pride themselves in offering the cheapest commission won't have the manpower or experienced staff to offer such a service. Therefore, unless you are proficient in all things markets, it is often a good idea to avoid choosing a firm simply because it can give you the lowest transaction cost. You would be surprised how far a little trading support can go toward happy and profitable trading.

Full Service Doesn't Have to Be Expensive

People tend to assume that *full service* is synonymous with *expensive*. Although this is sometimes true, it doesn't have to be. Some brokerage firms charge excessive commissions and fees; however, a good brokerage firm understands that higher transaction costs detract from the client's ability to profit and, in turn, prevent the client from becoming a long-term customer.

Be wary of firms that offer set commission rates to all clients, regardless of size, experience, volume, and account size. As discussed in Chapter 5, doing so results in a scenario in which certain types of clients are indirectly subsiding the trading practices of others. This logic can be compared to an insurance company that collects the same life insurance premium for a 60-year-old smoker and a 21-year-old athlete. Just as insurance firms realize that this type of practice isn't equitable to its policy holders, brokerage firms must adopt a similar policy. A quality brokerage firm understands that the needs of each client differ, and the cost of trading should reflect these discrepancies. Additionally, firms that offer blanket commission schedules are likely cutting corners in other places, too.

Only you can decide how much commission is too much to pay. However, you can't argue with the bottom line. If you rack up a large commission bill and your account isn't making progress, you might question whether it is worth it. On the other hand, you must also be aware of how much of your account drawdown is due to commission and how much can be attributed to trading losses sustained by your own hand. More important, are the excessive commission costs due to high round-turn charges, or is your trading volume simply out of hand? The easiest way to lower your trading costs is to trade less!

Be honest with yourself about whether the trading might have been better or worse without the help of your broker. This is difficult to do. By nature, we are always looking for someone or something to blame for poor trading results, and your broker is an easy target. Conversely, if you were able to negotiate a low commission rate at a discount broker but are losing money, it is fair to say that you might be better off paying a little more for better service and support.

> "In this business if you are good, you are right six out of ten. You are never going to be right nine out of ten."
> —Peter Lynch

Is Your Broker Working for You or for Your Commission?

There's a big difference between a broker who works for you and one simply looking to collect a transaction cost. If you feel as though your broker is putting his best interests ahead of yours, don't be afraid to confront him. It is your money, and you should be completely comfortable with how you and your account are handled.

Unfortunately, because the brokerage industry thrives on commission, it can be easy for account executives to succumb to the pressures of generating income *now*. After all, they have bills to pay, too, but I think we all agree that your broker's financial stability shouldn't have an effect on the trading in your account. I would like to think that brokers with this type of mentality are the exception rather than the rule, but it is important to fully understand the potential motivations behind the industry to avoid, or at least recognize, a compromising situation.

Why Using a Broker May Be a Good Idea

Many traders have a propensity to avoid commission without considering the consequences beyond saving a few dollars or cents in transaction costs. For instance, I have witnessed inexperienced clients lose several thousand dollars in the markets without blinking an eye but argue over 50 cents in commission. Similarly, I have been approached by traders who have offered to write a check to me for several thousand dollars in exchange for tutoring, yet they weren't willing to open a brokerage account with me because they could save a dime per trade somewhere else. Some quick math reveals that it would take a lot of trades to equal the money saved in commission that they were willing to pay me up front to teach them. Being knowledgeable and wise about the choice you make in terms of service and commission is commendable, but don't be foolishly stubborn. You get what you pay for—if you pay to the right person, slightly higher transaction costs in the short run might actually save you money in the long run.

Always remember, the goal of trading is to make money, not to save it.

Avoid Overtrading and Panic Liquidation

Working with a broker might mean having someone to "bounce" ideas off and hold your hand through good times and bad. Under most conditions, the trading decisions made in your account should be yours, but you can't deny that your broker will have an influence. If you are with the right account executive, it should be a positive influence.

This isn't to say that a good broker will always be right; remember, there are no crystal balls. Nevertheless, a second opinion from seasoned professionals can be priceless. They have the luxury of keeping fear and greed out of the decision-making process and hopefully have the market experience that you are paying for through commissions to aid in their advice.

Additionally, online traders are often tempted to trade unnecessarily by executing orders in multiple contracts or simply lacking the patience to wait for a proper opportunity. Those who choose online trading to save money in commission often end up paying far more in transaction costs due to a higher trading volume—often destructive trading. I've worked with some traders who have found placing orders by phone with an experienced broker to be an effective tactic in preventing them from succumbing to the human tendency to overtrade and take on too much risk. It might also work against the emotional toll of decision making because having someone to talk to keeps traders grounded.

Shifting Risk of Order Placement

You have likely heard the old adage, "Don't trip over dollars chasing pennies." This is the best way I can explain the idea of a traders pushing themselves to trade without the help of a broker before they're truly ready.

One of the biggest benefits of using a broker is that it shifts the risk of error in trade placement from yourself to your brokerage firm—or, more specifically, your broker. Too often a trader placing orders online does so to save a minimal amount of money in transaction costs, but the result can be expensive errors that can dwarf any potential transaction cost savings. After all, the minimum price tick in most futures contracts equates to several dollars while potential commission savings from firm to firm is a mere fraction of this.

If you aren't completely comfortable in your knowledge of the markets and trades, trading without the help of an experienced broker isn't wise. I can't emphasize enough that mistakes can be costly. I have seen online traders lose hundreds or thousands of dollars simply because they were unprepared for online trading but insisted on saving a few dollars in commission. Examples of common mistakes are unknowingly executing trades in extremely low volume markets, buying or selling the incorrect number of contracts, selling instead of buying (or vice versa), placing a stop order when it should have been a limit (or the other way around), and, most destructive, overtrading.

> "I wish it grew on trees, but it takes hard work to make money."
> —Jim Cramer

Many of the mistakes inexperienced online traders make stem from a lack of emotional stability. Whether looking to get out of a trade gone bad or seeking to take a profit on a well-speculated position, exiting a market can be psychologically challenging. I have witnessed many traders mistake wheat for corn (yes, it happens) or confuse buying and selling when it comes to verbally or electronically offsetting holdings. It sounds strange that anyone would mistake a buy order for a sell order, but it happens frequently. Beginning traders often equate selling with exiting the trade; obviously, if the trader is long, he would sell to offset his position. However, if the trader is short, he must buy back the contract to exit, not sell it.

A trader with a large profit or loss can often become disoriented in the heat of the moment. A good broker can't save you from yourself, but he might eliminate some of the risk by being aware of your positions.

Conversely, if you call your broker and ask her to buy July corn at the market and she inadvertently sells a contract, she is responsible for making your account whole again. In other words, your broker must liquidate the accidental position, execute your order properly, and compensate you for any damages incurred, including the commission charged on the mistaken trade. Of course, if you tell your broker to buy July corn at the market and she does, the rest is left to your ability to speculate, the timing of your exit, and fate.

Margin Calls

Although most retail traders don't fully understand the exchange's method of margining short options and option spreads known as SPAN (Standard Portfolio Analysis of Risk), a seasoned broker should. Putting a monetary value on the ability of relieving a margin call without wiring money or completely liquidating positions is difficult, but take it from me, it is substantial. Possible margin adjustments might include buying or selling options as a hedge against current positions, or it might involve purchasing or selling futures to do the same. If you are unaware of the mechanics of SPAN, working with a broker will be well worth the commission paid if you ever get into a tight margin situation.

Companionship

This might sound corny, but many traders find that the people they are closest to have either no interest in, or no knowledge of, the trading world. Thus, having a full-blown trading conversation with friends and family can be hard, but your full-service broker will always be there for you.

Ensure Limited Slippage

A full-service broker will work hard to make sure you get fair fills. Although slippage is inevitable, questionable fills can be contested and are often a simple error on the part of a floor clerk, a broker, or, less commonly, the electronic trading network. An online trader whose account is serviced by a deep discount broker must be more proactive in getting time and sales data to confirm fill prices and getting an adjustment on a previously reported fill relative to a full-service client that has the luxury of letting his broker do the dirty work.

Conclusion

The commodity industry has something for everyone; as a retail trader, you are free to choose your own transaction costs through both trading behavior and broker selection. Keep in mind that when you choose a commission rate, you are also choosing a service level. Absolutely nothing is wrong with negotiating an affordable commission rate, but be sure you are prepared to operate with the associated level of service.

Saving money in commission can actually be more expensive in the long run than paying a full-service broker or paying a slightly higher discount online commission than the basement rate. This is because a substantial amount of risk is involved in trade execution and market speculation. If you aren't comfortable with your knowledge of the markets and trading platforms, as well as your psychological stability when it comes to trading, you and your account might be an accident waiting to happen. Nevertheless, if you are an experienced and well-informed trader, you should be looking to trade online at a reasonable rate; don't pay for service that won't help you reach your goals.

chapter 7

Order Types and How to Use Them

Being properly familiar with order types and when to use them can make a profound impact on trading results. Market prices and dynamics are ever changing, making every second count. Regardless of whether you trade online or through a broker, knowing the type of order you need to place and placing it accurately is vital.

Later in this chapter, I discuss proper phone order etiquette when placing trades with a broker or a trade desk. Whereas an experienced full-service broker can typically translate the intent of his clients, an order taker at a trade desk can't—and it isn't a good idea to leave anything to chance. Knowing exactly what you want and how to communicate your wishes is critical.

Order Types

If you've done your research, you have likely come across excessive lists of "exotic" order types. Yet, due to the dawn of electronic trading and issues with floor broker liability, most exchanges no longer accept many order types. For all intents and purposes, the order types that you should be comfortable with are the market order, stop order, and limit order. For the most part, the others are more useful in academics than they are in reality. However, I go over some of the others for the sake of being thorough.

> "Things may come to those who wait, but only the things left by those who hustle."
> —Abraham Lincoln

Market Order

The market order is likely the most commonly used because of its convenience and the lack of uncertainty involved. A market order is a request to execute a trade at the best possible price at that particular time. In other words, the trader is agreeing to sell at the bid, synonymous with taking the other side of the best buy limit order. If the trader's intention is to buy, a market order agrees to pay the ask, which equates to taking the other side of the best available sell limit order. We discuss the details of limit orders later in the chapter.

In most cases, a market order guarantees that you will receive a fill, but it doesn't guarantee that you will enjoy the price. Sometimes the best possible price at the time of the order isn't the best price for your trading account. Beware of markets with low volume and large bid/ask spreads; in such markets, a market order can result in an unfortunate fill price. Also, if a market is so thinly traded that nobody is willing to take the other side of your market order, the exchange will reject it.

This happens only in extreme cases of illiquidity and is a sure sign that you shouldn't be trading that particular market anyway. If a market order to enter a trade is rejected for this reason, it is a blessing in disguise. If it were an order to exit an already open position, it would be an unnecessarily stressful and a potentially expensive predicament to be in. Once again, I don't recommend trading in markets that aren't capable of providing the liquidity necessary for seamless entry and exit.

Traders who place market orders have little control over the fill, but they do control the timing. In electronically executed markets such as the e-mini S&P, fills are instant. In open outcry trading environments, most exchanges and contracts abide by the policy that states that a market order must be filled within three minutes of reaching the floor broker's hands.

When to Use Market Orders

Although they should not be used in markets that have low levels of volume and open interest, market orders are useful when time is of the essence. Specifically, the trader feels as though ensuring that the order is filled is more important than stipulating the fill price. If a trader feels strongly about being long or short a particular contract, a market order might be the optimal entry choice because missing the trade isn't an option.

Limit Order

A limit order is often called an "or better" order because it is a request to initiate a trade at a specific price or better. The phrase "or better" is meaningful in many ways, some being less than obvious. First, *or better* has a different meaning for buyers than it does for sellers. A better price for a buyer is a lower price, whereas a better price for a seller is a higher price.

A limit order is synonymous with an "or better" order.

Don't make this simple concept more difficult than it is. Many beginning traders I speak to unnecessarily confuse themselves when it comes to limit orders. From the buyer's perspective, using a limit order in the futures or options market is no different than putting in an offer to buy a car or a house.

As a buyer, it would be *better* for you to pay less for the car. Therefore, after you issue your final offer, you are claiming that you will pay the stated amount or less, but no more, to purchase the car. You are probably thinking to yourself that it is rare to purchase a car for less than your offer, and you are right to be suspicious. Similarly, it is also relatively rare for a limit order to buy a futures contract to get filled at a better price than what is asked for, but it does happen from time to time.

From a seller's standpoint, the more he can sell the car for, the better. Therefore, the final offer that a salesman puts on the table is an agreement to sell the car for the stated price or more, but no less. As you would expect, the seller typically doesn't have the opportunity to sell a car for more than the named price but is happy with the offered price.

Let's go back to a commodity example: If a trader places a limit order to buy a September soybean futures at $14.95, the order states that he is willing to accept being long only from $14.95 or less. In other words, the trader would be happy to receive a fill price of $14.95 and would feel rather lucky to receive a better price. If the same trader wants to place a profit target after being filled in the previous example, he might place a limit order to sell September soybeans at $15.05. In this case, his instructions are to fill the order if it can be executed at a price of $15.05 or more, but not less.

Thus far, I have ignored an important point about an "or better" order. Contrary to what many assume, if the market reaches your price but never surpasses it, you are not owed a fill. If this happens, you might or might not receive a fill. This is because the bid/ask spread typically prevents an order from being filled at the limit price without the market trading beyond it. Using the previous example, if the high of the day in September soybeans were $15.05, the trader might have been filled on the limit order, but if he wasn't filled, he has no grounds for a complaint because he isn't owed a fill. In other words, the trades at that price might have been buys, not sells, in which a market maker was on the other side, or perhaps only a few contracts traded at that price and there weren't enough to go around to fill all working orders. Limit orders are typically treated on a first-in, first-out basis, so if a trader is last to enter an order at a specific price, he would be the last owed a fill. However, if the market ticks higher to $15.05'2 (or $15.05 and one quarter of a cent), he is owed the fill, and most likely it would have been reported. It is often said in the business that it "has to go through it to do it."

When to Use Limit Orders

Limit orders can be useful, but you need to understand that their purpose shouldn't be greed. I recommend that traders use limit orders as profit targets, or as entry prices, if they are looking for the market to travel a significant distance from the current price at which they would like to enter, or if they are trading a market with considerable bid/ask spreads.

In my opinion, limit orders should not be used as an attempt to save a small amount of money. With the exception of scalpers, if a trader truly wants to be long or short a market, saving a tick on the entry price likely won't have a profound impact on the overall result. On the other hand, missing the trade altogether might.

Imagine thinking that the e-mini S&P is going to rally sharply in the near term. With the market trading at 1,305.25, you place an order to buy a futures contract at 1,305.00, assuming that the natural ebb and flow of the market will allow you to enter the market at a slightly discounted price and, in turn, cover the cost of commission and fees. Now imagine the gut-wrenching feeling that overcomes you as you watch the market soar to 1,325.00 without you because your limit buy at 1,305.00 wasn't filled—or went *unable,* as insiders would say. In this example, you would have missed a potential profit of 20 points, or $1,000 ($50 × 20), while attempting to save a few dollars. The moral of the story is that if a tick—in this case, $12.50—isn't going to make a large difference in the profitability of your trading strategy, then it isn't worth the risk of not getting filled on a limit order. Simply put, if $12.50 will keep you out of a market, you likely aren't comfortable enough with the position in the first place and should look elsewhere for opportunities.

> "When I have to depend upon hope in a trade, I get out of it."
> —Jesse Livermore

Option traders, on the other hand, might find limit orders much more useful due to the breadth of the bid/ask spreads. In some option markets, the bid/ask spread is a substantial cost of executing a trade. Therefore, a practice known as *splitting the bid* is common. When traders split the bid, they place a limit order at a price between the bid and the ask, hoping that the market maker will budge in price and fill the order; in many cases, this does happen.

One of the most illiquid and difficult markets to trade options in is copper. For example, if a trader attempts to purchase a $3.00 call option in copper, she might find that the bid/ask spread is 2.00 bid at 4.00—in other words, it would cost 4 cents in premium to buy the option, and the seller would receive 2 cents in premium. With each penny representing $250 of profit and loss to the option trader, you can see that the intrinsic transaction costs are large. For this trader, it seems worthwhile to enter a limit order at 3 cents (splitting the bid) as a means of potentially reducing the cost of entering the market. In doing so, he will accept the risk of not getting filled. However, the potential savings of $250 might be substantial enough to justify placing a limit order instead of paying the market price. Nevertheless, markets with significant bid/ask spreads such as this are often better left untouched.

Stop Order (a.k.a. Stop Loss)

A stop order, often referred to as a stop loss or simply a stop, is an order to execute a contract at the market price when a specified price is reached. This might mean that the market trades at the stop price—or, more specifically, when the price falls within the bid/ask spread, at which time the ticket essentially becomes a market order.

Contrary to popular assumption, a stop order can be placed as a means of either entering or exiting a position. In most cases, stop orders are used to defend open positions from losses beyond the stated point or simply an attempt to lock in profits up to the stipulated price. However, some traders use stop orders as a method of entering a market after it has broken some sort of price barrier, with the anticipation of a continuation of the move.

Unlike a limit order that requires the price to become favorable before a fill is owed, a stop order requires that a market price become unfavorable before the trade is executed. For instance, a buy stop order would be placed at a price that is above the current market price, and a sell stop order should be placed below the current market price. As you can see, the buyer of a contract on a stop order will be filled only if the price goes up (unfavorable), and the seller of a contract on a stop will be filled only if the market goes down (unfavorable).

Because stop orders become market orders after the listed price is reached, the possibility of undesirable slippage on the fill exists. In other words, your fill price can be different than the stop price you originally named. In theory, the slippage can be favorable or unfavorable, but throughout my experience, I have found that stop order slippage almost always works against the retail trader.

When to Use Stop Orders

As mentioned, stop orders are most commonly used as a means of exiting a trade gone bad or to lock in open profits in an existing trade. Imagine a trader long a December corn futures contract from $7.45; he may decide that it would be prudent to place a stop-loss order at $7.10 to liquidate the position if the market goes against the original speculation in the amount of 35 cents. Assuming that this trader was actually filled on his stop at $7.10, the total loss would be $1,750 ($35 \times \$50$).

Many traders rely on stop orders to remove some of the psychological anguish involved in pulling the plug on a bad trade. Without a working stop order, some traders don't have the ability to take a loss and can end up letting a small loser turn into an account-devastating trade.

On the contrary, a stop order can also be used to enter a market. This strategy is often used by break-out traders who are anticipating the market to continue to move in the current direction following the penetration of technical support or resistance. Let's take a look at an example.

Markets generally spend most of their time trading in a range; many traders believe that the best time to make money is during the time when markets break out of their price envelope. As shown in Figure 7.1, a Japanese Yen trader might have attempted to profit from a breakout by placing a buy stop above resistance and a sell stop below support. This strategy is known as a *futures strangle* because the trader is indifferent to the direction of the market but would like to profit if prices make a large move one way or the other.

In this case, the trader is willing to buy a Japanese Yen future if the market rallies to 1.2995 because, at this point, he believes that the market will continue to move higher. The same trader is willing to sell a Japanese Yen future when the market drops to 1.2595 because he believes that, if this occurs, the trend will continue lower.

After the futures market breaks either support or resistance and reaches one of the working stop orders, the trader will enter the market. In Figure 7.2, the gold market broke through trend line resistance and traded through the price of the buy stop order. Assuming no slippage, the trader would now be long a gold futures contract from $1,622, in anticipation of higher prices. Keep in mind that when one of the stop orders is filled, the trader must cancel the other order, to avoid confusion and accidental fills. Most electronic trading platforms are capable of orders in which you can instruct the platform to cancel one order if another is filled. A full-service broker also would likely be willing to do this for you. These types of orders are known as OCO orders, or One Cancels the Other, and are discussed next.

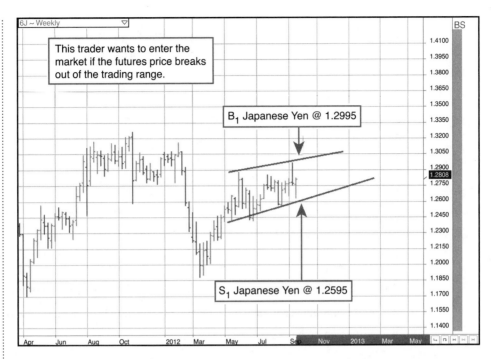

Figure 7.1 Breakout traders often use stop orders to enter a market, in hopes that the underlying move will continue.

One Cancels the Other (OCO)

An OCO order, or a One Cancels the Other order, is referred to as a contingency order because it requires that the broker—or your trading platform, if capable—cancel one of your orders if the other is filled. An OCO order can consist of a combination of any order type but most often involves a stop order and a limit order. However, there are several possible combinations of linked orders such as the futures strangle (see Figure 7.2).

When to Use OCO Orders

An OCO order makes trading more convenient and helps to avoid erroneous fills resulting from failure to cancel working orders that you no longer desire to be executed because another order has been filled. They are typically used by traders who want to manage an existing position by placing a profit target (limit order) and seek protection against an adverse market move (stop order).

Figure 7.2 **Placing stop orders on both sides of the market requires the trader to cancel the unfilled order once the opposite order is filled. Otherwise, the trader risks being filled on both orders.**

For instance, a trader who is long a June gold futures from $1,590 might place a limit order to sell the position at $1,620 and also place a stop order to avoid running losses at $1,570. When either the stop or the limit is filled, the trader would be flat the market (no longer have a position) and, therefore, likely wouldn't want to be filled on the outstanding order; that order should be canceled accordingly. Because an OCO order is an instruction to a broker or a capable platform to automatically cancel the unfilled order, a broker assumes a substantial amount of responsibility with this type of order and will likely do so only on either a full-service basis or a not-held basis via a trading platform. This simply means that, in extreme market volatility, if the platform is unable to cancel the appropriate order in time, traders cannot hold their brokerage responsible. Such instances are rare but worth being aware of.

Market If Touched (MIT)

This order is similar to a stop order, in that it becomes a market order when the specified price is "touched." However, it is also similar to a limit order because a sell order is placed above the current market price and a buy is placed beneath. In other words, this is a special type of limit order. The trader isn't simply asking for a price or better; the trader simply wants to be filled at the best possible price if the market hits the stated MIT price.

When to Use MIT Orders

Many platforms accept limit orders, but few accept MIT orders. Similarly, most floor brokers do not accept MIT orders due to the potential liability involved. This is because, unlike limit orders, MIT orders are subject to unfavorable slippage. Nonetheless, if you are provided the opportunity to take advantage of MITs, they can be useful if you're looking to buy at a lower price or sell at a higher price and are more interested in getting a fill than getting an exact price. Remember, with a limit order, the market must go through it to do it, reducing the odds of a fill.

Good Till Canceled (GTC)

Good Till Canceled (GTC) orders, often called open orders, are always considered active until filled, canceled, or replaced by another order. A GTC can be any order type but most often is a stop or limit order.

GTC orders really are good until canceled. Don't forget about them after you have placed them!

When to Use GTC Orders

GTC orders reduce the number of conversations with the broker or the number of times you must enter the trade online, if you are a self-directed trader. In each of these cases, a GTC order reduces the probability of error in trade placement.

Those who have determined their strategy in advance and would like the benefit of not watching the market on a constant basis might place GTC orders. However, beginning traders have been known to place GTC orders and forget about them, only to find that disaster has struck while they weren't watching. If you want to use GTC orders, make sure that you properly monitor them and cancel them when appropriate.

Fill or Kill (FOK)

These orders are limit orders sent to the pit to be executed immediately or canceled. For orders directed to the open outcry pits on the trading floor, the broker commonly attempts to execute the trade at the named price on three immediate occasions, at which time he either reports a fill or reports the order as unable (unable to fill).

When to Use FOK Orders

I have been in this business for a considerable amount of time and can count on one hand the number of times I called the pit and placed an FOK order. Likewise, many online trading platforms simply don't support this order type. However, for traders who are day trading—or, more specifically, attempting to scalp market prices—this might be a viable option, assuming that the performance of the strategy being utilized can be significantly altered by a tick or two in the fill price and, of course, the trading platform supports this order type. For example, a trader who enters the market with the objective of gaining only two ticks in price but is trading large multiples of contracts to make the two-tick profit substantial might find use in an FOK order.

FOK orders are sometimes used by option traders who attempt to execute a trade by placing a limit order to split the bid/ask spread. In a sense, they are telling the market maker, "Here is the price I am willing to pay—take it or leave it." This might also be a viable order in extremely illiquid futures markets with a wide bid/ask spread.

Immediate or Cancel (IOC)

An Immediate or Cancel (IOC) order is nearly identical in nature to the FOK order. The primary difference is that a trader who enters an IOC order is willing to accept a partial fill, whereas a trader who placed an FOK does not accept partial fills.

When to Use IOC Orders

Similar to the use of FOK orders, IOC orders are normally used by extremely short-term day traders. Because their intention upon entering the market is for very modest gains, a single tick in entry or missed entry might have a significant impact on the performance of a trade. However, those interested in using IOC orders might be trading high numbers of contracts. For instance, a trader wanting to buy 100 e-mini S&Ps would likely rather get a fill on some or most, as opposed to none of them.

Market on Open (MOO)

A Market on Open (MOO) order is an order to buy or sell a named contract marked for execution during the opening range of the market, usually in the first three minutes of open outcry pit trade. Unfortunately, the MOO order is becoming obsolete as the commodity markets migrate toward electronic execution because MOO orders are not typically accepted in electronically traded contracts.

The absence of the MOO order has taken away a considerable amount of convenience to the futures trader. However, some full-service brokers are willing to accept such an order for manual execution. In other words, the accepting broker would have to hold the ticket and send it to the exchange for execution upon the open of the market. As you can imagine, a lot of room for error and considerable liability is involved in a broker's acceptance of an order. Accordingly, many brokers opt not to take such orders. With that said, many trading platforms now have the ability to accept timed execution orders. For instance, a trader might instruct the platform to buy a crude oil futures contract at 9:30 a.m. Eastern Standard Time, the official start of the day session.

Keep in mind that with the advent of 24-hour markets, "the open" of trade can be left to interpretation and those placing MOO orders should clarify with the broker accepting the order. For instance, most markets open for trade in the afternoon for what is considered to be the next day's business, but the official day session open is considered to take place at a noted time in early morning trade.

When to Use MOO Orders

Many commodity traders prefer to use MOO orders as a means of eliminating some of the guesswork in entering a market. If they had conducted an extensive amount of research in the evening or over a weekend and feel confident in being long or short a market, they might use an MOO order to execute a trade. Such an order takes away the risk of not being filled on a limit order or the agony of staring at a quote board deciding when to pull the trigger.

On the other hand, many traders are reluctant to use MOO orders due to the potential price volatility that can occur during the first few minutes of a trading session. MOO orders might be subject to volatile and unexpected fill prices. However, it seems as though, in the end, favorable and unfavorable fills might end up being a wash relative to attempting to time trade entry in early trade.

Market on Close (MOC)

A Market on Close order, most often referred to as an MOC order, is one in which the trade is executed within a specified closing range, usually the last 3 minutes to 30 seconds, of the noted market. However, similar to MOOs, as the world of open outcry commodity execution has died, so has the MOC order. Electronic contracts do not accept MOC orders. If your full-service broker agrees to accept the order, she is doing so as a courtesy and, in turn, is facing a considerable amount of accountability. For this reason, brokers often accept MOC orders only on a "not held" basis. This simply means that the broker cannot be held personally liable if she cannot execute the trade during the closing range. Of course, traders with a platform capable of timed execution simply place an order to execute the trade near the close of the session.

When to Use MOC Orders

We now know that 24-hour markets have blended the boundaries between trading sessions. Nonetheless, futures traders most often use MOC orders as a method to avoid overnight risk. Because many of the commodity markets trade virtually 24 hours per day, many traders are not able or willing to hold positions and the corresponding risk beyond the confinement of a single trading session. Similarly, several brokerage firms that specialize in high-leverage day trading force-liquidate all client positions before the close. In other words, they do not allow their clients to carry overnight risk.

When a trader becomes a prayer rather than a player, the odds of a positive outcome are slim.

Some traders, although perhaps not wise traders, use MOC orders to liquidate positions necessary to meet margin calls. Frankly, when they become overmargined, they hope that any incremental exposure to the market will improve their position and, thus, their margin deficit. However, I have found that this type of wishful thinking often does more harm than good. Waiting until the last possible minute to satisfy a margin call usually implies that the trader has gone from being a player to a prayer, and nothing good can come of that.

Straight Cancel (Straight "Can")

Canceling an order completely eliminates a previously placed order. In electronic markets, the cancellation takes place immediately, but in open outcry markets, it might be subject to being "too late to cancel." Most traders will likely never encounter the challenges of trading open outcry, but those who trade options might, so it is worth noting. The difficulty in confirming a canceled order in pit trading is due to the amount of time that it sometimes takes to report a fill in an open outcry environment. To clarify, just because a fill hasn't been reported to you doesn't necessarily mean that your order has not been filled. Perhaps the filling broker has executed the trade but the pit clerk hasn't reported the fill electronically in your account; this is often referred to as a *keypunch*. If this is the case, he cannot cancel your order because it has already been filled.

Keep in mind that a market order cannot be canceled after it reaches the exchange floor.

Electronically traded markets such as the e-mini stock indices provide traders with instant fills and fill reporting. Thus, barring any technical glitches with the exchange or your trading platform, any order placed in an electronically executed market that has not been reported a fill can generally be canceled. That said, market orders are filled and reported so quickly that the only possibility of a trader canceling the order would be during a period of Internet or platform connectivity issues; that is the only instance in which the order might not immediately reach the exchange, giving the trader a short amount of time to cancel the order.

Brokers typically confirm whether you are straight-canceling a ticket or canceling a ticket and replacing it with an alternative order. If it is an outright cancel, you might hear your broker refer to it as *canning the order* or a *straight can*.

When to Straight-Cancel an Order

A trader who wants to completely eliminate a previously placed order, whether it a stop order or a limit order, straight-cans the ticket. Again, it is important to realize that a market order placed in open outcry cannot be canceled after it reaches the exchange floor—but this practice is nearly obsolete anyway. For electronic traders, when the trigger is pulled on a market order, the trader is forced to live with the consequences because quick execution times leave no time to cancel the order.

A trader wanting to cancel the existing order and place a new but similar order might be better off using a cancel/replace, otherwise known as modifying the order, instead of straight-canning the original and placing a new ticket.

Multiple Entry, Multiple Exit (MEME)

Most order-entry platforms enable traders to enter MEME (Multiple Entry, Multiple Exit) orders, or strategies. A *strategy,* when correctly entered into a computerized trading platform, is a collection of user-defined rules that create and manage a set of entry and exit orders applicable to a trading position. MEME orders can be simple entry orders with automatic profit targets (limit orders) and stops (stop-loss orders). They can also be highly complex orders in which traders enter the market with multiple contracts and automatically place various target prices and stop orders for each individual contract. In the case of a strategy, or MEME order, the platform is "intelligent": It is programmed to automatically cancel the stop order if the limit is filled, or vice versa.

Cancel/Replace (Modified Order)

A cancel/replace order eliminates the possibility of double fills on changed orders.

A cancel/replace cancels an existing order and replaces it with a similar order; some platforms refer to this as a modified order. The premise behind using a cancel/replace instead of straight-canning an order is to avoid being double-filled. For instance, if a trader has a limit order working to buy corn futures at $7.25 and wants to change the price to $7.24 [1/2], a cancel/replace order is necessary to avoid the possibility of being filled at both prices. Manually canceling the order and then placing a fresh limit order price involves a timely additional step which could lead to missing the trade altogether. Open outcry traders know that simply straight-canning the original ticket and entering a new ticket for the adjusted price doesn't necessarily guarantee that the first order won't be filled before the floor broker is able to cancel it. If this is the case, the trader might end up with two long positions, one from $7.25 and another at $7.24[1/2], if the market conditions allow for such fills. Similar to the discussion of straight-canceling orders, understanding the risks of not using a cancel/replace order in open outcry execution will likely be useful only to option traders; futures traders shouldn't trade pit contracts, under nearly all circumstances. Conversely, electronic trading platforms have greatly simplified the process of modifying an order via a cancel/replace. Most platforms enable traders to merely click a working order displayed on a chart and drag it to the new desired price.

When to Cancel/Replace an Order

Traders use a cancel/replace as a means of changing the price or quantity of an existing order. However, most brokers, exchanges, and platforms will not allow a cancel/replace to be used to modify the order type, commodity, or contract month. Traders wanting to change these characteristics of an order need to straight-cancel the previous ticket and enter a new order. This makes sense because, in these circumstances, double fills are not possible.

Placing a Trade with Your Broker

Now that you are familiar with the types of orders that are available, you must effectively communicate your intentions to your broker or efficiently enter the trade into a platform. In either case, being properly prepared could make the difference between profitable trading and the contrary. Aside from possible miscommunications or online errors, being knowledgeable and confident in your desires will

Timing is everything, in more ways than one.

help to mitigate the nerves and emotions that can work against the mental stability of any trader.

Even if it is your intention to place and execute trades through an online trading platform, sometimes you will need to place trades over the phone due to technical difficulties or other unforeseen events.

Before you even pick up the phone, you should have a good idea of what you want to do. Clearly, if you are working with a full-service broker, you are paying for the ability to ask questions and gather the broker's opinion on strategy and market speculation. Be sure to get your money's worth—that's what brokers are there for. However, don't assume that because someone is a broker, he is somehow a trading genius; relying solely on your advisor's advice isn't a good idea. After all, it is your money, not your broker's. You need to have an opinion and a plan of your own.

You should also have a good idea of the current market price. I realize that this isn't always possible; in fact, one of the primary reasons to use a full-service broker is to have the ability to call in to stay in touch with the markets. Nevertheless, not knowing where the market is sometimes leads to erroneous orders. For example, if a limit order names a price at which the market has already "traded through," either it will result in the equivalent of a market order that is executed immediately or, in some markets, the exchange will simply reject it.

A good broker generally notices an error before placing the trade on a client's behalf, but this isn't guaranteed. Additionally, if you made the call to a discount trading desk or a courtesy night desk, the order will be handled by a clerk, who will likely not offer the handholding that a full-service broker would. In any case, the client is responsible for the consequences of the order.

As a trader, you should also be aware of the opening and closing times of the markets that you place trades for. As an industry insider, I realize how difficult this can be due to constant revisions and various trading hours in each contract. Even so, you need to be aware for the purposes of placing and monitoring positions. If you place orders on off-market hours or when the market is closed, you are at risk of being exposed to gapping prices on the reopen of trade. Some platforms reject orders placed while the markets are closed, but others accept them, and this opens the door for surprises on fill prices. Being attentive of small details does matter!

Calling Your Broker

Confusion caused by miscommunication between you and your broker can be costly for both parties. A full-service broker will happily clarify your intentions and coach you along the way; however, it is a good idea to be aware of the proper procedures, to avoid compromising situations.

Most brokers can interpret your order in alternative formats, and that is fine, but it is in your best interest to know the proper format. This is the sequence of information that you should communicate to a trade desk clerk or broker.

1. State your name and account number.
2. If the order will be a futures or options spread, make that known in advance.
3. Specify whether you will be buying or selling.
4. State the quantity.
5. Identify the expiration month.
6. Identify the futures contract.
7. State the strike price (if applicable).
8. Specify the price and order type (that is, limit, stop, market).
9. Clarify the time horizon (that is, good until canceled, day order).
10. State any contingency orders, such as OCOs, or place a limit after the primary order is filled.

A verbal account of placing an oral order with a broker might sound something like this:

> Hi, this is Robin B. Good. For account 79700, I would like to place an order to buy 1 June T-note at the market with a stop order at one-thirty-one-eleven (131'11).

This is a market order to enter a long position in the June 10-year note with a stop loss to exit the position at 131'11, and it is implied that this is a day order only. If the trader wants the stop to be GTC, she must specify because it is assumed a day order if there is no mention.

> For account 79700, I would like to place an order to sell 5 December gold on a stop at fifteen-seventy-five ($1,575.0) for the day only.

This trader is placing an order to sell five futures contracts of December gold if the market drops to the price of $1,575.00. The trader also specifies that this order is good for the day only, meaning that if it is not filled during the session that it is placed, he wants the order to "die." Again, if a trader does not state whether an order is good for the day or GTC, it is assumed to be a day order. Therefore, if you enter a market and place a stop order, be sure to state that it is intended to be GTC. Otherwise, you could be in store for an unpleasant surprise.

> For account 79700, I would like to place an order to buy 5 July corn 760 puts for 5 cents or better GTC.

As you should recall, a limit order is the same as an "or better" order. Therefore, the preceding order instructs the broker to try to buy five July corn puts with a strike price of $7.60 at 5 cents on a limit good till canceled. Note that the execution price denoted in an order with multiple contracts is based on the individual contract price, not the cumulative price. Simply put, this trader is buying five options at 5 cents per option, not five options at 1 cent per option.

> For account 79700, I would like to place an order to buy 2 March orange juice at 98 cents (98.00).

This trader is instructing his broker to purchase two March orange juice futures on a limit at 98 cents. Even though a limit order was not specified, nor were the words *or better* used, any time a price is mentioned without a specific order type, it is assumed to be a limit order.

Placing a Trade Online

Experienced traders might determine that placing orders through an online trading platform is a great way to increase efficiency; after all, doing so saves time and lower transaction costs. However, this can be a detrimental scenario for those who aren't mentally capable of controlling their trading or simply aren't knowledgeable enough about the markets to take on so much responsibility.

When it comes to actual trade placement through an online platform, the procedure varies widely from application to application; many of them even offer multiple ways to enter orders. Almost all futures and options platforms offer drop-down menus to guide traders, and many advanced trading environments provide point-and-click capabilities in which orders can be placed with a few quick clicks. For example, some platforms enable you to place trades directly from a price ladder or a chart, whereas a right-click triggers a buy order and a left-click triggers a sell. As convenient as these functions are, they can be *too* convenient for those who are restless or, worse, careless.

Order entry with drop-down menus is designed to guide traders and reduce errors, but there is a downfall. Many have default settings that reset in between orders or after minimizing a trading window, and so on. In other words, traders must be careful to ensure that the contract, month, and price are as they want them to be before placing the order. I have lived through the horror of having a platform default to a December S&P futures while I was trading the June. These types of blunders are scarring from both a monetary and a psychological standpoint.

Some platforms even enable orders to be entered by typed text. This might sound cumbersome, but I actually prefer it. After you learn the format, and assuming that you have strong typing and 10-key skills, this can be a fast and efficient way to place trades. To give you an idea of how it works, the following text would instruct some platforms to buy a December 2012 electronic bond futures contract at the market:

B 1 ZBM12 M

Similarly, the following text is a command to buy a June Euro currency 135 call for 30 ticks:

B 1 6EM11 13500C 30 O

You might be wondering what the O at the end of the command stipulates. For option trades, many platforms require that you disclose whether you are attempting to enter or exit a trade. Therefore, the O indicates that this order is to open the position. If it were a closing order, the command would have a C at the end.

The purpose of denoting option orders as "open" or "close" is to aid the brokerage firm's risk-management department in approving client orders. This is because option sellers face unlimited risk, but the risk to buyers is limited to the premium paid. Consequently, it is helpful for the brokerage firm to know whether a trader is selling an option to get out of an existing long position or is selling to enter a new short option trade.

Keep in mind that each platform has a slightly different format and maybe even contract symbols. Unfortunately, if you want the benefits of trading online, you have a lot of learning to do before you can start.

chapter 8

Making Cents of Commodity Quotes

Too many stock traders or aspiring commodity traders are discouraged from participating in the futures markets by the complexity of the pricing. Even worse, others venture into the markets relying on their trading platform to calculate their trading results after they execute the trade.

> "Risk comes from not knowing what you are doing."
> —Warren Buffet

I believe that becoming comfortable with commodity quotes and calculating profit and loss in each market is even more critical than accurate market speculation. In fact, until you are proficient in determining position and contract value, you shouldn't be risking money in the markets. After all, if you can't measure your reward, how can you possibly manage your risk?

Unfortunately, quoting and calculating commodities is also the most frustrating aspect of trading commodities. Unlike stocks, in which all securities and options are calculated in the same manner, each commodity contract has its own set of rules.

Even though each futures contract is standardized, comparing commodities to those with differing underlying assets reveals that the values and corresponding calculations involved are worlds apart. As you can imagine, this can be extremely overwhelming for beginning and even seasoned traders. To complicate matters, many of the quote vendors use slightly different formats to display futures prices and option premium. The ability to quickly and accurately sift through the chaos to derive the information and figures desired takes a considerable amount of experience. The following explanations will hopefully lessen your learning curve as you begin your journey into the challenging yet potentially lucrative trading arena known as options and futures.

The futures industry is notorious for a lack of uniformity. Mergers of the CBOT, CME, and NYMEX have improved continuity among various commodity markets, but quoting and calculating in futures will always be a challenge for newcomers.

Some of the differences in quoting and calculating among commodity contracts stem from the underlying product itself. However, a substantial number of discrepancies in price format and quoting methods have occurred due to differences in the creators of the contracts.

Until recently, the U.S. commodities industry was dominated by four individual exchanges, all with four individual views on how to conduct business. Failure of the industry to adhere to congruent policies led to mass confusion among the trading public. Even brokers had a hard time keeping up. Inconsistencies between exchanges and products included (and, to a lesser extent, still include) opening and closing times, accepted order types, order-handling policies, price limits, expiration dates and delivery rules, and holiday trading hours. A handful of exchanges working independently of each other created an environment in which traders found it unwise to assume anything. Luckily, the creation of the CME Group has resulted in a single entity controlling three of the major exchanges.

Although the mergers of the CBOT, CME, and NYMEX brought a sense of uniformity to the industry, the complexity surrounding contract size, point value, and quoting format still exists. Regrettably, reading and calculating commodity prices will likely never become easier. For example, some commodities are referred to in fractions, whereas others use decimals. Additionally, some decimals depict the difference between dollars and cents—others between cents and fractions of a cent.

Rule #1: Use Multipliers, Not Contract Sizes

Most of the futures trading literature written encourages beginning traders to calculate contract values and profit-and-loss figures via the contract size. However, I feel that using contract multipliers results in a simpler calculation. This is because doing so typically involves smaller numbers, less confusion over decimals and fractions, and, hopefully, less room for error.

A multiplier is simply the dollar value of a specific price move in the underlying commodity. Any change in price can be multiplied by the multiplier to find the value of the price change per contract. A similar calculation can be made to determine the risk between the entry price and the stop order placed or the entry price and the profit order (limit order) placed. Most commodities use a penny as the multiplier, but others use a dollar in price change. This distinction will become clearer with a few examples.

Also supporting our assumption that beginning traders will be more comfortable using multipliers, remembering a multiplier is generally easier than remembering the contract size. For example, you might remember that a 1-penny price move in corn is worth $50 before you can recall that a corn futures contract represents 5,000 bushels of the underlying commodity. After all, you trade commodities in hopes to make money, not make or take delivery of corn.

With that said, it is necessary to realize that each of the conclusions reached using multipliers could also be achieved through alternative calculations that involve contract size. Using the corn example, it is easy to see that the $50 multiplier is the result of multiplying the contract size by 1 cent ($5,000 \times .01$); therefore, you can determine the value of a futures price change using it. However, for reasons that we soon point out, doing so seems to create confusion, not solve it.

Rule #2: Stay Positive

This might sound elementary, but you need to have a full grasp of the concept. I believe that traders benefit from working with positive values; negative figures often create confusion and breed calculation errors. Accordingly, traders should always be subtracting the smaller number from the larger number to derive a positive value. However, this means that, before a calculation begins, you should determine whether it was a profit or a loss.

Any time that a trader can buy low and sell high, whether with an option or futures contract, it is a profitable venture. On the contrary, selling an option or futures contract low and buying it back at a higher price always results in a net loss. This is true regardless of the order in which it is executed.

Knowing this, determining which trades are losers and which are winners is easy at a glance. From there, it is possible to easily subtract the smaller price from the larger price to determine the magnitude of the position and apply that number to the win or loss column.

Quoting Grain Futures

As we have learned, the U.S. futures trading industry began in Chicago and was formed to facilitate grain trade. Speculation in the grain complex has been popular throughout the years, and participation and interest is growing. Much of the appeal of the grain complex is the cyclical nature of the markets.

Grain prices fluctuate on what is often referred to as a *crop year*. Each grain has a specific time of the year in which planting and harvesting takes place and traders are aware of the time frames in which the crops are most vulnerable to damage. For instance, during spring planting of corn and soybeans, too much rain can delay fieldwork or, in extreme cases, make it impossible. On the other hand, too little rain can have a negative impact on proper germination of the crop and lead to sharply reduced production. In anticipation of something going wrong with either planting or harvesting, the grain markets tend to trade higher in the spring. The increase in prices is known as a *risk premium* and tends to deflate as harvest approaches in late summer or early fall. Despite what seem like obvious and tradable price cycles, grain trading continues to be challenging. After all, timing is everything, and that is all but certain. Early entry or late exit could turn somewhat accurate price projection into a losing proposition. Due to the difficulties involved, market participants must have a solid understanding of what is at stake before putting their money on the line.

Grain prices are seasonal, but don't mistake this for "easy." Cyclical price patterns are evident in agricultural markets, but guarantees are not.

In regard to math, the grain complex is the easiest of the commodities to work with simply because four of the major contracts included are similarly calculated and quoted. In the next section, "Calculating Profit, Loss, and Risk in Grain Futures and Options," I discuss the fact that wheat, corn, soybeans, and oats are all referred to in cents and fractions of a cent per bushel. This holds true for both the futures contracts and the corresponding options and should be a breeze for anyone comfortable in adding and subtracting fractions.

Because corn, soybeans, wheat, and oats are quoted in cents and eighths of a cent, the fractions always use 8 as the denominator. Grain fractions are never reduced, despite the fact that they could be. This helps to create continuity and avoid some confusion among traders.

The minimum tick is the smallest increment of price movement allowed in a particular contract. In the case of the grain futures previously listed, the minimum tick is one-quarter of a cent, or [2/8]. Options, on the other hand, can move in increments of [1/8], although they are typically traded in quarters, similar to the underlying futures.

Commodity quotes generally refrain from showing the denominator of the fraction because it is always assumed to be 8. Thus, if corn were trading at seven-fifteen and a quarter cent ($7.15[1/4]), you would see it displayed on a quote board as 715'2, where the number 2 represents the unreduced fraction [2/8]. Note that the cents and fractions of a cent are separated by an apostrophe or, in some cases, a hyphen (-). Less commonly, you might see grain quotes in terms of a decimal (for example, 715.25).

Knowing this, you have probably realized that half of a cent is denoted by [4/8], and three-quarters of a cent is displayed as [6/8]. Of course, if you were looking at a quote board, you wouldn't see the denominator of 8. Instead, you would see a 4 or a 6, respectively. This is in contrast to how you verbally state the price. To demonstrate, corn trading at 741'4 would be stated as "seven forty-one and a half," or $7.41[1/2].

Similarly, if wheat futures were trading at $8.50[3/4], it would be displayed as 850'6 and verbally expressed as "eight fifty and three quarters"; wheat futures at "eight seventy and a half" would be listed as 870'4 ($8.70[1/2]). If you are the type of person who cringes at the thought of fractions, you might want to simplify your calculations by replacing the fractions ([2/8], [4/8], and [6/8]) with .25, .50, and .75, respectively, and simply punching the digits into your calculator.

Calculating Profit, Loss, and Risk in Grain Futures and Options

Corn, soybeans, wheat, and oats all share the same multiplier because they also share the same contract size (see Table 8.1). Accordingly, aside from the underlying commodities and the value that the market places on them, each of these grain contracts trade identically.

> With the exception of U.S. Treasury options traded on the CBOT division of the CME Group, all commodity options are valued and calculated in the same manner as the corresponding futures contract.

Table 8.1 Contract Size and Specifications for Similarly Quoted Grains

Contract	Multiplier	Size Contract	Minimum Tick Value	Quote Terms
Corn	$50	5,000	$12.50	Cents per bushel
Soybeans	$50	5,000	$12.50	Cents per bushel
Wheat	$50	5,000	$12.50	Cents per bushel
Oats	$50	5,000	$12.50	Cents per bushel

The multiplier in the grain futures discussed (corn, soybeans, wheat, and oats) is always $50. This is because each contract represents 5,000 bushels of the underlying commodity; 1 penny multiplied by 5,000 is equal to $50. In other words, each penny of movement in the futures price of any of these grains is worth $50 to a futures trader. For example, a trader long a December corn futures contract from $7.40 would be profitable by $50 if the price of corn increases to $7.41. Conversely, if the price of corn drops to $7.39, the same

There's more than one way to skin a cat, and the same applies to calculating profit, loss, and risk in the futures markets.

trader would be losing exactly $50 on the position. Thus, the minimum tick of a quarter-cent ([2/8]) results in a profit or loss of $12.50 ($50 × [2/8]). When you are armed with this knowledge, computing profit, loss, and risk in terms of actual dollars in your trading account is relatively simple. Let's take a look at a few examples.

A trader who is long March soybean futures from 1320'4 ($13.20[1/2]) and later decides to offset his position by selling a March soybean futures at 1354'6 ($13.54[3/4]) would have netted a profit of 34'2 cents, or $1,712.50 before commissions and fees. We know that if a trader buys low and sells high, the trade is a profit. Thus, the profit is figured by subtracting the entry price from the exit price and multiplying that number by $50. Note that if this trader had been short beans from 1320'4 and bought it back at 1354'6, the trade would have been a loser by the same amount.

In the same way, as portrayed in Figure 8.1, a wheat trader who sells a December contract at a price of 741'6 and buys a December wheat contract at 660'0 is profitable by $4,087.50, or 81'6. This is figured by subtracting the buy price from the sell price and multiplying by $50 ((741'6 – 660'0) × $50). We know to add this to the winning column. Buy low, sell high, remember?

Figure 8.1   **Knowing that markets tend to overreact to fundamental changes only to revert back to an equilibrium, a trader might have sold a futures contract in hopes of the possibility of buying it back at a lower price later, to take a profit on the trade. (Chart courtesy of QST).**

The same result could have been figured through the use of contract size. Knowing that the preceding trade was profitable in the amount of 81[3/4] cents (741'6 – 660'0), you could have multiplied the contract size, 5,000 bushels, by $0.8175 (81[3/4] cents expressed in decimal format), to arrive at a profit of $4,087.50. As you can see, using the contract size instead of the multiplier requires converting the fraction by shifting the decimal point two spots. You can probably also see that although this version of the equation yields the same result, it creates confusion and opens the door to errors.

An option trader faces the same math. If it is possible to purchase a March soybean call option with a strike price of $19.00 for 15 cents, or $750 ($50 × 15), and later sell the option for 21'4 cents (21[1/2]), the net profit would be 6[1/2] cents. Converted to a dollar profit, it would equate to $325 before commissions and fees.

Not All Grains Are Created Equal

Not all grains share the same convenient contract specifications as corn, soybeans, wheat, and oats. Although they are less talked about and less traded, two futures contracts are written on byproducts of soybeans.

A "crush spread" involves a speculative or hedge position in which a position is taken in soybeans and the opposite position is taken in its respective products.

Soybeans are often crushed to extract oil used in many food products, known simply as *bean oil*. The substance left after extracting the oil from the beans is soybean meal and is often used as animal feed. Each of these products trades in the futures markets as a vehicle for hedgers to reduce price risk and for speculators to attempt to profit from price movements. As displayed in Table 8.2, soybean meal and soybean oil have unique contract sizes and multipliers; therefore, they require a bit more care when it comes to calculating profit, loss, and risk.

Table 8.2   Contract Size and Specifications for Bean Byproducts

Contract	Multiplier	Contract Size	Minimum Tick Value	Quote Terms
Soybean meal	$100	100	$10	Dollars and cents per ton
Soybean oil	$600	60,000	$6	Cents per pound

Soybean Meal Futures

Even though both bean oil and bean meal are derived from the same bean, when it comes to trading them in the futures markets, they have little in common. Soybean meal is quoted and traded in dollars and cents per ton, with a contract size of 100 tons. You might see soy meal futures trading at 430.2; this is referring to four hundred thirty dollars and twenty cents per ton, or $430.20. The minimum tick or incremental price movement is a dime. In other words, it could go from 430.20 to 430.30, but it can't trade at 430.25. Each dime in price movement represents a $10 profit or loss per contract for a futures or options trader. Likewise, each dollar in movement represents a $100 ($1.00 × 100 tons) swing in account equity to a trader with an open position. This makes sense because each dime of movement results in a $10 profit or loss, so a full dollar in price change would yield an amount ten times the minimum tick. Thus, the multiplier for soybean meal futures is $100.

As shown in Figure 8.2, if a trader shorts December soybean meal futures at 540.0, or $540.00 per ton, and later buys it back at 492.0, she would be profitable by $4,800 before considering transaction costs. The profit can easily be figured by subtracting the price at which the trader offsets the position from the price at which it was originally sold and then multiplying the difference by $100 ([540 − 492.0]) × $100).

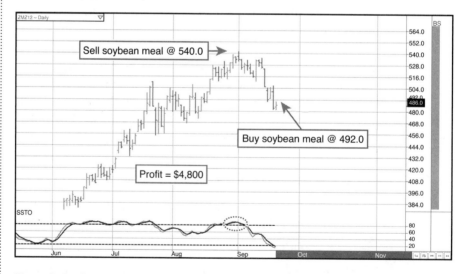

Figure 8.2   Soybean meal futures are conveniently priced, in that they have a multiplier of $100. The simplicity of calculation and the mitigated leverage relative to soybeans attracts many beginning traders. (Chart courtesy of QST.)

Calculating the results of a soybean meal option trade is identical to calculating the results for the futures. Had the same trader opted to buy a put instead of sell a futures contract, he might have purchased the December 540 put for 26.70 in premium, or $2,670, and later sold the option for 33.20 in premium, or $3,320. The net result would have been a realized profit of 6.5, or $650 before transaction costs. This is derived by subtracting the purchase price of the put option from the sales price and multiplying it by $100. Keep in mind that the same principles of buying low and selling high apply to option premium. We knew to subtract the purchase price from the sales price because the trader bought at a low premium and sold at a high premium, to create a profitable trade. Had the purchase price been higher than the sales price, we could have subtracted the sales price from the purchase price to determine the loss.

Soybean Oil Futures

Traders often refer to soybean oil futures as bean oil. Soybean oil futures are traded in contracts of 60,000 pounds and are quoted in cents per pound. Looking at a quote board, you might see bean oil futures priced at 49.20. This is actually referring to $0.4920, or 49.20 cents per pound. The minimum tick for soybean oil futures is .01, which represents a price change in the amount of [1/100] of a cent. Each tick is valued at $6, making the multiplier $600 ($0.01 × 60,000 pounds) for a full penny of price movement. In other words, if the futures price went from 48.00 to 49.00, those holding short positions would have lost $600, whereas those with long futures positions would have been profitable by the same amount.

Case in point: If a trader went long December bean oil from 47.00 and was forced to sell a December bean oil to cover the position at 46.20, the total damage to the trading account would have been $480. This can be figured by subtracting the sales price from the purchase price and multiplying the difference by $600 ([47.00 − 46.20] × $600).

An option trader uses a similar calculation to determine the net results of a trade. The same trader might have chosen to buy a put option instead of selling a futures contract. If this is the case, it might have been possible to buy a December put with a strike price of 47.00 for .70 in premium, or $420 (.70 × $600). After an adverse price move, the trader might have liquidated the option at .20, for a loss of $300 before commissions and fees. This can be figured by subtracting the premium collected from the sale of the put from the premium spent to purchase it and multiplying it by $600 ([.70 −.20] × $600).

The Meats

The complex known simply as "the meats" is traded on the CME division of the CME group. It consists of feeder cattle, live cattle, and lean hogs. The United States is the largest producer of high-quality grain-fed beef in the world.

Looking at Table 8.3, you can see that the CME has made an effort to keep the meat futures and options complex standardized in terms of contract size and point values. However, the feeder cattle contract has unique characteristics that can cause confusion for those unfamiliar with it.

Table 8.3   Contract Size and Specifications for Meat Futures

Contract	Multiplier	Contract Size	Minimum Tick Value	Quote Terms
Feeder cattle	$500	50,000 lbs.	$12.50 (2.5 points)	Cents per pound
Live cattle	$400	40,000 lbs.	$10 (2.5 points)	Cents per pound
Lean hogs	$400	40,000 lbs.	$10 (2.5 points)	Cents per pound

Because there are two cattle contracts, live cattle and feeder cattle, it is necessary to distinguish between them. Live cattle futures represent the going price for calves and young cattle weighing about 600 pounds up to 800 pounds. A calf typically needs about six months to reach this weight range, at which time it is transferred to a feedlot. When transferred, it is considered feeder cattle.

Each meat is quoted in cents per pound, and there are 100 points to each cent. With the exception of feeder cattle, which have a contract size of 50,000 pounds and a point value of $5, the meats have a contract size of 40,000 pounds and a point value of $4. Therefore, a penny move (100 points) is equivalent to $400 in profit or loss in live cattle and lean hogs. This can also be figured by multiplying the contract size by a penny ($0.01 × 40,000). An equivalent move in feeder cattle would yield a profit or loss of $500. Thus, the penny value of each of these contracts is used as the multiplier in any calculations.

Some confusion stems from the format of meat futures pricing. The meats are commonly quoted with decimals, causing some to infer that the price depicts dollars and cents. Conversely, the digits beyond the decimal point refer to the fraction of a penny in which the price is trading. Specifically, if January feeder cattle futures are trading at 131.25, this is equivalent to 131 [25/100] of a cent. When this is understood, calculating the profit and loss is easy. Let's review an example using live cattle futures.

In Figure 8.3, a trader sells an October live cattle futures at 128.525, in hopes of a price recovery from overbought status. Note that the final digit in the quote represents a half. Accordingly, 128.525 is quoted as "one twenty-eight, fifty-two and a half."

Figure 8.3 Meat futures are notorious for having low margins, but they are also prone to violent and one-directional price moves. This trader is attempting to profit from a countertrend move. (Chart courtesy of QST.)

The same trader decides that the market has potential to decline to the previous area of support, near 123.50. Consequently, he places a limit order to buy an October live cattle contract at 123.50. As you should recall, with a limit order, the markets must "go through it to do it." To determine the profit potential of the trade, the exit order price must be subtracted from the entry price, and the difference must be multiplied by $400. In this particular case, if the trader gets filled on his limit order to exit the position, the realized profit would be 5.025 cents, or $2,010 (5.025 × $400).

The same trader might not be willing to face the theoretically unlimited risk presented by being short a futures contract. As a method of mitigating the risk of an adverse price move, the trader can place a buy stop-loss order. Although stop orders are not guaranteed in terms of price, the use of stops can be effective in exiting a trade that has gone badly without the psychological turmoil of pulling the plug manually.

As you can see in the Figure 8.4, a trader short an October live cattle from 128.525 with a buy stop at 129.625 would be risking $440 before considering transaction costs and potential slippage. The risk of $440 is calculated by subtracting the futures entry price from the buy stop price and multiplying the difference by $400 ([129.625 – 128.525] × $400).

As you should recall, a stop order becomes a market order when the price is hit. Therefore, the reported fill might be better or worse than your stated stop price. Any potential difference in actual prices relative to the named stop price is referred to as *slippage* and can be substantial in volatile market conditions.

Figure 8.4   This trader is willing to risk $440 plus commission and slippage to potentially make $2,010. (Chart courtesy of QST.)

Foods and Fiber

Unlike other commodity groups, the complex known as the *softs* doesn't consist of homogenous products. Coffee, orange juice, cocoa, sugar, and cotton all fall into this category and are all traded through the Intercontinental Exchange, also known as ICE. Although a majority of the contracts have food as an underlying product, cotton is primarily used as a fiber. However, cotton oil is often listed as an ingredient in many of the foods that you eat.

Cocoa prices often catch unsuspecting traders off guard. Don't turn your back on this market.

It might seem as though these contracts were grouped together for a lack of anywhere else to put them, but they are categorized as such because a majority of production in the softs markets takes place outside the United States. Keep in mind that, just as production is done overseas, so is compilation of statistics. Many of the softs are grown in third-world countries, and the data is far less reliable than that published by the United States Department of Agriculture (USDA) on domestically produced commodities.

The softs are among the most complicated commodity sectors to calculate in; each contract within the category has an exclusive contract size, tick value, and, thus, multiplier (see Table 8.4).

Table 8.4   **Contract Size and Specifications for the Softs Complex**

Contract	Multiplier	Contract Size	Minimum Tick Value	Quote Terms
Coffee	$375	37,500 lbs.	$18.75 ([5/100] cent)	Cents and hundredths of a cent
Cocoa	$10	10 metric tons	$10	Dollars per metric ton
Orange juice	$150	15,000 lbs.	$7.50 ([5/100] cent)	Cents and hundredths of a cent
Cotton	$500	50,000	$5	Cents and hundredths of a cent
Sugar	$1,120	112,000 lbs.	$11.20	Cents and hundredths of a cent
Lumber	$110	110,000 bd. ft.	$11	Dollars and cents

With the exception of cocoa, each contract is quoted in cents per pound. Consequently, although the multiplier is different, the methodology in figuring

Brazil is the largest exporter and producer of sugar.

profit, loss, and risk is similar to that of the meats. Cocoa, on the other hand, is quoted in even dollar amounts per ton; therefore, prices are not broken down into cents. This concept is sometimes overwhelming for beginning traders who have grown accustomed to commodities quoted in cents. For example, if a quote source shows that the price of December cocoa is 2,100, this infers that the price is $2,100 dollars per ton. Your broker would simply say "twenty-one hundred" to communicate the quote verbally.

Each cocoa contract represents 10 tons of product; therefore, the dollar amount of a market move is figured by merely adding a zero or multiplying by 10. To illustrate, if the daily price change is +22, a trader would have made or lost $220, depending on whether he was long or short the market. Likewise, a

Coffee futures are prone to rallies during the summer months because of freeze threats in Brazil. However, a freeze occurs only about once every five years.

trader who goes short December cocoa at 2,975 and places a buy stop at 3,000 is risking a total of 25 points, or $250 plus commissions, fees, and potential slippage. This is figured by subtracting the entry price from the stop price and multiplying by 10 ([3,000 − 2,975] × 10). If the same trader places a limit order to take a profit on the trade at 2,940, it would be profitable by 35 points, or $350 ([2,975 − 2,940] × 10), if filled.

Coffee futures trade in contracts of 37,500 pounds; accordingly, each penny of movement in price is worth $375 to the trader ($0.01 × 37,000 pounds). For example, if March coffee rallies from 155.00 to 156.00, a trader long through the move would have benefited by $375 before accounting for transaction costs. The minimum tick in coffee is .05, or [5/100] of a penny. Note that 155.00 represents a price of $1.55 per pound and would be verbally quoted as "one fifty-five." If the price were 155.55, the verbal quote would be "one-fifty-five-fifty-five."

Similar to the meat complex, the decimal point in a coffee price isn't intended to separate dollars from cents. Instead, it's a way of breaking each penny into fractions of a penny. To clarify, if prices rise from 163.50 to 164.00, the market has appreciated by a half-cent.

Orange juice futures are written on 15,000 pounds of the underlying commodity, frozen concentrated orange juice, and has a multiplier of $150 ($0.01 × 15,000). As previously mentioned, orange juice futures are priced in cents per pound. The minimum tick value is [5/100] of a cent, so you might see orange juice trading at 135.05, or 135 and [5/100] cents. The price could move to 135.10 or 135.00 but could never trade at 135.02. At 135.05, your broker would verbally quote the contract as "one-thirty-five-o-five." Don't forget that orange juice and coffee futures are similar to the meats, in that the decimal is intended to separate not dollars and cents, but cents and fractions of a cent. Consequently, 135.05 is actually $1.35 and [5/100].

As you have likely inferred from the multiplier, each penny movement in price is equivalent to a profit or loss of $150 for a futures trader. In other words, if the futures price moved from 135.00 to 136.00, a long trader would have made $150 and a short trader would have lost the same amount.

Imagine a trader who goes long orange juice futures at a dollar forty, or 140.00; with the current market price at 147.50, he has an unrealized profit of 7.5 cents, or $1,125. This is calculated by subtracting the purchase price from the current price and multiplying the difference by the multiplier ([147.50 – 140.00] × $150). Because the trader bought the contract at a lower price, we know that the trade is a winner in this amount.

Sugar #11 (not #14) futures are a worldwide benchmark based on a contract size of 112,000 pounds. With that said, each tick in sugar is worth $11.20 to the trader; each full handle of price movement (or penny) is equivalent to $1,120 and acts as the multiplier ($0.01 × 112,000). Don't make the potentially costly blunder of trading sugar #14 or its newer version, sugar #16—those contracts are based on domestically grown sugar and are extremely illiquid futures contracts.

Also similar to orange juice and coffee futures, don't mistake the decimal for separation of dollars and cents. Sugar is denoted in cents and hundredths of a cent per pound. If your quote vendor shows that March sugar is trading at 21.50, it is worth 21[1/2] cents per pound, and your broker might say that sugar is trading at "twenty-one-half" or "twenty-one—fifty."

Sugar used to be considered an ideal market for beginning traders. In the past, margins were relatively low, as were volatility and risk. However, in recent years, sugar futures have experienced large and violent price moves, making participation much more difficult—and perhaps more expensive—than it once was. For example, in Figure 8.5, October sugar futures dropped more than 5 cents, from 23.98 to 18.81. A trader lucky (yes, lucky) enough to have sold at 23.98 and bought the contract back at 18.81 would have realized a profit of 5.17 cents, or $5,790.40. As shown in Figure 8.5, this was calculated by subtracting the price at which the contract was purchased from the price it was originally sold and then multiplying the difference by $1,120 ([23.98 – 18.81] × 1,120). Such a move would be considered relatively mild for those accustomed to trading higher-leveraged contracts such as crude oil futures. However, for a market that has been historically tame, the late 2000s molded sugar into a volatile marketplace.

Figure 8.5 Selling the high and buying the low isn't as easy as it sounds, but if it were possible to sell the high and buy the low of this move, the trade would have netted nearly $6,000 before commission and fees.(Chart courtesy of QST).

Seasonally, the highest prices for cotton futures normally occur between March and July. The lowest prices typically occur between September and November.

Cotton isn't a food; it is a fiber. Nonetheless, it is most often grouped with the softs because it trades on the same exchange and, like the other contracts in this category, is primarily produced overseas. Cotton futures trade in 50,000-pound contracts and are quoted in cents per pound. Again, the decimal point isn't intended to separate dollars and cents; rather, it separates cents from fractions of a cent. In other words, if cotton is trading at 68.50, it is read as 68[1/2] cents. Due to the contract size, each minimum tick of price movement is worth $5 to a trader, and each penny in price movement is equivalent to $500 ($0.01 × 50,000). Therefore, if a speculator sells July cotton at 60.35 and is later stopped out of his position with a loss at 67.30, the total damage to his trading account would be 6.95 cents, or $3,475. This can be determined by subtracting the entrance price from the stop price and multiplying by $500 ([67.30 – 60.35] × $500).

With the exception of Treasury options, all commodity option calculations work the same as with the corresponding futures. The same trader might have purchased a July cotton 80 put for 1.25 and decided to sell it at a loss when the value had depreciated to .70. In this case, the trader would be out the difference, which is $275 ([1.25 − .70] × 500).

Lumber futures are not traded on ICE with the other softs, but they are often categorized with the group because lumber is a fiber. For reasons unknown to me, lumber futures attract beginning traders. Perhaps it is because it is the epitome of the definition of a commodity due to its widespread usage. Nonetheless, it is a sparsely traded contract by speculators, and until liquidity improves, I don't recommend trading it.

I have walked by the lumber trading pit only once (at the CME before merging floors with the CBOT), and there were three market makers passing the time by reading a newspaper. As a speculator, it is never a good idea to trade in a market in which your order will be one of a handful of fills in the entire trading day.

If you insist on trading lumber, you must be willing to accept wide bid/ask spreads and a considerable amount of slippage getting in and out of your position. The contract size for lumber is 110,000 board feet, and it is quoted in dollars and cents. Therefore, each tick of price movement represents $11, and each dollar move equates to $110, which is what you use as the multiplier. In the case of lumber futures, the decimal is used in its usual context. If the market is trading at 216.80, it is interpreted as $216.80 per 1,000 board feet. Likewise, if a trader sells September lumber at 209.50 and is forced to buy back the contract at 218.60, the realized loss would be $9.10 in the futures market and would incur a drawdown of $1,001 to the trading account before commissions and fees ([218.60 − 209.50] × $110).

Precious Metals Futures

By definition, a precious metal is a rare metallic element of high value. To a futures trader, it is simply gold, silver, platinum, and palladium. Copper isn't typically described as a precious metal but is often lumped into this category.

Be aware of the dangers involved in trading what many call a safe haven.

Historically, precious metals are best known for their currency uses but are also utilized in art and jewelry. However, in a post-Bretton Woods world that took the U.S. dollar off the gold standard, gold has lost most of its banking appeal. Despite this, droves of traders insist on speculating on gold prices, with the theory that it holds some monetary value. Accordingly, gold futures tend to trade at an inverse relationship to the dollar in the long run; as one increases, the other falls, and vice versa.

Two Products, Two Versions

Before the NYMEX became part of the CME Group, gold and silver futures contracts with nearly the same specifications (size, point value, and such) traded on both the CBOT and COMEX (now a division of NYMEX). With the exception of the minimum tick value, the contracts were identical. Beginning in fall 2008 the former CBOT metals contracts began trading on NYSE Euronext, a new up-and-coming domestic futures exchange.

Before the CBOT relinquished rights to the alternative version of gold and silver futures, the contracts maintained a healthy amount of liquidity. After being listed on NYSE Euronext, traders seemed to migrate back to COMEX, the original provider of such products. COMEX gold and silver have always maintained leadership when it comes to volume and open interest. As a result, it is generally a good idea to execute metals speculation using the version listed on the COMEX division of the CME Group most often identified by GC (gold) and SI (silver)—some platforms might denote them as EGC and ESI, respectively. Nevertheless, some traders migrate back and forth between the COMEX and NYSE Euronext metals contracts, to take advantage of differences in margin.

Gold, Platinum, and Palladium Futures

Silver prices can be volatile; 20- to 30-cent moves from the previous day's close are common. At $50 a penny, profits and losses add up quick.

The precious metals futures complex attracts a lot of attention from beginning traders. Some of the appeal might be attributed to the fact that they are relatively easy to price, quote, and calculate.

Gold, platinum, and palladium are quoted just as they appear. The decimal included in the quotes is intended to separate dollars and cents. The numbers to the left of the decimal are dollars, and the numbers to the right are cents. In other words, a point in these metals contracts is synonymous with a cent. As shown in Table 8.5, we use even dollar increments as the multiplier for gold, platinum, and palladium futures.

Table 8.5 Precious Metals Contract Specifications

Contract	Multiplier	Contract Size	Minimum Tick Value	Quote Terms
Gold	$100	100 troy ounces	$10	Dollars and cents
miNY Gold	$50	50 troy ounces	$12.50	Dollars and cents
E-Micro Gold	$10	10 troy ounces	$1	Dollars and cents
Mini Gold	$33.33	33.33 troy ounces	$3.30	Dollars and cents
Platinum	$50	50 troy ounces	$5	Dollars and cents
Palladium	$100	100 troy ounces	$5	Dollars and cents

A gold futures contract represents 100 ounces of the underlying commodity and is quoted in terms of price per ounce. Accordingly, each penny of price movement results in a profit or loss of $10 to the trader, and each full dollar movement in price represents $100 of profit or loss ($1.00 × 100 ounces). If gold is trading at $1,530.20 and rallies 60 cents, the price will be $1,530.80. One dollar in futures price movement represents a $100 profit or loss to a trader. Therefore, a 60-cent move would translate into a $60 gain for someone long gold futures and a $60 loss for anyone short before considering transaction costs.

You might have heard gold referred to as a safe haven, or a hedge against inflation or systemic risk, but I encourage you to challenge this premise. The purchase or sale of gold futures is highly speculative and can result in large profits and losses, despite what you might have heard on television. Figure 8.6 displays just how volatile prices can be.

Had a trader bought into the $2,500 gold banter flooding the airwaves in fall 2011, the result would have been disastrous. In three trading sessions, a single contract traded might have lost approximately $20,000. Specifically, a futures trader who went long gold in late August at $1,920.0 and later liquidated the position by selling the contract at $1,720.0 would have lost $200 per contract, which equates to $20,000 to a trader. Once again, this is figured by taking the difference between the entry and the exit price and multiplying it by $100 to account for the fact that a single contract represents 100 troy ounces.

Figure 8.6 Despite being known as a safe haven, gold prices can be extremely volatile. Those on the wrong side of a price move might be unpleasantly surprised.

When I think of a safe haven, Treasury bills and Eurodollars come to mind, not trading a highly leveraged futures contract that is capable of losing the value of a well-equipped economy car in a matter of days. Even if you remove the leverage component, the price exposure is substantial. On the other hand, a trader who sold at $1,920.0 and bought back the contract at $1,720.0 would have been nicely compensated for the risk taken. As shown in Figure 8.6, the bulls would have had a second opportunity to make a tragic mistake a few days later, as the market attempted to rally again but succumbed to a similarly dismal outcome. Unfortunately, traders playing without stops and with horrible timing on their entry might have suffered a loss well in excess of $30,000 per contract.

The massive market moves in metals going into and following the financial crisis of the late 2000s spawned the popularity of "mini" and "micro" gold futures contracts. These are lower-margined and lower-risk ways of gaining exposure to the gold market while still maintaining the simplicity and benefits of trading futures contracts outright. For instance, the COMEX division of the CME Group lists what it calls miNY Gold, which is half the size of the original. No, *miNY* is not a typo; the CME Group lists the contract this way because it is traded in New York, as opposed to its Chicago divisions.

Knowing that the miNY version is half the full-size version, you've probably inferred that the contract size is 50 troy ounces and the multiplier is $50. In other words, for each dollar the price of gold moves, a miNY trader makes or loses $50. The COMEX division of the CME also lists an E-micro gold futures, which is one-tenth the size of the original. Therefore, each dollar movement in gold price equates to a $10 profit or loss to the trader.

Believe it or not, the commodity confusion continues. Along with the miNY and E-micro gold futures traded through the CME Group, a viable mini gold contract is traded on the NYSE Liffe exchange. This contract represents 33.3 troy ounces, or one-third of the original contract size. Accordingly, traders face risk of $33.33 per dollar movement in gold prices.

Platinum and palladium are the less-traded metals contracts. They are treated the same as gold in terms of reading and interpreting quotes; there are no surprises here. However, their point values and multipliers do differ. Palladium has an equivalent point value as gold, $100 per dollar of price movement, but the point value and contract size of platinum is half of that of gold and palladium.

The Other Metal Futures

Silver and copper futures are quoted in cents per ounce instead of dollars and cents per troy ounce, as gold, palladium, and platinum are. Table 8.6 shows that silver calculations are conveniently similar to the grains; however, copper specifications are exclusive to that particular futures market.

Table 8.6 Industrial Metals Futures Contract Specifications

Contract	Multiplier	Contract Size	Minimum Tick Value	Quote Terms
Silver (COMEX)	$50	5,000	$25 (.5 cents)	Cents per ounce
miNY Silver	$25	2,500	$31.25	Cents per ounce
Mini Silver	$10	1,000	$1	Cents per ounce
Copper	$250	25,000 lbs.	$12.50	Cents per pound

Silver Futures

If you're comfortable working with grain quotes and values, silver shouldn't be a problem. Silver is quoted in an identical fashion to corn, wheat, and soybeans. The similarity in pricing and multipliers is directly related to the similarity in contract size. Although a grain futures contract represents 5,000 bushels of the underlying commodity, silver futures are written on 5,000 ounces. As a result, for every penny that the futures market moves, a trader makes or loses $50 ($0.01 × 5,000).

Also similar to the grains, silver futures trade in fractions of a cent. In the case of COMEX silver, the minimum tick is a half-cent, but the former CBOT (now NYSE Euronext) version of the contract trades in dimes. For example, if the price of silver is quoted at 30.305, it is valued at $30.30[1/2] per ounce and can tick up to 30.310 or down to 30.300 in the COMEX version. Keep in mind that the price always has five digits, even if the contract is trading at a whole cent value. NYSE Euronext silver, on the other hand, could move from 30.305 to 30.306 or 30.304. At 30.304, the price is at $30.30 and [4/10] of a cent.

If a trader sells silver at 32.450 ($32.45) and places a buy stop order at 32.600, the risk is $750 plus transaction costs and possible slippage ([32.600 – 32.450] × 50). By the same token, if a limit order is placed at 32.330, to take a profit on the trade if the price of silver reaches the named price, the realized gain is 12 cents, or $600 ([32.450 – 32.330] × 50).

Both the COMEX division of the CME Group and the NYSE Liffe list a mini version of their silver futures contract. However, no micro-size version exists. The COMEX miNY silver futures contract represents 2,500 ounces, which is half the full-size contract. The NYSE Liffe is far more "mini," in that it accounts for 1,000 ounces. At 2,500 ounces, the COMEX miNY silver exposes traders to a profit or loss of $25 per penny in price movement, but the NYSE Liffe risk equates to $10 per cent. You should know, however, that the COMEX miNY silver has a minimum tick of 1.25 cents, or $31.25.

Copper Futures

Many people are surprised to learn that copper futures and options are thinly traded. This creates sizable bid/ask spreads and uncomfortable amounts of slippage in fills in the futures market—and even more so in copper options. The lack of liquidity combined with the excessive price volatility witnessed in the late 2000s has made copper a treacherous venue for speculation.

In contrast to gold and silver, copper is almost primarily used for industrial purposes. Also unlike the other metals that are referred to in terms of cents per ounce, copper is quoted in cents per pound.

The contract size is 25,000 pounds, making the multiplier $250 for a penny move ($0.01 × 25,000 pounds). Simply put, if copper rises or falls by 1 cent, a futures trader makes or loses $250. This makes sense because if the price of copper goes up by 1 penny, you make 25,000 pennies on a long futures position. Also unlike gold futures, copper prices trade in fractions of a cent. If you see copper quoted at 3.6825, it is trading at $3.68[1/4]. Likewise, if copper rallies from this price to 4.050, it represents a gain of 36.75 cents, or $9,187.50 ($250 × 36.25) per contract. This is great if you happened to be long, but a short trader during this move likely lost a lot of sleep.

The Energies

Crude oil and its distillates are among the most talked-about commodities but are also among the most difficult markets to navigate successfully. Futures traders face incredibly high margins and price risk, whereas retail option buyers must overcome extremely large premiums to turn a profit. This doesn't mean that these markets should be off-limits; the leverage they provide makes them among the most exciting commodities to trade and as an advocate of an option selling strategy, experienced traders might find crude oil to be an ideal market-place for short option trading. However, traders should be aware of market characteristics and, as in any market, should conduct due diligence in regard to their chosen strategy. Petroleum futures have become a hotbed of speculation due to global political tension, OPEC policy, volatile demand from emerging markets, and the subsequent price records. If you plan to trade in these markets, you had better be willing to accept large amounts of risk because you are chasing potentially lucrative rewards. To put the stakes into perspective, after peaking at nearly $150 per barrel in 2008, crude oil quickly dropped below $50 per barrel. The move occurred in approximately five months and represents a ballpark value of $100,000 per contract. In other words, had someone been either long or short during the entire move, he would have made or lost $100,000 per contract.

They don't call it "crude" for nothing. Energy futures are highly leveraged, and price changes can be fierce.

Looking at Table 8.7, you can see that WTI, West Texas Intermediate (not to be confused with brent crude traded on the ICE exchange and representing European held oil), is quoted in dollars and cents per barrel. From a trading standpoint, calculating profit, loss, and risk is relatively simple because it is quoted in a format that we are accustomed to in everyday life. The contract size is 1,000 barrels, so each penny of price movement in crude represents $10 of risk to a commodity trader ($0.01 × 1,000 barrels), and each dollar in price movement is equivalent to $1,000 ($1.00 × 1,000 barrels). This number is used as the multiplier.

Table 8.7   Energy Futures Contract Specifications

Contract	Multiplier	Contract Size	Minimum Tick Value	Quote Terms
WTI crude oil	$1,000	1,000 barrels	$10	Dollars and cents
Natural gas	$10,000	10,000 mmBtu	$10	Dollars and cents
Unleaded gasoline (RBOB)	$420	42,000 gallons	$4.20	Dollars and cents
Heating oil	$420	42,000 gallons	$4.20	Dollars and cents

A price quote of 90.00 is just as it appears, $90.00 per barrel of crude. A drop in price from 90.00 to 88.00 is equivalent to a $2,000 profit or loss for a futures trader. Remember, each penny is worth $10 to a trader, and a $2 move in price is 200 cents. Knowing this, calculating option values is a cinch. If a July crude 70 call option is quoted at 1.20, it is valued at $1,200 (1.20 × 100).

Heating oil and unleaded gasoline are much more complicated to figure. Both are quoted in cents per gallon, similar to how prices are displayed at a gas station pump. Consequently, in both cases, the decimal point separates the dollars from the cents, and each trades in fractions of a cent. Both have a contract size of 42,000 gallons; each point in price movement is worth $4.20 to a futures trader, and each penny (100 points) is worth $420 ($0.01 × 42,000). To demonstrate, if heating oil is trading at 2.9120 ($2.91 [20/100]) and rallies to a price of 3.2140 ($3.21[40/100]), the futures contract has gained 30.2 cents, or $12,684 (30.2 × $420). By this example, you can see how easily money can be made or lost in the futures market. A price move of less than 31 cents could result in a profit or loss of several thousand dollars.

Natural gas is one of the most volatile commodity markets. As a result, options written on the commodity are extremely expensive.

Natural gas is quoted in BTUs, or British Thermal Units, which is a measurement of heat. *Nat gas,* as insiders call it, has a contract size of 10,000 mmBTU, or million BTUs. Each tick of price movement in this contract is valued at $10, and there are 1,000 ticks in a dollar. Thus, for every dollar move in natural gas, the value of the contract appreciates or depreciates by $10,000 ($1 × 10,000 mmBTU). To illustrate, if the market rallies from 6.505, or $6.50[1/2], to 7.505, a trader would make or lose $10,000 (multiplier) on one futures contract. This might be enough to deter you from this market, unless you have deep pockets and a high tolerance for risk.

Energy option traders can expect the same computations. For example, if the March natural gas 7.00 call option is quoted at .492, it is worth 49 and [2/10] of a cent. Knowing that $1 is equivalent to $10,000, we can figure that this option has a value of $4,920. This is likely too pricey for the average retail trader; even those who can afford it would likely have a difficult time making money with such a purchase due to wide bid/ask spreads and the massive amount of premium that one must overcome to be profitable on a long option play. However, this is a popular market for hedge funds and some CTAs that have the proper amount of capital to trade in such an environment.

chapter 9

Figuring in Financial Futures—Stock Indices, Interest Rates, and Currencies

The Boring But Necessary Basics

When most people think of commodities, they imagine fields of grain or bars of gold; however, not all commodities are grown or mined. A futures contract might be written on any commodity in which the underlying asset can be considered interchangeable, often referred to by the term *fungible*. In essence, fungible products are those for which an end user would have no preference in choosing one over another. In other words, you wouldn't prefer one bushel of wheat over another. Assuming that the bushel meets the exchanges definition of a deliverable grade, wheat is wheat.

A commodity is any interchangeable product.

Most people don't realize that financial products can be looked at in much of the same way. One Treasury futures contract or unit of S&P futures is just as valuable, or invaluable, as the next. Consequently, financial products also can be considered commodities and trade accordingly in futures markets worldwide.

If you are like most people, you work hard for your money; the last thing you want to do is see it evaporate in a trading account. Unfortunately, I have not yet found a foolproof way to guarantee profitable trading. What I *am* certain of is that you owe it to yourself to fully understand the products and markets that you intend to trade before risking a single dollar. This is true even of products

Leverage, lack of borrowing costs, and transparency make stock index futures popular among speculators, relative to their equity market counterparts.

that seem to be somewhat familiar, such as stock index futures. What you learn from this chapter is merely a stepping stone. After reading it, you won't know when to buy or when to sell, but you *will* have the basic information you need to lay the foundation necessary to become a successful trader.

Stock Index Futures

Stock index futures have become a popular vehicle for speculation because of the leverage involved, efficient electronic trading execution, and perhaps the ability for people to relate to them. Unlike corn or soybeans, most people are aware of the basic fundamentals involved in the equity markets. Therefore, they view stock index futures trading as a venture that might not require as much homework as an unfamiliar commodity contract would. Whether this assumption is accurate is up for debate, but it undoubtedly has contributed to their popularity.

Four primarily traded futures markets exist, based on U.S. stock indices: the S&P 500, NASDAQ 100, Russell 2000, and Dow Jones Industrial Average (see Table 9.1). With that said, you rarely see them referred to in this context. Instead, they are simply referred to as the S&P, NASDAQ, Russell, and the Dow. You might also hear the S&P called "the big board." Several other stock index futures are available, but as a speculator, you want to be where the liquidity is, and many of the other futures simply don't offer that.

Table 9.1   Stock Index Contract Specifications

Contract	Multiplier	Contract Size	Minimum Tick Value	Quote Terms
S&P	$250	$250 × Index Value	$25 (.10 points)	Dollars
e-mini S&P	$50	$50 × Index Value	$12.5 (.25 points)	Dollars
Dow	$10	$10 × Index Value	$10 (1 point)	Dollars
e-mini Dow	$5	$5 × Index Value	$5 (1 point)	Dollars
NASDAQ	$100	$100 × Index Value	$25 (.25 points)	Dollars
e-mini NASDAQ	$20	$20 × Index Value	$5 (.25 points)	Dollars
Russell 2000 mini	$100	$100	$10 (.10)	Dollars

Most of the stock index futures contracts trade on CME Group exchanges. Specifically, the S&P and NASDAQ trade on the CME division of the CME Group, whereas the Dow is a CBOT division product. The Russell 2000 is currently traded on ICE, but before fall 2008, it was a contract cleared by the CME.

> *In general, attempting to trade financial futures contracts in distant expiration months is a bad idea.*

As is the case with all stock index futures contracts and other financial futures products, expiration occurs on a quarterly basis. In other words, each year four stock index futures contract expirations take place, in March, June, September, and December. Conversely, options written with financial futures as the underlying asset often have expirations in each of the 12 months of the year. The options with different expiration months as the futures contracts are commonly referred to as *serial options*. Serial options include January, February, April, and so on.

In both the futures and options markets, contracts with expirations other than the front month have dramatically lower liquidity. This is especially true in the case of the futures contract. Therefore, in most circumstances, futures traders should avoid trading distant-month contracts because the lack of liquidity creates large bid/ask spreads and an unnecessary hurdle to overcome. I have found that beginning traders interested in holding a position for a considerable amount of time often want to trade in a back month, to avoid the hassle and costs involved in rolling into the next contract month. In my opinion, this is destructive behavior because the hidden transaction costs faced in illiquid contracts can often far exceed the money saved in commission.

Electrifying Minis

As I discuss in detail later in the chapter, with the exception of the Russell and the Dow, each major stock index future has two versions, a mini contract and the original full-size contract. In the case of the Dow, a third version is known simply as the Big Dow. This created some confusion at first because traders often referred to the original Dow as "the big Dow," as a way to differentiate it from the mini contract. However, insiders now refer to the complex as the mini Dow, the Dow, and the Big Dow, respectively.

Along with the benefits of lower margins, risk, and enhanced transparency, the mini versions of the stock indices offer increased liquidity and generally recognized better trade execution.

Compliments of lower transaction costs in the futures markets and better trading technology, few traders opt for the full-size versions of the stock index futures. In most scenarios, traders are better off executing their trades in the mini contracts, even though it requires a higher quantity of contracts traded.

Although any market will have a bid/ask spread and some slippage (variance in the fill price and what is expected on stop and market orders), orders in the e-mini Dow, e-mini S&P, e-mini NASDAQ, and mini Russell are electronically routed and executed, making fill quality favorable over similar products traded in open outcry. The ease of entry and exit makes these contracts very appealing to trade and, without a doubt, has contributed to their popularity.

Also contributing to the convenience of trading the mini contracts as opposed to their open outcry counterparts is ease of access to real-time streaming quotes and what is known as a *price ladder*. As discussed in Chapter 3, "The Organized Chaos of Open Outcry and the Advent of Electronic Trading," a price ladder is simply a display of working limit orders surrounding the current market price. From here, you can see market depth (the number of limit orders working) on both the bid (the "Buy" column) and the ask (the "Sell" column). Table 9.2 represents a sample price ladder for the e-mini S&P. Price ladders, or DOM (Depth of Market) panels, display the current market price and the number of working sell limit orders (Ask Size) and buy limit orders (Bid Size). Remember that, as a trader, you can buy at the ask and sell at the bid to take the opposite side of the working limit orders. Contrary to many assumptions, seeing the market in real time—and, better yet, seeing where others are placing orders—hasn't improved the odds for retail traders, but you can understand how it can be useful. In this case, there are more buy orders beneath the market price than there are sell orders above it.

Table 9.2   Price Ladder

Bid Size	Bid	Ask	Ask Size
359	**1,339.00 (2)**	1,339.25	577
1,194	1,338.75	1,339.50	744
1,388	1,338.50	1,339.75	1,400
1,364	1,338.25	1,340.00	877
1,812	1,338.00	1,340.25	911

The Dow is the only futures contract that is offered in three different sizes.

The minority that choose to trade stock index futures using the larger versions of the contracts most often executes positions in an open outcry environment, although overnight sessions in each of the contracts mentioned in this book do offer electronic execution. There are definitely great aspects of open outcry, and I believe that they provide a necessary function. However, when it comes to obtaining live data for an open outcry traded contract, justifying the expense is often difficult; thus, the electronic versions tend to be much more transparent and convenient to trade. Regardless of the contract or version you decide fits your needs as a trader, be sure to know exactly what you are getting into before entering a trade. After all, it is your money.

Stock indices are highly correlated in terms of price simply because, as the market moves up or down, as a whole, each sector follows, to some degree. However, each index has a distinct personality and, at times, is exposed to various risks in various degrees relative to the others. For instance, if a tech giant such as Intel reports negative earnings while the broad-based stocks are profitable, NASDAQ futures might be under selling pressure as the S&P 500 futures are basking in the glory. As a trader, you must be comfortable with the characteristics and contract specifications of the futures you trade and the underlying asset itself.

Dow Jones Industrial Average Futures

As mentioned, Dow futures are listed and traded on the Chicago Board of Trade (CBOT) division of the CME Group. The CBOT's version of the index closely follows the more commonly known Dow Jones Industrial Average, which consists of 30 blue-chip stocks. The CME enables traders to speculate on price changes in the Dow in three increments of risk and reward. Despite the fact that the Dow is the most commonly quoted index in mainstream media, it is not the most-traded futures index: Most traders opt for the liquidity and smoother nature of the e-mini S&P.

E-mini Dow Futures

The most popular of the three listed Dow futures is the e-mini Dow, referred to as the mini-sized Dow before the merger between the CME and CBOT. Industry insiders regularly refer to this contract simply as the mini Dow or even the nickel Dow. The nickel reference stems from its lessened margin and risk, and the point value of the contract, which is $5 of profit or loss per tick.

Most Dow traders flock to the e-mini version due to lower margin requirements and lower risk and reward potential. Those unfamiliar with the realities of risk and reward might wonder why you would choose a contract that offers less leverage. Those privy to speculation realize that too much of a good thing can be disastrous.

The e-mini Dow trades exclusively via electronic execution. An open outcry pit does not exist for either futures or options on this version of the contract. Because of its method of execution, the e-mini Dow can trade continuously for nearly 24 hours per day.

Unlike some of the true commodity futures contracts, the contract size of a stock index is not fixed. In fact, there is no contract *size;* instead, the contract *value* fluctuates with the market and is calculated by multiplying the index value by the point value.

For instance, if the e-mini Dow futures contract settled at 13,100, the value of the contract at that exact moment would be $65,500 ($5 × 13,100). Although $65,500 is the market value of the underlying asset, it is far more than the margin required to buy or sell a mini futures contract. Margins are subject to change at any time, but the average required deposit to trade the e-mini Dow seems to average between $3,000 and $4,000; in addition, day-trading margins are often as low as $500, making this a highly leveraged market. As you can imagine, being responsible for the gains and losses of roughly $65,000 worth of Dow stocks for less than $4,000 could create large amounts of volatility when it comes to the value of your trading account. Nonetheless, the leverage has attracted many futures traders to the markets and keeps them coming back for more. Unfortunately, leverage has also been a major contributor in the experiences of many bitter ex-futures traders.

Calculating profit and loss in the e-mini Dow—or any of the Dow futures contracts, for that matter—is relatively easy. Unlike many other commodities or even financial futures, the Dow doesn't trade in fractions or decimals; one tick is simply 1 point equal to $5. Consequently, if a trader goes long a March mini-Dow futures contract at 13,272 and can liquidate the trade the next day at 13,345, the realized profit would have been 73 points, or $365 (73 × $5), before accounting for transaction costs. This is figured by subtracting the purchase price from the sale price and multiplying the point difference by $5 ([13,345 − 13,272] × $5).

Not bad for a day's work. Regrettably, it isn't always this easy. Had the trader taken the exact opposite position by selling a March e-mini Dow at 13,272 and buying it back at 13,345, the loss would have been $365 plus commissions and fees.

The Original Dow

Although the e-mini Dow is the most popular version of the index among futures traders, the original is still available and is the second most liquid in the

Dow complex. The Dow futures contract is double the size of the mini version, making each tick valued at $10 instead of $5.

Aside from tick value and, thus, contract size, the mini Dow and the Dow are similar in nature. When you are comfortable doing the math on the e-mini Dow, you can easily apply the same principals to the other two contracts, the Dow and the Big Dow, respective to their point values. With that said, each of the CBOT-listed Dow products is fungible. In other words, if you were long two mini contracts and short one regular Dow ($10), you would have the ability to call your broker and request that these positions offset each other.

The method of figuring risk, profit, and loss for Dow futures is identical to that of Dow options. Let's take a look at a simple example. A trader who believes that Dow futures are poised for a large rally might consider buying call options. Assuming that a trader could buy a June Dow 14,000 call option for 54 points, or $540 ($10 × 54), the total risk on the trade would be $540. This is because option buyers, not sellers, face limited risk in the amount of premium paid. If it were later possible to sell the option for 89 points, the trader would be profitable by 35 points, or $350 ([89 – 54] × $10), before subtracting commissions and fees.

Big Dow

In March 2006, the CBOT launched its Big Dow futures contract in an attempt to meet the needs of larger capitalized hedgers and speculators. The Big Dow is exclusively executed on an electronic trading platform. However, higher margins and risk seem to have prevented this contract from becoming a popular venue for retail trader speculation. Open interest and volume remains low, and until this changes, I believe that this contract should be left alone.

Nonetheless, calculating profit and loss for the Big Dow is similar to doing so for the other contracts in the complex. Each point in the Big Dow is valued at $25. Therefore, if a trader goes short a September Big Dow from 13,205 and buys back the contract at 13,125, the realized profit would be 80 points, or $2,000 ([13,205 – 13,125] × $25).

NASDAQ 100 Futures

NASDAQ futures are a CME product that closely tracks the NASDAQ 100 equity index. If you are unfamiliar with the NASDAQ 100, this is an index of the 100 NASDAQ–listed stocks with the largest market capitalization. Unlike the Dow, NASDAQ futures come in only two sizes: an e-mini version and a

NASDAQ futures and the commonly quoted NASDAQ composite typically have drastically different values because the futures index accounts for only 100 stocks.

full-size version. In the case of the CME stock indices—namely, the NASDAQ and the S&P 500—the e-mini versions of the contract are one-fifth the size of the original. Thus, the e-mini multipliers are also one-fifth the size.

Of the major index futures, the NASDAQ complex seems to be more popular among speculators than the Dow but still falls behind the S&P and the Russell in terms of market participation as measured by open interest. However, daily volumes suggest that NASDAQ futures are a vehicle of choice for many day traders. This is likely due to attractive margins and low point values relative to other stock index futures; accordingly, e-mini NASDAQ traders are afforded more room for error.

The Original NASDAQ

It is often said that tech stocks lead the market in and out of bull and bear cycles. As a result, the NASDAQ can be extremely volatile. Therefore, traders must be nimble—and brave.

In my opinion, the original NASDAQ futures contract is ambitious for beginning traders, in that the leverage is high and so is the point value. Even those with substantial risk capital should be cautious when trading this contract because it typically moves fast, resulting in large equity swings in a trading account.

Note that "big" NASDAQ futures and options are highly illiquid and involve large bid/ask spreads. In most cases, it seems as though this is a market that is best to avoid. Although a broker with access to the trading floor can provide optimal execution in this market, the electronically traded e-mini NASDAQ might be a preferable vehicle.

Full-size NASDAQ 100 futures trade in an open outcry environment during the trading day on the CME. However, they are available for trade via an electronic execution platform during an overnight session. This allows for the contract to be tradable nearly 24 hours a day.

Each point of fluctuation in the original NASDAQ results in a profit or loss of $100 for any trader with an open futures position. Keep in mind that 10- to 20-point days are somewhat common, and 50- to 60-point days aren't necessarily rare events. Thus, those willing to accept exposure in this market have a lot at stake. Also take into account that, in the stock indices, the contract size is the point value multiplied by the index value. With the NASDAQ trading at 2,620, traders expose themselves to the profit and loss potential equivalent to $262,000 of the underlying NASDAQ 100 equity index. Unless a trader is well margined and even tempered, he should likely look toward the more manageable e-mini version of this contract.

NASDAQ futures prices (both e-mini and original contract) trade in minimal increments of a quarter of a point, depicted by a decimal, or simply .25. Therefore, each tick in the original full-size contract is worth $25 (.25 × $100). If a trader went short a December NASDAQ from 2,540.25 and placed a stop loss at 2,560.00, she would be risking 19.75 points, or $1,975 ([2,560.00 – 2,540.25] × $100). I believe that this is typically too much for the average retail trader to risk on any given trade but I wanted to portray the realities involved in trading this market. The NASDAQ is capable of seeing such a price move in the blink of an eye and then taking it back in another blink; realizing this, the CME wisely created a mini version of the NASDAQ 100 futures contract. I suspect that the CME Group will eventually delist this version of the NASDAQ, perhaps within the next few years.

e-mini NASDAQ

Similar to the e-mini Dow, the e-mini NASDAQ futures contract is fully electronic, making price ladders displaying the quantity of working limit orders and streaming real-time quotes an affordable possibility. This also makes it possible for trading to commence nearly 24 hours per day.

Again, e-mini CME stock index futures are one-fifth the size of the original contracts. Therefore, the point value per full unit of movement in an e-mini NASDAQ futures contract is $20 (one-fifth of the original $100), reducing the contract size considerably. With the futures market at 2,560.00, an e-mini NASDAQ contract is equivalent to $51,200 of the underlying index. Profit, loss, and risk calculations are also much easier on the eye and the heart.

At $20 per point, it might seem as though trading the e-mini NASDAQ is relatively tame. However, as Figure 9.1 shows, profits and losses can add up quickly. For example, a trader who went short a December e-mini NASDAQ at 2,689.00 might have found himself in a horrible situation about four weeks later, as the market approached 2,900.00. At a price of 2,876.00, the unrealized loss would have been 187 points, or $3,740 ([2,876.00 – 2,689.00] × $20). Of course, a trader who had taken the opposite position would have been profitable by the same amount.

This is a rather extreme example, but it shows that even mini futures contracts shouldn't be taken for granted. The risks and rewards are high, so always respect the market. That said, during times when trade resembles its historical norms more, the e-mini NASDAQ is a relatively attractive arena for stock index speculation.

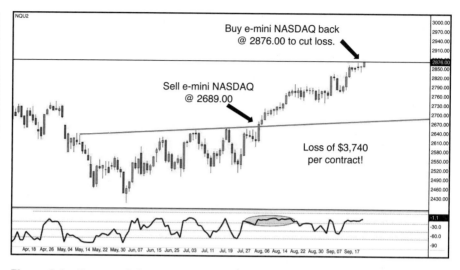

NQU2

Buy e-mini NASDAQ back
@ 2876.00 to cut loss.

Sell e-mini NASDAQ
@ 2689.00

Loss of $3,740
per contract!

Apr, 18 Apr, 26 May, 04 May, 14 May, 22 May, 30 Jun, 07 Jun, 15 Jun, 25 Jul, 03 Jul, 11 Jul, 19 Jul, 27 Aug, 06 Aug, 14 Aug, 22 Aug, 30 Sep, 07 Sep, 17

Figure 9.1   Even e-mini products deserve respect: Profits and losses can mount quickly. (Chart courtesy of NinjaTrader.)

S&P 500 Futures

One of the busiest open outcry option pits is that of the big board S&P. Hedge funds, institutions, and speculators enjoy the leverage and favorable trade execution the product offers.

The S&P 500 is by far the most popular speculation vehicle among stock index futures. Volume and open interest in both the options and futures markets for each denomination (e-mini and full-size) dwarf that of the NASDAQ, Dow, and Russell. The original full-size S&P 500 futures are often used by institutions as a means of hedging portfolio risk and, in some cases, even speculation. However, this pit, in particular, experienced a dramatic drop in trading volume following the demise of MF Global simply because many of the S&P floor traders either were affiliated with MF Global or used the brokerage to clear the trades.

The S&P futures complex is the most widely traded stock index market on U.S. exchanges and, arguably, the most traded in the world.

The attraction to the S&P is likely the fact that it is a broad-based index that best represents the market as a whole and is, therefore, seen as a benchmark of large-capitalization stocks in the U.S. The S&P 500 futures contract represents the widely followed Standard and Poor's 500 index and is a CME product that is now traded on the combined CME/CBOT trading floor.

The Original S&P 500

The full-size S&P 500 futures contract trades in an open outcry environment during the day and electronically by night, making it available to traders nearly 24 hours per day. It is one of the few contracts that has managed to avoid going electronic during the day and, up until late 2011 (the anniversary of the MF Global failure), had one of the more active trading pits on the exchange floor.

The full-size S&P futures contract has a multiplier of $250 with a minimum tick of .10 or $25 to a trader. Therefore, for every dollar, or point, of price movement in the S&P, the trader makes or loses $250. In other words, if the price moves from 1,400.00 to 1,401.00, the index has moved a dollar and would represent a $250 gain for those long the market and a $250 loss for those short the market.

Knowing this, we can easily calculate the contract value of the index. Assuming that the futures price was 1,325.00, one full-size S&P 500 futures contract would be valued at $331,250. Although margins vary with market conditions, the average margin in the S&P tends to be between $20,000 and $25,000. As you can imagine, being responsible for the profit or loss for a contract valued at more than $300,000 with a deposit of less than $30,000 results in a highly leveraged endeavor. Both the rewards and the risks are magnified considerably, and traders must be willing to accept the consequences. That said, traders can essentially eliminate the leverage by depositing the full value of the contract being traded with leverage, profits, and losses add up quickly.

For instance, a trader who goes long an S&P futures contract at 1,389.40 and is forced to sell it due to margin trouble at 1,253.20 would have sustained a loss in the amount of 136.2 points, or $34,050, plus the commissions paid to get into the trade ([1,389.40 − 1,253.20] × $250). Likewise, a trader short the market would have benefited in the same amount. Accordingly, many traders aren't willing to accept this type of volatility in their trading accounts and look to the e-mini version of the contract. Nonetheless, I doubt that even plentifully capitalized S&P traders would allow a loss to extend to such a degree, but it would be nice if a trader had the fortitude to let the winners run in this way.

Open Outcry S&P Options

Perhaps one of the most respected option trading pits on the newly combined CME/CBOT floor is that of the S&P. Institutions and large speculative traders are lured in by the ample liquidity and massive contract size. Because the options are written on such a large underlying contract, the premiums can be high. Accordingly, option sellers and option spread traders often find that this market offers favorable circumstances. However, the opportunities do not come without risks and hefty margin requirements for option sellers.

E-mini S&P 500

Those trading the original full-size S&P 500 futures contract have a lot at stake; both the point value and the margin are high. As a result, many speculators have turned to the e-mini version of the contract, which is exactly one-fifth of the size. For the average retail trader, the reduced contract size supports more effective risk management.

Trades in the e-mini S&P 500 futures market are executed exclusively electronically; an open outcry pit does not exist. As with the larger version of the contract, the e-mini S&P is open for trading nearly 24 hours per day. The minimum tick in the e-mini S&P 500 is a quarter of a point, or .25, which differs from its full-size counterpart's ticks valued at a dime, or .10. Because the point value of the e-mini S&P is $50, the minimum price movement is worth $12.50 ($50 \times .25$) to a trader.

At $50 per handle, if the e-mini S&P 500 futures are valued at 1,350.00, the contract would represent $67,500 of the underlying asset. Now that's more like it. An e-mini S&P futures trader is exposed to risk, but relative to the "Big Board" contract, the risk is much more manageable. When it comes to leverage, less is sometimes more. Let's take a look at an example.

If a trader opts to buy a March e-mini S&P at 1,401.50 but would like to protect himself from runaway losses by placing a sell stop order at 1,385.00, he would be risking 16.50 points, or $825 ([1,401.50 – 1,385.00] $\times$ $50).

E-mini S&P options are also popular among retail traders because of ample amounts of liquidity and the transparency of electronic execution. Unlike open outcry options, in which quotes are expensive and hard to come by without having a contact on the trading floor, electronic option quotes (bid/ask spreads) are readily available at a discounted price, or perhaps free if you're with the right brokerage firm. In addition, the relatively low multiplier creates affordable options and attracts traders of all capitalization levels.

The financial crisis of the late 2000s ushered in a unique opportunity for option buyers in the e-mini S&P. In fact, most traders might not see that magnitude of volatility again in their lifetimes. For instance, it was possible to buy a December e-mini S&P 500 1,050 put for $10.50 in premium, or $525 (10.50 × $50), in mid-September 2008. Option buyers face a maximum risk in the amount paid for the option; therefore, the absolute worst-case scenario was a loss of $525 plus the commissions and fees, and maybe a little bit of confidence. However, the profit potential of a long option is theoretically unlimited, as Figures 9.2 and 9.3 show.

Figure 9.2 Long-option traders tend to migrate to the e-mini S&P due to affordable option premiums and perceived risks. In this example, a trader buys a 1050 e-mini S&P put for a total risk of $525. (Chart courtesy of Gecko Software.)

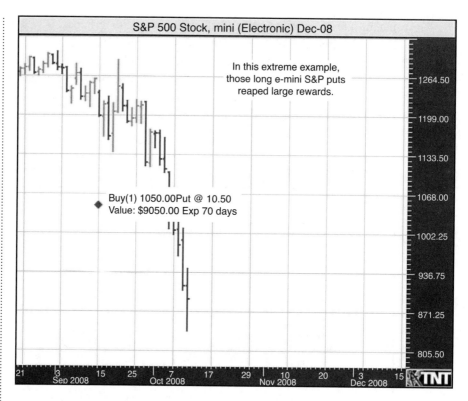

Figure 9.3 This particular "lottery ticket" proved to be a winner, but it isn't always this easy for long-option traders. More often than not, options expire worthless. (Chart courtesy of Gecko Software.)

As Figure 9.3 shows, by mid-October, it might have been possible to sell the December e-mini S&P 1050 put for as much as $181.00 in premium, or $9,050. Calculating the profit and loss of a e-mini S&P option trade works identically to calculating for futures; the purchase price is subtracted from the sales price and multiplied by $50. Assuming these fills, the trader would have realized a profit of $170.50, or $8,525 ([181.00 – 10.50] × $50).

This would have been an exciting and lucrative trade to be a part of. Nonetheless, it is an extreme example of how a long option play can result in large returns to a trader. In fact, this particular instance might be categorized as a once-in-a-lifetime event: The market move that occurred during this period was one of the largest in history. In more normal market conditions, something like this might not be possible. In my opinion, most long options can be thought of as a lottery ticket that has the *potential* to return abnormal rewards but isn't necessarily likely to do so.

Arbitrage

The price at which the large version of the S&P and the e-mini S&P are trading at any given time is nearly identical, aside from the differences in minimum tick values. This is made possible through the practice of arbitrage trading. As you should recall from Chapter 1, "A Crash Course in Commodities," the term *arbitrage* describes a risk-free opportunity. That said, we all know that truly risk-free trades are nonexistent. Nonetheless, there's no shortage of traders who will try to beat the odds, and in some circumstances, the very quick stand to profit on the difference between valuations on two related contracts.

> Constant arbitration between the large and small contracts in each of the stock index futures ensures that all versions of a particular contract trade at or near identical prices.

Some arbitrage traders attempt to profit on differences in price between the large S&P contract and the e-mini version. For instance, if the e-mini is trading at 1,350.50 and the full-size version is at 1,350.60, a trader might look to buy the cheaper version and sell the expensive version. Don't forget that it would be necessary to buy five e-minis against every original S&P contract.

Assuming fills at the noted prices, the trader is locking in a profit of .10, or $25 (.10 × $250), before considering transaction costs. The constant search for such opportunities ensures that the spread between the prices of the two contract remains narrow.

Russell 2000 Futures

Russell futures have grown in popularity perhaps because of the leverage offered, or maybe because of the ease in calculating profit, loss, and risk. This index is considered to be a benchmark for small-cap stocks, a market sector that is notorious for experiencing volatility and leading markets in and out of secular bull and bear markets. Do not confuse the Russell 2000 futures with the Russell 1000 futures. Although the 1000 version is offered, it does not have enough market liquidity for efficient trading. Therefore, any time brokers or traders refer to the Russell, they are speaking in terms of the Russell 2000.

Unlike the other indices, the Russell futures do not have a full-size counterpart. Before the move to from the CME to ICE, a large version of the contract was traded in an open outcry environment. However, ICE does not have a trading floor and opted to drop the large Russell 2000 altogether.

The Russell is relatively easy to calculate. Each tick is worth $10 to the trader, and each full point is worth $100; this is what we use for the multiplier.

Therefore, if the Russell drops from 851.00 to 850.00, a trader short the market gains $100. Had it dropped to 849.90, the profit would have been $110.

Interest Rate Futures

As discussed, the term *commodity* can describe a wide array of assets, including financial products. The formal definition of *commodity* is a physical substance or asset that is "interchangeable" in trade. From a general standpoint, a commodity is simply any product that trades on a futures exchange, and interest rate products fit the bill. Just as you wouldn't prefer one bar of gold over another, you likely wouldn't have a preference between one T-bill and another. The CBOT recognized this and created a complex of U.S. Treasury futures products. Each of the standardized Treasury contracts represents government-issued fixed-income securities ranging from short-term T-bills to the 30-year bond.

Interest rate futures do not earn interest; they are simply a speculative play on the direction of interest rates.

Not all interest rate futures are based on government-issued securities; the CME division of the CME Group is home to the Eurodollar futures contract. In its simplest definition, a Eurodollar represents U.S. dollars deposited in commercial banks outside the United States. Due to liquidity and affordability, it is a popular tool for hedging interest rate risk, specifically the London Interbank Offered Rate (LIBOR).

The Eurodollar is the most heavily traded futures contract in the world. Much of the appeal comes from relatively affordable margin requirements and typically low levels of volatility. However, during times of economic turmoil or uncertainty, price moves can be uncharacteristically large.

A Complex "Complex"

Several widely traded contracts are available in the realm of interest rate futures and options. Each of these contracts carries slightly differing market characteristics and, in some cases, different contract sizes, point values, and so on. For those unfamiliar with the futures markets, these discrepancies can be overwhelming. However, I hope to deliver the pertinent information clearly to make your journey into financial futures trading as pleasant as possible.

Before I cover the basic specifications of each contract, it is important to be aware of a few facts regarding bond valuation and the characteristics of each underlying asset. Although thoroughly covering the details here is impractical, my intention is to give you the foundation needed to understand the mechanics of Treasuries.

Inverse Relationship Between Price and Yield

The value of a bond or note (the price in which it is trading) is inversely corre-lated with interest rates or yields. Accordingly, if interest rates go up, the price of Treasury securities drops, and vice versa. This can be explained by the value of the bond or note's stated interest rate. If market rates go up, any securities issued with lower interest rates are less valuable. Likewise, if market rates decline, the value of bonds and notes issues with higher stated interest rates increases.

Long Maturities Versus Short Maturities

Because a fixed-income security is one in which the value is derived from the future cash flows (coupon and face value at maturity), its market price fluctuates along with current market interest rates. These futures cash flows are coined *coupon payments* and are fixed based on the yield at the time of the bond or note issue. I discuss the cash flows of bonds and notes in the next section, "Treasury Bond and Note Futures." For instance, if the market rate at the time the Fed sells 10-year notes is 2%, the investor would receive periodic interest payments based on that rate and the size of the investment. This is true regardless of fluctuations in market interest rates.

Bonds tend to be more volatile in nature than notes, and notes more so than T-bills.

The possibility of market interest rates changing after the issuer sells a bond or the buyer invests is referred to as *interest rate risk*. Naturally, if you purchase a bond at face value with a coupon at 2% and interest rates go up to 4%, you will feel a bit of buyer's remorse. However, this is the risk (interest rate risk) that bond investors and sellers must accept and adapt to.

As mentioned, if current interest rates go up from the time of issuance, the value of the coupon payments on the existing bond goes down, as does the market price of the security itself. It is important to realize that bonds with longer maturities face increased levels of interest rate risk; accordingly, the prices of these securities react much more quickly and more violently to changes in market interest rates.

Cash market bond securi-ties are often quoted in yield, but futures are quoted in price.

Keep these points in mind as you review the details of each contract because they can help you determine which avenue best suits your risk tolerance and personality when trading interest rate futures products.

Treasury Bond and Note Futures

Treasury futures are similar to agricultural-based futures contracts, in that they represent the future delivery of the underlying asset. Therefore, a Treasury futures contract enables the buyer and the seller to agree upon a price today for delivery and payment of the asset at a specified date in the future. Confusion often stems from the fact that the underlying asset of Treasury futures is much more difficult to define than it is for a physical commodity such as corn or soybeans. This is because of the wide variation in expiration dates available in each Treasury category eligible for delivery and the various yields of similar securities.

The terms *bond* and *note* are commonly used in finance and even among the less informed investment community, but the details of the instruments are often overlooked. I believe that it is worth the time to review some of the basic concepts behind the mechanics of bonds and notes, to give you a better grasp of the instrument being traded in the futures market.

Treasury futures are futures contracts written with U.S. government–issued coupon securities as the underlying asset. The U.S. government issues three instruments based on the time to maturity: bonds, notes, and bills. The bond is often coined the "long bond" because it has the longest time to maturity, at 30 years; this contract also is referred to as the T-bond or the 30-year bond. Notes can have maturities ranging from 10 to 2 years, whereas bills have a life span of a year or less. The most commonly quoted note is the 10-year note, which is often referred to as the T-note or simply "the note," and is considered to be the benchmark interest rate.

Bonds and notes are collectively referred to as fixed-income securities or coupon bonds. This is because they are a claim on a specified periodic stream of interest income known as coupons.

The textbook definition of a bond or note is a debt security in which the authorized issuer is indebted to the holder. In essence, the bond issuer is obligated to repay the principal and interest (coupon) to the holder at a later date, termed *maturity*. In its simplest form, a bond or note is a loan with a fancy name. The issuer (seller) is equivalent to the borrower, and the buyer is the lender. The seller pays the buyer the coupon payment, or interest, to compensate the buyer for the funds borrowed. In essence, the seller collects money from the buyer and issues an IOU to be payable in the form of periodic coupon payments (interest) throughout the life of the bond and a lump sum paid at maturity equal to the principal paid to acquire the bond. This principal amount is also known as the *face value* or *par value*. In the case of Treasury bonds and notes, the issuer is always the U.S. government. Therefore, Treasury buyers are believed to be virtually free of default risk because the U.S. government has never defaulted on its obligations. Nevertheless, massive government borrowing in the late 2000s sparked questions on the ability of the U.S. Treasury to pay back its obligations.

To illustrate the point, a 30-year bond with a par value of $1,000 and a coupon rate of 5% ($50) might be issued to a buyer for $1,000. At this point, the buyer agrees to hand over $1,000 in exchange for an annual income stream equivalent to 5% of the par value ($50) for the life of the bond. At maturity of the bond, the holder receives the original $1,000.

Discount Securities

The U.S. government refers to its discount securities as Treasury bills, or simply bills. Treasury bills have maturity dates of up to one year. Although T-bill futures contracts are available, they are not widely traded, creating illiquid and undesirable market conditions. Nonetheless, I feel it necessary to point out their existence because, outside the futures markets, they are a relevant piece of the financial market puzzle.

Discount securities are those that have no coupon or interest payment; instead, the bondholder can purchase the security at a discount to par, with the expectation of receiving the full par value back upon maturity. With this form of security, the interest isn't paid in coupon payments; it is paid at maturity as the difference between the face value and the purchase price. For instance, if an issuer sells a security with a face value of $1,000 for a price of $950, the holder will receive a 5% return upon maturity of the security because he will be receiving more at expiration than he paid to purchase the security. Unfortunately, 5% discount bonds seem to be a thing of the past; government-manipulated interest rates and the Great Recession have driven discount yields to nearly zero at the time of this writing.

What Does a Treasury Futures Contract Represent?

The CBOT has declared that the underlying assets for its 30-year bond, 10-year note, and 5-year note futures contracts are $100,000 worth of the respective

U.S.-issued Treasury securities. Unfortunately, this isn't as simple as it seems. Certainly, more than one maturity date exists for each of the fixed-income securities, with various coupon payments and so forth. The question you are probably asking is, which exact security is reflected by the price of the corresponding futures contract?

Instead of assuming that a Treasury futures contract represents a single bond or note (it doesn't), look at it as a proxy. Simply, it trades as an index for a variety of issues within a range that the exchange specifies. This noted range is commonly referred to as *deliverable securities*. The range of deliverable bonds or notes includes all those eligible for delivery based on CBOT standards. Here's where many people get lost: The CBOT has developed a conversion factor system to enable the futures contract price to reflect the full range of available fixed-income issues.

The exchange assigns a conversion factor to each bond or note eligible for delivery based on the CBOT specifications. Specifically, conversion factors are assigned to each cash market bond or note that meets time maturity specifications for the particular futures contract expiration.

The conversion factor allocated by the CBOT represents the price in terms of percentage, based on the price that the par value of the security would trade if it had a 6% yield to maturity. Specifically, a conversion factor is the approximate decimal price at which a $1 par of a security would trade if it had a 6% yield-to-maturity. As a result, government bonds or notes that have a coupon less than 6% are assigned a conversion factor that is less than 1. A conversion factor less than 1 signifies that the issues are returning a coupon that is at a discount to the 6% standard. Bonds and notes with a coupon greater than 6% have conversion factors greater than 1, to reflect that the security's coupon payment is priced at a premium.

Based on this brief discussion, it is probably obvious that the intricacies of the conversion factor can get somewhat complicated and are beyond the scope of this text. However, you should gain from this description of the process that the net effect of the conversion factor is to link the different prices of the bonds and notes eligible for delivery, to create a single price at which the corresponding standardized futures contract can trade. Simply put, the conversion factor enables Treasury bond and note futures to trade as if they were an index of the underlying securities eligible for delivery.

Knowing that the futures contract is based on conversion factors using a 6% yield, it is easy to see why the price of the futures contract typically doesn't correspond to the prices seen in the cash market. This is especially true in extreme cases such as the summer of 2012, when yields on the 30-year traded well under

3%. It is important to recognize that the current market yield will always be similar in reference to the futures market versus the cash market.

T-Bond Futures

Several years ago, the long bond, or the 30-year Treasury bond (a.k.a. the T-bond), was the primary interest rate product traded on the CBOT. During its prime, it was considered the only contract for experienced traders to be involved with. However, the Federal Reserve's failure to issue new 30-year bond contracts on a regular basis has worked against the popularity of the contract. In the meantime, shorter maturities, such as the 10-year note, benefited in terms of volume and open interest.

The Treasury bond and note futures complex is the only one in which options are quoted in different terms than futures.

Similar to the other financial futures contracts, such as currencies and stock indices, all interest rate products are on a quarterly cycle. This means that there are four differing expiration months, based on a calendar year: March, June, September, and December. Unlike true commodities, traders typically avoid distant expiration months. For example, if the official front-month 30-year bond contract were March, the volume and open interest in the June contract would generally be sparse, and there would be even less trading activity in the September contract.

As is the case in the stock indices, a mistake beginning traders often make is to try to enter the market using a distant contract month, with the intention of holding the position for a considerable period of time. Their reasoning in doing so is

Bond and note futures values are referred to in fractions.

typically to avoid the additional transaction cost associated with entering the front month contract and being forced to roll into the next contract month upon expiration of the current month. This thought process is flawed. As I have mentioned, the lack of liquidity in the distant expiration months results in wide bid/ask spreads; therefore, the hidden transaction cost paid by the trader is often far greater than the commission saved. Accordingly, this practice might be much more harmful than helpful.

We've noted that the 30-year bond is often referred to as the long bond because of its lengthy maturity, but you might also know it simply as "the bond" because other Treasury issues are known as notes or bills.

Because the 30-year bond has the longest maturity of the Treasury complex, it is situated at the end of the yield curve and typically carries the highest yield. The yield curve is simply a plot of the relationship between interest rates and their time to maturity. As for the rest of the yield curve, under normal circumstances, the notes carry less of a yield relative to the bond, and the bills pay less than the notes. This scenario has been dubbed a *normal curve* and makes sense because an investor who locked into a security for 30 years would demand more compensation than one who invested for 10 years.

As Table 9.3 shows, the face value of a single T-bond futures contract written with the bond as an underlier is $100,000. Knowing this, it is easy to see that a contract can be looked at as 1,000 points, or trading handles, worth $1,000 a piece. What isn't very obvious is that each full point or handle can then be looked at as a fraction.

Table 9.3   Treasury Futures Contract Specifications

Contract	Multiplier	Contract Size	Minimum Tick Value	Quote Terms
T-bond	$1,000	$100,000	$31.25 (1 point)	Fractions of par
T-note	$1,000	$100,000	$15.625 (.5 points)	Fractions of par
Five-year note	$1,000	$100,000	$15.625 (.5 points)	Fractions of par
Two-year note	$2,000	$200,000	$15.625 (.25 points)	Fractions of par

The term *handle* often describes the stem of a quote. This usage began in reference to currency futures to describe a penny move but is now commonly used as slang in nearly all futures contracts. For example, if the Euro rallies from 121.00 to 122.00, some might say that it has moved a handle. Likewise, if the T-bond drops from 131'00 to 130'00, it is said to have moved a full handle.

Treasury bond futures trade in ticks equivalent to 1/32 of a full point, or $31.25, figured by dividing $1,000 by 32. Adding to the confusion, in early 2008, the CBOT decided to alter the contract by allowing traders to buy or sell bond futures in half-ticks, or $15.625. In other words, this change made a minimum price movement in the T-bond futures .5/32. Ironically, in fall 2009, the exchange opted to return to the original format, which no longer permitted trading in half-tick increments.

The futures and options trading arena can be frustrating because it seems as though the rules are constantly changing. Nonetheless, it isn't the trader's job to analyze why or how the exchange determines contract specifications; traders must simply be aware and accept them.

Bonds are quoted in terms of their $1,000 handles. Thus, a typical bond quote can be 132-24. This is read as "132 handles and 24/32nds" and is equivalent to a contract value of $132,750. It is calculated by multiplying 132 × $1,000 and then multiplying 24 by the point value of $31.25. You could also come to the same conclusion by multiplying the fraction 24/32 by $1,000. In my opinion, this method causes the least amount of confusion, so we use $1,000 as the multiplier. On a quote board, you might see something that looks like this: 137'24. It is read simply as "one-thirty-seven-twenty-four."

Those comfortable with the process of adding and subtracting fractions can easily derive profit, loss, and risk; those who are fractionally challenged might find trading Treasuries frustrating. Yet I am confident that anyone can quickly become proficient in bond futures calculations after looking at the following examples.

I don't expect you to understand or even remember bond futures prices by simply looking at a quote and the multiplier, but the following examples should add some clarity. If a trader buys a December T-bond futures contract at 137'22 and can later offset the position by selling the contract at 138'24, the trader realizes a profit of 1'02, or 1-2/32. We know that the trade was a positive one because the purchase price is below the sales price. Therefore, subtracting the entrance price from the exit and multiplying the result by $1,000 results in a gain of $1,062.50 (1-2/32) × $1,000). If dealing with both full numbers and fractions is confusing, it is possible to split them up before multiplying and add the results of each. For example, we know that the profit was at least $1,000 (1 × $1,000) because of the full handle of gain. To calculate the remaining portion, we simply multiply the fraction by $1,000 (2/32 × $1,000) to arrive at $62.50; together, we get $1,062.50.

The multiplication involved in bond futures calculations is relatively standard, but people tend to be unjustifiably intimidated by fractions. If you recall the concept of borrowing, you will be fine. In the preceding example, it wasn't necessary to borrow. The numbers were convenient enough to simply subtract the numerator (the top number in the fraction) of the buy price from the numerator of the sell price and multiply the result by $1,000. Likewise, you would have subtracted the handle of the buy price from the handle of the sell price and multiplied the result by $1,000.

The math isn't always this opportune. Sometimes you need to borrow from the handle to bring the fraction to a level at which you can properly figure the profit or loss; this is where many opt to trade another market. For example, a trader who sells a June bond at 138'12 and buys back the contract at 136'27 might have a challenge when it comes to calculating the exact profit. In this case, it is easy to see that the trade was profitable because the trader bought low and sold high, in the opposite order. However, unless you have been doing this for a while, it deriving the net profit takes a little work.

In this example, the numerator of the sell price, 12, is much smaller than the numerator of the buy price, 27. Therefore, we know that we must borrow from the handle to properly net the fractions; otherwise, we would end up with a negative number and, likely, mass confusion. The least complicated way of coming to a fraction that is easily workable is to reduce the selling price handle to 137 from 138 and increase the fraction by 32/32. In other words, after reducing the selling price by a handle, we add 32/32nds to the existing fraction of 12/32nds, to arrive at 44/32nds.

Then we can easily subtract 27/32 from 44/32 to determine a profit of 1'17

The 2-year note is the only contract in the Treasury futures complex with a differing contract size and point value.

([137 – 136] + [44/32 – 17/32]). From here, we can convert the fraction to dollar value by multiplying by $1,000. Assuming these fills, this trade would have been profitable by $1,531.25 before commissions and fees ([1-27/32] × $1,000).

T-Bond Options

As if trading and calculating bond futures weren't difficult enough, the CBOT created options written on Treasury futures with a slight twist to the valuation. Instead of quoting bond options in 32nds as the futures contracts are, the exchange opted to value them in 64ths. The multiplier remains $1,000, so each handle still carries the same value; the only difference in figuring the options as opposed to the futures is the fraction it is multiplied by. Let's look at some examples.

One of the most memorable and dramatic bond rallies of all time occurred late in 2008 and caught a majority of traders by surprise. The example that we visit is strictly for the sake of understanding how bond option values are calculated and in no way represents a trading strategy that I recommend employing. However, as you will see, doing so would have worked out very well in this instance. Dramatic market conditions make this a fun trade to imagine happening to you, but based on my experience and conversations with others, most traders were speculating in the wrong direction. Instead of the windfall of profits you are about to witness, some had the opposite experience.

Let's revisit the events of late 2008 in which many of the financial markets experienced volatility that might never be matched. In mid-November of that year, T-bond futures successfully broke out of a trading channel that began in September. However, with yields at historically low levels, many traders doubted the ability of the market to make considerable gains; remember, when bond prices are high, interest rates are low. Many were treating the breakout as a potential bull trap in which prices would quickly reverse and trade lower into the trading range. Those who were keen enough to see what was coming next might have opted to purchase a March bond 125 call option for 1'58, or $1,906.25 (1-58/64 × $1,000), as shown in Figure 9.4. Normally, I wouldn't recommend spending such a dollar amount on an option that could very well expire worthless. After all, most options are worthless at expiration. Once again, this is simply being used as a mathematical example.

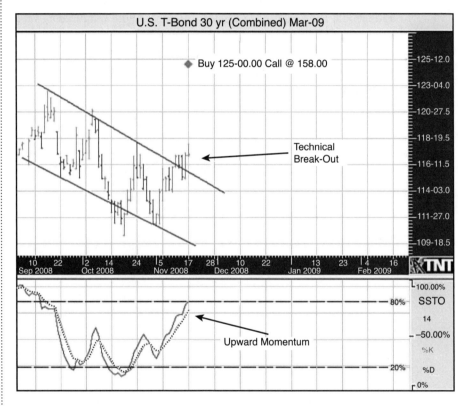

Figure 9.4 Whether trading options or futures, the goal is to buy low and sell high; there is no need to complicate things any more than that. If this trader pays 1'58 for a call option, he is hoping to sell it for more at some point in the future. (Chart courtesy of Gecko Software.)

What happened next could have never been predicted. The March 30-year bond futures swiftly rallied above 135 to crush previous standards of what was then an all-time high in price and low in yields. This particular rally was the ice breaker for what the market eventually came to know as the "new normal." By the early 2010s, 30-year bond futures frequently traded in the 150s. Back to the example at hand, a trader willing to risk nearly $2,000 on an option with a strike price well above and beyond levels normally seen in the T-bond would have been compensated handsomely for what seemed like a long shot.

Looking at Figure 9.5, you can see that, by mid-December 2008, approximately a month later, the option once purchased for 1'58 was valued at 11'51. Assuming that the option could have been sold for such a premium, the dollar value of the sale would be $11,796.88 ($1,000 × 11-51/64). Accordingly, this trade would have resulted in a net profit of $9,890.63, figured by subtracting the purchase price from the sales price and multiplying the difference by $1,000. To make the fractions "workable," it is necessary to borrow a handle from the entry price and add 64/64 to the exit price. When this is done, the following equation can be easily figured to arrive at $9,890.63.

$$([10\text{-}115/64 - 1\text{-}58/64]) \times \$1,000) = \$9,890.63$$

Figure 9.5 Strictly long option strategies don't necessarily provide traders with optimal odds of success, but for those in the right place at the right time, the payoff can be large.

The purpose of these examples is to give you an idea of how T-bond traders can calculate their trading results. Obviously, not all bond trades or traders make money, but I hope that giving you the proper background in the basics of futures trading allows you to focus on your speculative skills and increase your odds of success as a result.

10-Year Note

The 10-year note, or simply "the note," has many similarities to the long bond. The contract size, the point value, and the manner in which options are quoted are all common characteristics. Similarly, if you can come to peace with the 30-year bond calculations, the 10-year note won't pose any hurdles.

To reiterate, the contract size of the note is $100,000, which is split into 1,000 handles equivalent to $1,000 and a tick value of 1/32, or $31.25; however, the T-note futures and options trade in half-ticks (.5/32), valued at $15.625. Therefore, if you see notes priced on a quote board as 132'295, they are trading at 132'29-1/2, not 132-295/32.

Calculating profit, loss, and risk for the 10-year note is identical to calculating for the 30-year bond. To demonstrate, if a trader goes short the 10-year from 128'29.5 and places a buy stop to defend himself from an adverse move at 130'15.0, the risk on the trade would be 1'17.5, or $1,546.87. This is calculated by subtracting the entrance price of the short position from the potential fill price of the buy stop, at 130'15.0. Once again, the math requires borrowing from the handle to properly subtract the fractions. This is done by adjusting the stop price from 130'15.0 to 129'47 ([130 − 1] + [15/32 + 32/32]) before doing the math. After this, you can easily subtract 128'29.5 from 129'47.0 to arrive at 1'17.5 of risk, equivalent to $1,546.87.

As with bond options, note options are quoted and calculated in 64ths rather than 32nds. Thus, if a trader sells a June 133 10-year note put for 35/64, she is collecting $546.88 (35/64 × $1,000). If she is later forced to cover the position by buying it back for 52/64, the net loss would be 17/64, or $265.63 (17/64 × $1,000).

5-Year Note

In many aspects, the 5-year note is identical to the bond and the 10-year note. As with the others, each futures contract represents a face value of $100,000 of the underlying security. The 5-year note is also broken into handles valued at $1,000 each, and each of these is divided into 32nds. Unlike the bond and the

10-year note, each point (32nd) in the 5-year note is traded in quarter-ticks. In other words, each 32nd moves in increments of .25/32. As you should recall, the bond and note (10-year) have a minimum price fluctuation of 1/32 and .5/32, respectively. If 1/32 is equal to $31.25 and .5/32 is worth $15.625, then we know that .25/32 must be $7.8125. Nobody said this would be easy. The futures markets can be potentially lucrative, but there is no such thing as easy money.

Other than the fact that they trade in quarter-ticks, there aren't any surprises when it comes to 5-year note calculations. Although the process remains the same, the tick increment requires an additional digit to be typed into your calculator.

A trader who goes short a December 5-year note from 122'24.25 and subsequently places a limit order to take profits at 121'21.50 will be profitable in the amount of 1'02.75, or $1,085.94. This is figured by subtracting the limit order price from the original sell price and multiplying the difference by $1,000 ([122'24.25 – 121'21.50] × $1,000).

2-Year Note

The 2-year note is the "oddball" of the Treasury complex. Likely in part due to the CBOT's anticipation of commercial hedgers and speculators using the 2-year note as a trading vehicle, they adjusted the contract size in a way to cater to larger transactions. Unlike the others, this contract has a face value at maturity of $200,000. Thus, the value of a point (handle) is $2,000, and 1/32 is equivalent to $62.50. As with the 5-year note, the minimum tick is a quarter of a 32nd, or simply .25/32. In dollar terms, this is $15.625.

Another reason for the difference in contract size of the 2-year note relative to the other notes and bonds is that the U.S. government issues significantly more debt in the 2-year maturity. Accordingly, more 2-year Treasury notes are traded in the underlying cash market. In other words, the CBOT opted to list the contract with a $200,000 maturity face value to provide "economies of scale" for market participants. This translates into saving the hassle of paying an additional commission, which is interesting and noble logic for an organization that thrives on trading volume in the form of exchange fees charged on a per-contract basis.

With the diversity in contract size and point value relative to the other Treasuries, calculating profit and loss in the 2-year note must be slightly adjusted. A trader who is long a September 2-year note futures at 108'10.75 and is later stopped out of the trade at 106'02.25 would have realized a loss of 2'08.50, or $4,531.25 (remember, 1 handle = $2,000).

Eurodollar Futures

Many traders confuse Eurodollars with the Forex currency pair Euro/dollar. They might sound the same, but that is where the similarities end. A Eurodollar futures contract is written on a 3-month interest rate vehicle denominated in U.S. dollars but is deposited in off-shore banks (see Table 9.4). At its simplest, it is an interest-bearing deposit of U.S. funds in a foreign bank and is based on the London Interbank Offered Rate, or LIBOR. Consequently, the interest rates offered to Eurodollar holders (in the cash market) are relatively low due to the minimal perceived risk of default.

Table 9.4   Eurodollar Futures Specifications

Contract	Multiplier	Contract Size	Minimum Tick Value	Quote Terms
Eurodollars	$25	$1,000,000	$6.25 (.25 points)	100 - Yield

It is important to note that Eurodollars have nothing to do with Europe; dollar-denominated deposits in Asia are also deemed to be Eurodollar deposits. The *Euro* prefix merely indicates any currency held in a country in which it is not the official currency. An example is the commonly discussed Euroyen, which are Japanese Yen-denominated deposits held in banks outside Japan.

Eurodollar futures have become wildly popular among speculators and commercial hedgers. Their appeal stems from the fact that they are extremely liquid and, although highly leveraged, typically see less trading volatility relative to other futures contracts. Unlike the other financial futures markets, the liquidity in Eurodollars ranges well into distant expiration months. It is possible to actively trade Eurodollar futures with maturity dates spanning from several months to years. This seems like an opportune time to warn you that distant-month Eurodollar futures move much more quickly than do the closer months. Therefore, the benefit of reduced volatility diminishes as you choose contracts with longer expiration dates.

> *Eurodollars are a great place for beginning traders or for those who are simply risk averse.*

Together the CME Eurodollar futures and options lead the worldwide industry in open interest. The daily volume averages 3 million, making this the most liquid futures market in the world. A large majority of Eurodollar volume is executed electronically though the CME Globex platform, enabling efficient and timely fills. However, at one time, the CME's Eurodollar pit was just as enormous in square footage as it was in trading and audio volume. Unfortunately, the advent of electronic trading has been detrimental to the world of open outcry, and the Eurodollar pit was no exception.

A Eurodollar futures contract represents $1,000,000 of the underlying asset. To put the amount of leverage into perspective, the margin on a Eurodollar futures contract is typically near $1,000. Thus, a trader can enjoy, or suffer from, the profits and losses based on a million dollars deposited overseas with a mere $1,000.

Eurodollar futures involve a considerable amount of leverage due to low margin requirements and a large contract size. However, the short-term nature of the underlying interest rate product works to keep prices relatively slow moving.

Similar to the other interest rate products, Eurodollar contract expirations are quarterly: March, June, September, and December. Fortunately, the point values and minimum increments are quoted in decimals rather than fractions, as is the case with the other interest rate products.

The Eurodollar is typically quoted in five digits, with the last representing a fraction of a point. Eurodollar prices are verbally communicated just as they look. For instance, if the December Eurodollar is trading at 98.450, it is said that it is "ninety-eight forty-five." However, 98.455 would be spoken as "ninety-eight forty-five and a half." Each trading handle of a Eurodollar futures contracts represents $2,500 to a trader. Accordingly, each individual point in price movement results in a $25 gain or loss in a trading account. Therefore, the full handle value of a Eurodollar is $2,500, and the tick value is $25. This contract has a minimum price movement of a half-tick, or $12.50 for most months, but it is a quarter-tick, or $6.25 for the nearest expiring month. Simply put, if the price of a June Eurodollar futures rallies from 98.550 to 98.560, a profit or loss of $25 would have occurred. For a plunge from 98.550 to 97.550, the move would represent a profit or loss of $2,500.

The difference in minimum tick increments between contract months is likely because the near-month Eurodollar futures contract doesn't typically see much in the way of price change. The daily price change in the front month is typically less than five ticks, making it a great place for beginning speculators to get their feet wet. However, as previously mentioned, the deferred Eurodollar contracts react more violently to changes in interest rates or climate. If your risk tolerance is low to moderate, stay with the near months.

Eurodollars are quoted in handles and decimals and are simply an inverse of the corresponding yield that is tied to the LIBOR. For example, a Eurodollar price of 98.500 implies a yield of 1.5%. This is figured by subtracting the contract price from 100 (100 − 98.500). Rates this low are somewhat rare but can and do happen. For example, the now infamous credit crisis of the late

2000s sparked a massive flight to quality in which the Eurodollar was a beneficiary. Naturally, Eurodollar futures rallied to compensate for increased demand
in the spot market. The result was incredibly high valuations and low yields.

Before the financial meltdown of 2008, I was convinced that yields couldn't
go to zero. However, massive buying of Treasury bills in fall 2008 and well
beyond did create a scenario in which investors were essentially *paying* to park
their funds in a security guaranteed by the federal government because T-bills
were trading at a negative yield (their market price was higher than the par value
received at expiration). On the other hand, Eurodollars are not backed by the
U.S. government—or any government, for that matter—so there is some
perceived risk of default. Conceivably, we can infer that the Eurodollar will
probably never trade at 100.00, which would imply a yield of zero. Thus, in
general, as the futures price approaches 100.00, you should consider the
technical setup of the market and fundamental forces to construct a bearish
strategy.

Calculating in Eurodollars is much less cumbersome than that of the
Treasury complex because it lacks fractions. A trick simplifies the process.
Before you begin your calculation, merely move the decimal point two places to
the right and multiply each (full) tick by $25.

As always, the process involves determining whether the trade is a profit or
loss, subtracting the lesser number from the greater, and multiplying it by the
appropriate figure, but don't forget to move the decimal point. Consider an
example: If a trader buys a December Eurodollar futures contract at 98.035
(98.031/2) and later sells it at 98.220, the realized profit on the trade is 18.5
ticks (9,822 – 9,803.5), or $462.25 (18.5 × $25).

In my opinion, beginning traders and those who simply prefer a slower-
paced market should strongly consider trading Eurodollar futures and options.
With that said, even Eurodollars experience periods of excessive volatility,
making it important that traders in this market consciously avoid complacency.

Additionally, Eurodollar traders often make the mistake of letting losers run
simply because of the slow-paced nature of the market. For instance, if an open
position is consistently losing $25 to $50 per day, it isn't going to break the bank
in the beginning. However, if this is persistently the case, losses can mount, and
pulling the plug on such a trade might be psychologically difficult.

Currency Futures

Most have heard of the Forex or FX market in which cash market currency
transactions take place. Fewer are aware that currency futures are traded every

day at the CME via its electronic Globex trading platform. In stark contrast to the FOREX market, which is mostly an unregulated marketplace, currency futures have always fallen under the jurisdiction of the NFA and the CFTC. Accordingly, some of the regulatory and counterparty risks that exist for FX traders are irrelevant to currency futures traders. Nevertheless, U.S. regulators have made significant strides in enforcing compliance rules in the FOREX markets. If you are interested in an in-depth look at currency trading in various venues, my book *Currency Trading in the FOREX and Futures Markets* (FT Press, 2012) discusses the advantages and disadvantages of trading currencies using FX, futures, and ETFs.

Currency futures are mostly traded in "American terms." This simply means that the prices listed in the futures market represent the dollar price of each foreign currency, or how much in U.S. dollars it would cost to purchase one unit of the foreign currency. To understand the point of view of the futures price, ask yourself, "How much of our currency does it take to buy one of theirs?"

Euro, Franc, and Yen

Euro and Yen futures have little in common except that they have identical profit-and-loss calculations. Each of these currencies has a minimum tick value of $12.50 and a multiplier of the same value. Therefore, every tick of either the Euro or the Yen creates a profit or loss to the trader of $12.50. Despite this, the contract size of the two contracts is vastly different. The size of a single Euro futures contract is 125,000, whereas a Yen futures represents 12,500,000 Yen (see Table 9.5).

Table 9.5   **Currency Futures Contract Specifications**

Contract Terms	Multiplier	Contract Size	Minimum Tick Value	Quote
Euro	$12.50	125,000 Euro	$12.50 (1 tick)	Tick
Yen	$12.50	12,500,000 Yen	$12.50 (1 tick)	Tick
British pound	$6.25	62,500 British pounds	$6.25 (1 tick)	Tick
Canadian dollar	$10	100,000 Canadian dollars	$10 (1 tick)	Tick
Australian dollar	$10	100,000 Australian dollars	$10 (1 tick)	Tick

To clarify, if the Euro has a value of 1.2539, it is equivalent to saying that a single Euro could be purchased for $1.2539 U.S. dollars. Notice in Figure 9.6 that the decimal is shifted two places to the right. Unfortunately, it is not uncommon in commodities to run across slightly different methods of quoting any given contract. Another variation of the Euro quote is one with an extra zero at the end of the quote. In this case, you might see something like this: 1.25390. Nonetheless, you can always use $12.50 multiplied by each tick (the fourth digit to the right of the decimal) to determine the value of any position.

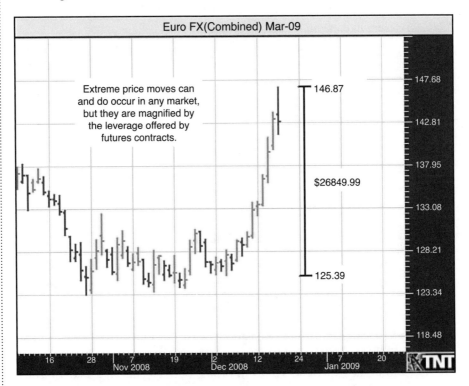

Figure 9.6 Don't be fooled by seemingly quiet currency markets; they have the potential for explosions. Traders should utilize proper risk management to avoid devastation in extreme scenarios such as the rally witnessed in December 2008. (Chart courtesy of Gecko Software.)

The Euro is a relatively new phenomenon; it was introduced to the world financial markets in January 1999 and replaced the former independent European Currency Units. The Euro is the official currency of 16 of the 27 member states of the European Union, known collectively as the Eurozone.

Another currency has a tick value of $12.50: the Swiss Franc. Many traders refer to this contract simply as the "Franc," and it is identical to the Euro in terms of size and point value. Before the Euro, the Franc was a widely traded futures contract. However, in the current environment, the volume traded in the Swiss Franc is a fraction of that seen in the Euro.

When figuring profit and loss for the Euro, the Franc, and the Yen, the tick value is best used as the multiplier. As mentioned, for each tick higher or lower that the futures price moves, a long trader would have made $12.50, and a trader short the market would have lost $12.50. Although $12.50 might not seem like much, it adds up quick.

Going back to what will perhaps be the most exciting year ever in the financial markets, 2008; beginning on December 4 and running through December 18, the Eurocurrency made history. The March futures contract rallied from 1.2539 to 1.4687, representing a profit and loss to a single lot trader of nearly $27,000, as depicted in Figure 9.6. As you can imagine, it was the move of a lifetime for those fortunate enough to be long—and a disaster for those left short. To calculate the exact profit and loss of the trade, you simply subtract 1.2539 from 1.4687 and multiply the difference by $12.50, to reach $26,850 ([14,687 − 12,539] × $12.50).

Aussie and Canadian Dollars

Known as the commodity currencies simply because their valuations tend to be correlated with commodity prices, the Australian dollar and the Canadian dollar future contracts are similar in nature. Both have a stated contract size of $100,000 of the corresponding currency (not the U.S. dollar) and a tick value of $10. Similar to our calculations with the Euro, the Franc, and the Yen, the multiplier is the tick value. Accordingly, for every tick that a trader gains or loses, he experiences a profit or loss of $10. Thus, if a trader buys a September Aussie dollar futures contract at 0.9300 and places a limit order to sell it back at 0.9310, the realized profit would be $100 (before commissions and fees) after the profit target is executed. This is figured by subtracting the purchase price from the selling price and multiplying the difference by $10 ([9,310 − 9,300] × $10).

British Pound

The British Pound is in a league of its own, in that its specified contract size and tick value are vastly different from any of the other currencies. The British

Pound, sometimes referred to as the "cable," when paired against the U.S. dollar, trades in contracts of 62,500 British Pounds. Accordingly, each tick in price movement results in a profit or loss of $6.25 for any trader with exposure in this market. You might have noticed that the contract size and the tick value are exactly half that of the Euro, the Franc, and the Yen. Despite much different contract specifications, calculations of profit and loss are similar to the other currencies. Therefore, if a trader is short a December British Pound futures from 1.4950, meaning that it would take $1.4950 in U.S. dollars to purchase a single Pound, and is later stopped out at 1.4975, the loss on the trade would be $156.25. This is figured by subtracting the original sales price from the fill of the stop loss order and multiplying the difference by $6.25 ([1.4975 – 1.4950] × $6.25).

Don't let the lower tick value fool you into thinking that there is relatively lower risk in trading the British Pound; this is far from the truth (Figure 9.7). In fact, the Pound is capable of unbelievably volatile moves. I have personally witnessed a single trading session in which the British Pound futures market traded in an approximate range of 1,000 points, or $6,250 per contract. This type of move is extremely rare—it has happened only once—but anything is possible at any time.

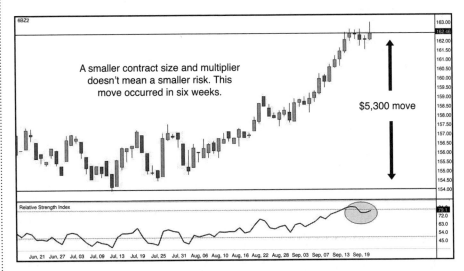

Figure 9.7   Traders should respect the potential for sizable moves in the British Pound—and any other market—despite the relatively small tick value. It isn't uncommon to see moves that equate to several thousand dollars of profit or loss to a trader in a matter of weeks, such as this rally from about 1.5400 to just over 1.6200.

Conclusion

The information in this chapter certainly won't carve your fate as a trader. However, without familiarity of the basic contract specifications and corresponding risk and reward, you aren't giving yourself a fair shake. The odds of successful trading are characteristically unfavorable, making it imperative that you do everything in your power to shift them in your direction. I believe that awareness and experience will do just that. After all, being properly educated about the "boring" details might prevent emotional trading decisions that could endanger your hard-earned money.

chapter 10

Coping with Margin Calls

Thanks to movies and other media outlets, many beginning traders have become overly frightened by the idea of a margin call. Truth be told, if you trade responsibly, you shouldn't receive many, but it can—and eventually will—happen. When it does, there's no need to panic; most margin calls can be alleviated via position adjustment instead of adding funds to the account or outright liquidating trades.

What Is Margin?

Unlike equity accounts, in which margin is granted only to a few, all futures accounts are margin accounts.

Margin is simply a specified amount of funds stipulated by the exchange and required to be held in a brokerage account to enter and keep open positions in a futures market. In its simplest form, it is a good-faith deposit or financial collateral used to cover credit risk. By demanding margin required to trade in any given contract, the exchange mitigates the possibility of traders defaulting on their trading or losing more money than they have on deposit and not meeting their obligations to those on the other side of the trade.

Futures traders are not charged interest on money borrowed, as equity traders are.

Although the exchange sets margin requirements, brokerage firms have the authority to increase rates. That said, brokerage firms are forbidden from decreasing margin or allowing undercapitalized traders to hold positions in the long term. We soon discuss that this rule does not apply to day traders.

Additionally, keep in mind that margin requirements are dynamic. The exchange and brokerage firm can change them at any time and without notice.

Initial Margin

You can use the terms *initial margin* and *margin* synonymously. Specifically, initial margin is the amount of capital that the exchange expects a trader has in a corresponding trading account to hold a given futures contract, or option spread, beyond the close of trade of the session in which the order was executed. Simply put, if the initial margin on a T-Note futures contract is $3,000, a trader should have at least this much in his trading account to buy or sell, and hold, a single contract.

Maintenance Margin

Maintenance margin, on the other hand, is the minimum account balance that must be maintained at the close of trade to avoid a margin call. The maintenance margin is typically 70% to 80% of the initial margin. When the account equity dips below the maintenance margin measured on the close of trade on any particular day, a margin call is triggered, and the trader is required to bring the account equity above the *initial margin* requirement by either liquidating positions, adding funds, or mitigating the margin through position adjustment. Bringing the equity above the maintenance margin level is no longer enough.

Day Trading Margin Versus Overnight Margin

A big misconception looms concerning how margin is levied by the exchange. Most people assume that traders must have the proper exchange-required margin to enter a position. This isn't necessarily the case; instead, the brokerage firm, or your individual broker, determines whether you have adequate margin to initiate a trade. Exchange-stipulated margin doesn't come into play until the end of the trading session. At this time, the exchange margins any open positions accordingly. Many traders are surprised to discover that the exchanges have little say on the margin charged for day trading activity.

Depending on a trader's established relationship with a brokerage firm—or, more important, an individual broker—the margin charged on any intraday positions can be anywhere from 10% to 50% of the exchange's stipulated overnight rate. Naturally, only clients who are believed to be responsible enough to have access to excessively low margin requirements are granted the privilege because irresponsible traders are a credit risk to the brokerage. This is similar to the threats posed to credit card companies by consumers with low credit scores. With that said, some platforms can now automatically liquidate the account if it is in danger of going negative or losing more than what is currently deposited.

When it comes to margin, just because you can doesn't mean that you should. Remember, a fool and his money are soon parted.

If autoliquidation is a capability of the platform, more lenient margin policies might be offered to day traders. After all, similar to the way a trader analyzes the market in terms of risk and reward, a brokerage firm assesses clients on a risk/reward basis and proceeds accordingly. Brokerage revenue is commission based; they want you to trade, but not if it isn't worth the potential consequences.

Therefore, traders with little money in an account can trade with margin well below the exchange's stated margin level without ever receiving a margin call, assuming that they always exit their positions before the close. For instance, a broker might permit a trader with an account balance of $2,000 to day-trade one e-mini S&P futures contract even though the overnight margin requirement is upward of $3,500. In extreme cases, brokerage firms have been known to extend discounted margins to traders to the tune of 5% to 10% of the overnight rate. Thus, assuming an exchange stipulated margin of $5,000, a trader might buy or sell the futures with as little as $500—or maybe less. Keep in mind that although it is not a good idea, aggressive traders have been known to abuse leverage because they have the freedom to do so.

Again, once a trader holds a position beyond the closing time of the day session, overnight margin rates are imposed and, if appropriate, margin calls are issued.

What Are Margin Calls?

The term *margin call* seems to infer that a trader is contacted by phone about a margin deficiency, but margin calls are typically communicated by email, thanks to modern technology. Brokerage firms provide clients with daily activity statements in which a margin call is noted, if applicable. A separate margin call notice might also be emailed to stipulate the amount of the margin deficiency and a countdown of the days.

How to Handle a Margin Call

Beginning traders are prone to panic when a margin call is received; however, this is an unnecessary emotion that can cause poor trading decisions. Margin calls can be eliminated in one way or a combination of three ways:

1. **Partial or total account liquidation.** In many cases, traders who have received a margin call notice are holding several positions. They might be spread across a handful of markets or all in the same contract. Nonetheless, a margin call doesn't require that all the positions be offset; the trader must liquidate enough of them to bring the account into good standing.

   With partial liquidations, it is important to monitor the positions throughout the day and pay special attention to the closing prices of the contracts in your account. This is because the exchange levies margin requirements based on your positions at the close of the day session in conjunction with the closing prices of all the positions in your account. If values of the remaining positions change from the time the original margin deficit was calculated, the time the partial liquidation took place, and the close of trade, it is possible that the actions taken were not enough to eliminate the margin call.

   For instance, consider a trader who is long two e-mini NASDAQ futures in which the initial margin requirement is $3,300 per contract and an account equity balance is $4,000 at the time one of the two contracts was offset. All else being equal, the trader faces an initial margin requirement of $3,300 and has approximately $700 in excess of the required funds. However, if the market drops sharply from the time the first contract was liquidated into the close, the margin call might remain an issue. In this example, this would occur if the e-mini NASDAQ drops approximately 35 points, causing the account balance to drop below $3,300.

2. **Margin adjustment through trade and risk alteration.** Although the exchange-required margins for any given futures contract is relatively fixed, it is possible to adjust the margin of your overall portfolio of positions using options or even futures. For example, a trader who is long a futures contract can purchase a put option in the same market as a method to reduce the risk—and, therefore, the margin requirement—on the futures contract. The same trader can also look to sell a call option for a similar but less effective impact on margin. If you are unfamiliar with

options or these types of strategies, you might be interested in reading my book *Commodity Options* (FT Press, 2009). Unfortunately, the scope of this book does not permit paying proper attention to these somewhat complicated strategies. Nonetheless, you need to realize that there are ways to alleviate margin issues, aside from throwing in the towel and liquidating the account or depositing additional funds.

Similarly, futures traders might look to reduce their risk and, more important, margin requirement by taking the opposition position in a highly correlated contract. For instance, a trader long March corn can sell a July corn contract to mitigate margin and hopefully alleviate a margin call. This is effective because the July contract tends to move in the same direction as March. However, after such an adjustment is made, a trader faces tough decisions on how to move out of the spread. At some point, completely exiting the trade or lifting one leg at a time will be necessary. This type of strategy can be compared to putting a Band-Aid on a wound. It conceals the injury but doesn't necessarily heal it. Moreover, the Band-Aid eventually needs to be removed—and this could be painful.

3. **Wired funds.** This is the most straightforward method of bringing an account within margin. Still, it is not without its complications due to the timing in which the margin is measured and levied. For example, the exchange charges margin on any positions being held at the close of trade, but margin calls are expedited late in the evening or early in the morning on the subsequent day. The trader then has the entire trading session to act before margin is calculated again.

Market conditions frequently are drastically different from the time the initial margin deficit is calculated to the time the margin call is received—even more so by the close of trade the following day, at which point the account is reassessed. Therefore, it is possible for traders to wire funds to meet the stated margin call, only to find out that, due to adverse price changes in the remaining positions, the wired amount was not sufficient to meet the call. For this reason, it is a good idea to wire more than the stated margin deficit.

The Margin Call Countdown

Similar to the manner in which margin is imposed, margin calls are measured in terms of days. As we have mentioned, measurement of whether a margin call has been met takes place at the close of day session trade. Any accounts that have failed to meet the initial margin requirement go into the next day with an aging margin call.

The amount of time a firm gives for eliminating the margin call varies but is most often within one to three days. If you find yourself in the midst of a margin call, it might be a good idea to follow a timeline, as outlined next; carrying a margin call too long or putting the account in danger of going negative could result in forced liquidation by the margin department. Simply put, if the margin department of a brokerage firm must step in to bring an account in line with required margin, it pays no attention to the prices or circumstances of liquidation. Its goal is to get the account under "control" in the quickest manner possible. As a trader, you never want to put your account in a situation in which third parties have a say in when and where you exit a trade.

Note that many deep discount brokerage firms are much stricter when it comes to margin calls. Due to their ultralow commissions, they can't afford to accept the risk of account debits as much as a balanced firm might. As a result, they might practice tight controls that could have a negative impact on overall trading results. Once again, sometimes saving money on transaction costs is actually more expensive when looking at the big picture.

Day One

A *first-day call,* issued the day the margin call is given, is a friendly warning that you have gotten in a little over your head and should reevaluate your positions. Unless the account is in danger of losing more than what is on deposit, known as going negative (you might also hear this referred to as *going debit*), a brokerage firm generally allows you to treat the first day as a freebie. In other words, even in the absence of any action taken by the trader, the broker should avoid liquidation of the positions.

Although action might not be immediately required, during the course of the first-day margin call, a trader should determine a plan of action that includes either wiring money, liquidating some or all the positions, or, preferably, adjusting current positions to meet the pending margin call. With that said, if the trader intends to adjust the margin by using hedges with futures and options, he should begin the adjustment process on day one of the margin call.

Some brokerage firms charge margin call fees to accounts that allow the margin deficiency to go beyond the close of trade on the first day of the margin call. Fees typically range from $25 to $50 per day, starting on day two. Additionally, some firms put the account on liquidation-only status.

Day Two

Hopefully traders take care of the problem on the first day; if not, on the second day of a margin call, traders are *expected* to take some action to alleviate the margin call. Additionally, adding positions to the account is considered irresponsible, so traders should refrain from trading unless the broker handling the account has granted consent. Excessive abuse of trading privileges can lead to tighter controls on the trading account, thus creating an undesirable situation for both trader and broker. Clearly, brokers and brokerage firms prefer that you trade more, not less, but they are also second-party risk bearers to their client's trading accounts. Not only do they have to answer to the exchange about margin deficits, but they also are responsible for seeing that any debit (negative) account balances are covered, even if this means withholding broker commissions until the client brings the account whole again.

If a trader fails to eliminate the margin deficit but has made an effort through position adjustments and/or partial liquidation, the brokerage firm generally sees it as cooperation and might grant the trader some freedom going into the third day of the margin call. Nonetheless, it is recommended that traders take care of their margin responsibilities within the first day or two of the margin call.

> "The safe way to double your money is to fold it over once and put it in your pocket."
> —Frank Hubbard

Day Three

If at all possible, a trader should avoid taking a margin call into the third day. However, it is understandable that, in certain circumstances, it can happen. In this situation, hopefully the trader used the second day wisely and reduced the margin deficit. Doing so makes it much easier to assess the actions necessary to get margin under control. Therefore, on the third day of a margin call, traders should be seriously focused on *eliminating* the margin deficit, regardless of the consequences. Most brokerage firms begin to take action on an account when a margin call is carried into the third day. This means that they have the authority to liquidate the account as they see fit to bring the account within margin. Trust me, this is not something that you want to experience. To reiterate, margin clerks aren't traders. Their sole purpose is to get the account compliant, which means they are not necessarily concerned with getting you the best fill price. Additionally, they tend to be heavy-handed, in that they sometimes liquidate above and beyond what is necessary to compensate for possible market movements in other positions.

Accepting Margin Calls

I thoroughly believe that psychology plays the largest part in determining whether a trader is successful, and margin calls are an important part of the equation. It is imperative that traders recognize that margin calls can, and do, happen; traders should be properly prepared to cope with them. Margin call management for clients is an area in which a good broker will earn his money.

Traders who understand the process and have reviewed contingency plans for margin issues stand a much better chance of defeating the overwhelming sense of panic that occurs when time and capital limits are applied to a position. Also, just as consumers are better off living within their means, traders should make every attempt to speculate within the confines of the capital available. Too often, beginning traders assume that more leverage will result in quicker profits; in reality, this couldn't be further from the truth.

chapter 11

The Only Magic in Trading—
Emotional Stability

As an industry insider, I am repeatedly confronted by those looking for a magic indicator, trading system, or newsletter. They want somebody, often me, to tell them where to buy and where to sell, and do it with impeccable accuracy. Regrettably, I am forced to bring them into reality.

> "If all the economists in the world were laid end to end, they still wouldn't reach a conclusion."
> —George Bernard Shaw

In my years as a broker, I have come across droves of retail and institutional traders and just as many trading strategies and methodologies. I have yet to discover any individual system or style that is capable of making money in *all* market conditions all of the time. Those who find a way to make money more often than not require excessive dedication to research and adjustment. In other words, there is no Holy Grail or easy money. Simply reading a few books on trading or subscribing to a signal service isn't going to ensure that you will trade profitably, but doing so could point you in the right direction. If you are looking for magic, go to Disneyland; you will not find it in a trading seminar, a book, or a newsletter—at least, not without putting your blood, sweat, and tears into it.

The only "magical" tool I have found in trading is the ability to keep emotions under control; without that, the best indicators or trading recommendations in the world won't be helpful. For instance, if in late 2007 I told you to sell the S&P futures at 1,500 and continue to roll over the position to avoid delivery until you have the opportunity to buy it back at 688, do you really think that you would have had the emotional stability to hold the position through all the peaks and valleys—or, better yet, the faith in my recommendation to do so?

Clearly, very few people, if any, would have the fortitude to execute a trade of this magnitude. Even if psychic powers were involved, in 2007, it would have been difficult to imagine that the value of the S&P would be cut in half. After all, to reap the entire reward of 812 points in the S&P ($203,000 per contract in the full-size version, $40,600 in the e-mini), the trader would have had to resist liquidating the trade prematurely at any point in the roughly 1 1/2-year time period that it took to complete the recommendation.

This is obviously an extreme example, but the same difficulties and emotions are involved in following a trading signal, recommendation, or idea of your own. The argument I am trying to make is that perhaps trading success is equally, or more so, reliant on psychology because it has a large influence on the implementation of the actual trading technique, philosophy, and indicators used or systems purchased.

Most trading literature emphasizes the impact that fear and greed can have on trading decisions and, ultimately, the bottom line. However, I believe that another emotion has the potential to wreak havoc on traders and their account balances: frustration. Each of these emotions is necessary but, in excess, can be catastrophic.

Warren Buffet's take on the subject is incredibly insightful. According to the "Oracle of Omaha," traders should "Be fearful when others are greedy and greedy when others are fearful." This is simply saying that traders should buy low and sell high in terms of market sentiment rather than price.

Traders who flock to the latest craze or newsworthy buzz are likely to get burned. This is because, after a market has attracted attention, there is a good chance that the move has run its course. On the contrary, the best opportunities can often be found in markets that have fallen out of interest with the general public.

The study of emotion and trading is ongoing, and an unlimited number of theories focus on managing the sensations that one feels before, during, and after any given trade. Believe it or not, as a broker I have seen many futures and options traders get more satisfaction out of the rush of being exposed to the markets than they do making money. I have to admit, part of what sparks me to get up in the morning is seeing what the markets have in store for our clients and me. Whether it is good or bad, it keeps us all coming back for more. Nonetheless, my motivation is money rather than thrill.

More to the point, studies have shown that traders with the ability to stabilize their emotions, in both winning and losing situations, see more positive trading results than traders who are less capable of managing their feelings. Unfortunately, unless you are born with a natural ability to effectively cope with the excitements of trading, the ability to do so will come only with experience.

Three Emotions in Trading: Fear, Greed, Frustration

In this chapter, I briefly discuss a few of the most influential emotions traders experience. Expecting that you will walk away from this book with all the insight that you need to control your emotions while trading is impractical. Yet I do believe that by getting a broad-based overview of what you can expect and some of the common traps that traders fall into, you will at least be able to identify such emotions; this is the first step toward managing them.

> "When everybody starts looking really smart, and not realizing that a lot of it was luck, I get scared."
> —Raphael Yavneh (*Forbes*)

Fear

If you have ever participated in the financial or commodity markets, you are well aware of the fears associated with them, such as the fear of losing money, being wrong, or leaving money on the table. Fear is a natural and necessary emotion, especially when money is involved. After all, if you are completely fearless when it comes to your trading, the odds are in favor of taking excessive risks and eventually losing your trading capital. Despite financial theory that suggests additional risk is equivalent to additional profit potential, the correlation diminishes when a certain threshold is met. The line in the sand is difficult to draw, but when you cross it, you will know—and at that point, it might be too late.

In my experience, *fearless* traders might have intermittent success simply because they are swinging for the fence and will achieve their goals from time to time. However, long-term success for such traders is unlikely because unnecessary risks will eventually haunt irresponsible traders.

Instead, traders should give the markets an appropriate amount of respect and approach them with a modestly fearful attitude. I believe that some fear of loss can work to keep traders humble and emphasize that, regardless of the countless hours of research performed and even an Ivy League education, traders can lose money trading commodities. In theory, a controlled fear of the markets and the devastation they are capable of can encourage more objective and sound trading decisions.

Although I speak of having a moderate amount of fear as though it is as simple as hitting a switch, managing that fear is far from being this easy. The general public and even seasoned traders often have difficulties managing their emotions. Thus, keeping feelings of fear at a controlled level is much more difficult than it sounds. In reality, many traders need years of practice before they can avoid the feeling of panic in an adversely moving market or even a profitable trade in which they are wrestling with the fear of giving back some of the gains or missing out on potential earnings.

Now that I have established that fear of the markets can be positive if kept at a reasonable level and addressed the difficulty in managing such emotions, I point out the influence of being too fearful. Traders who aren't capable of properly managing feelings of trepidation are prone to making irrational trading decisions, such as panic liquidation or failure to act. Either scenario has the ability to cause considerable harm.

> "A market is the combined behavior of thousands of people responding to information, misinformation, and whim."
> —Kenneth Change
> (*The New York Times*)

As a broker, I have had the unfortunate experience of having a front-row seat to the carnage that ill-timed panic can cause. Many traders have a strong tendency to exit a trade "gone bad" at the exact worst possible time. For example, they often ignore the well-known reality that prices are inclined to overshoot their equilibrium level before coming back to a more sustainable price. In the heat of the moment, fearful traders might exit their trade prematurely only to find the market traded favorably without them.

Undercapitalization Breeds Fear

Traders who are underfunded are typically more prone to fearful trading and, thus, poor results. This is because the less available margin that is in an account, the less room for error there is. Whether the lack of breathing room is the result of too many positions, not enough money on deposit, or a combination of the two, one big mistake could take the trader out of the game, and he knows this.

As a result, the trader is more likely to liquidate positions prematurely, causing unnecessary losses and, in many cases, avoidable transaction costs. Inexperienced traders have been known to rack up a large commission bill trying to trade in and out of a market while being dominated by the fear of loss or even fear of missing an anticipated price move.

This is not to say that it is necessary to deposit hundreds or even tens of thousands of dollars in an account. Regardless of the funding, traders should trade within their means. Thanks to products such as mini and micro futures and options on futures, this is possible even for the smallest of accounts. I remind you that this is not unlike the concept of living within one's means when it comes to budgeting personal finances.

Greed

As Gordon Gecko would say, "Greed is good." Without greed, you wouldn't be reading this book, and in all likelihood, the futures markets wouldn't exist. Greed is the emotion that inspires speculators to enter the markets in hopes of abnormal profits as opposed to investing in Treasury bills. However, with all the opportunity that greed creates in the world of trading, it also breeds misery.

Greed is a word that is used frequently to describe the personal desire for monetary wealth. In fact, the formal definition of *greed* is the excessive desire to acquire or possess more material wealth than one needs or deserves.

Anyone who has ever had money at risk in the market understands that greed works in two ways. On any given trade, the goal before entering the position is to bring profits to the trading account. Nevertheless, when the trade becomes a losing proposition, the yearning for profits quickly turns into the need to be right, or at least not wrong, by avoiding locking in a loss. At this point in time, greed turns from being solely monetary based to also involving ego. The combination of these two types of greed can be extremely powerful and often leads to financial ruin—or at least a depleted trading account.

> "It is an unfortunate human failing that a full pocketbook often groans more loudly than an empty stomach."
> —Franklin Delano Roosevelt

Those who cannot accept humility have the odds of productive trading stacked against them. There is little room for ego in the markets because it can be the biggest enemy to a trader; it can prevent a trader from cutting losses when wrong and taking profits when right. A trader driven by greed and ego tries to justify losses as being too early as opposed to being wrong and, therefore, is susceptible to an account-draining defeat on a single trade. Similarly, traders might also believe that the winners will obtain infinite gains, deterring them from taking profits while they are available. This outlook often leads to a scenario in which winning trades turn into losers.

A perfect example of greed in the marketplace is the Internet boom of the late 1990s. Investors with a get-rich-quick mentality were flocking to any stock that had a *.com* at the end of it. Greed and speculation drove share prices to unrealistic and unsustainable levels. As we all know, those who allowed greed to suck them into the euphoria paid dearly when the tech party ended.

Commodities are not immune to the same irresponsible price swings. The commodity rally that began in 2007 and consumed much of 2008 before coming to a screeching halt was arguably the result, at least in part, of greedy speculation as stock investors who were bored of flat-lining returns looked to the commodity markets for alternatives. A similar occurrence took place in 2011 in the gold and silver markets. Although strong commodity fundamentals lured money into the metals, irrational greed and ego kept the money flowing to a point at which unsustainable prices were reached. Similar to the dotcom craze, the commodity bubble eventually popped, leaving many market participants wishing that they hadn't taken part in the latest investment trend. Unfortunately, this is a long-term recurring phenomenon, and few markets have been spared its wrath.

Frustration

The influence of frustration on trading decisions is often overlooked, but having the ability to avoid letting disappointment take over is priceless. This is perhaps the single most important difference between a profitable trader and the masses.

Frustration can be a part of any trading scenario but primarily stems from one of two events: exiting a position with a loss or exiting a position with a profit but leaving potential gains on the table. An irrational trader repeatedly allows the emotions experienced in these scenarios to trigger an attempt to recoup what he believes the market "wrongfully" took from him. Such conduct is often the beginning of the end of a trading career.

The Angst of Taking Profits "Early"

For those who have never executed a trade, it might seem odd that aggravation could arise from a profitable speculation. However, imagine being a trader with the insight and gumption to sell crude oil short near the all-time high, at $147 per barrel, in mid-2008 and subsequently taking a profit on the trade at $137 per barrel to lock in a gain of $10,000 minus commissions and fees. This was clearly a great trade. Conversely, the personal anguish felt by the same trader who later watched crude prices plummet to less than $40 per barrel by early 2009 is indescribable.

From the outside, a $10,000 winner is a triumphant victory, but from the inside, a trader who hasn't developed the ability to control her emotions might see it as a loss. After all, had the trader continued to hold the position, she might have walked away with a six-figure winner. I have personally witnessed many traders who simply could not deal with the reality of cutting a winning trade too early and, as a result, began making unfounded trading decisions in their quest to get back what was lost—or, at least, not won.

A trader in this frame of mind isn't considering what it would have taken to hold the position to the end. She might react similarly to a contestant on the TV game show *Deal or No Deal* who just realized the million-dollar prize was in her case after settling for a deal of $235,000 by putting herself through the mental agony of questioning the decisions that led to the winnings earned.

The reality is, there is no way to predict how far a market will go, just as there is no way to know which case you are holding on *Deal or No Deal*. Additionally, it is unfair for a trader to agonize over what could have been, simply because it is impossible to predict what decisions would have been made as the market moves from point A to point B.

Going back to our *Deal or No Deal* analogy, few contestants can take the game all the way to the end because there are a lot of tough decisions to make in the meantime. Those who do take it to the final two cases often come up empty-handed. The same is true in trading. From my experience, the successful traders are those who can live with the fact that they will almost never pick the top or bottom of a market but are happy to take a piece out of the middle.

The Pain of Taking a Loss

One of the most difficult things to do as a trader is to exit a losing trade. This is because doing so confirms incorrect speculation, timing, or both. Accordingly, locking in a loss not only does damage to a trading account, but also takes its toll on the psyche of the untrained trader.

While a position is still open, regardless of the size of the paper loss, the trader is consumed with hope that the market will turn around and the losses will be erased. There is a sense that if there is no harm in the end, there is no foul. However, large losses often don't correct themselves; instead, they get even larger. Although taking a small loss is financially and mentally painful, don't forget that *large* losses can be nearly unbearable from both a mental and a monetary standpoint.

The biggest fear traders have in taking a loss is the possible subsequent market reversal that might have eventually allowed the position to be profitable. In a situation such as this, the frustration can be multiplied to a point at which an out-of-control trader can cause a lot of harm via poor trading decisions and maybe even poor personal decisions.

> As stated by Max Amsterdam, "Business is the art of extracting money from another man's pocket without resorting to violence." I believe that the same can be said of trading.

As a broker, I often communicate with traders and brokers located on the floor of the exchanges and have heard some extremely heartbreaking stories of traders who couldn't deal with their losses and chose to take their own lives. In October 2008, during the infamous equity market crash, a CME local trading his personal account took his life after sustaining losses to the tune of several millions of dollars on a short S&P play. The trader's account was force-liquidated by the clearing firm due to a margin deficiency. As it turns out, he was correct in being short the market but unwisely had too many positions on and was unable to ride out the volatility simply because he ran out of money. Subsequent to the premature liquidation of his positions, the market moved in the anticipated direction without him.

Clearly, this is an extreme and unfortunate case. However, all traders who have taken a substantial loss can relate to the emotions involved. The most common reaction is an irrational attempt to get back losses from the very market that took them. This mindset can wreak havoc on a trader and, although we will never know for sure, might have been the catalyst causing this trader to over-leverage his account.

After a devastating loss has occurred, the trader might have difficulty analyzing the market objectively and sticking to the original trading strategy or theory. Too often the story ends in out-of-control and mindless trading that benefits the brokerage firm, thanks to excessive commissions, but does even more damage to the trading account and the trader's ability to behave rationally.

Another instance in which I have noticed that traders allow their emotions to get the best of them is subsequent to being stopped out of a trade. Describing a filled stop order as premature is appropriate if, after the order is filled, the market moves in the intended direction. Unfortunately, this is a common occurrence and is one of the biggest arguments against using stop orders.

For example, a trader who is long a March crude oil from $95.60 per barrel with a stop loss placed at $94.60 in an attempt to limit the potential losses on the trade to $1,000 plus slippage is anticipating higher prices but is also allowing the market some amount of freedom. The emotional turmoil caused by a situation in which March crude futures drop to exactly $94.60 to trigger the working stop order, forcing the trader out of the market, and then stage a large rally can destroy the emotional stability of an untrained trader. Although the total loss on such a venture would be $1,000 plus transaction costs, assuming that the stop order was filled at exactly $94.60, in the mind of an undisciplined trader, the loss is considered to be that which was realized plus any potential profits that would have occurred by being long during the successive rally.

This type of market approach creates the dismal odds that retail traders face. An unseasoned speculator, and even a well-experienced and successful trader, can easily fall into the trap of vengeful trading. However, doing so generally leads to unreasonable trading decisions and even more losses.

Vengeful Trading Is Counterproductive

The act of revenge is described as inflicting punishment in return for injury or insult and is typically sparked by an event that leaves a person feeling as though he was wronged. It isn't hard to imagine why or how a trader would feel victimized by the market, causing vengeance to emerge.

Traders who have experienced one of the preceding scenarios or have had been part of similar incidents in suffering losses or potential gains foregone often seek revenge. Feelings of revenge typically begin as losses are mounting, well before the damage is realized by exiting the trade. However, in many cases, the yearning for retribution never subsides. Even those "lucky" enough to recoup what was lost from the very market that took it have a hard time satisfying their craving to settle the score. As you can imagine, traders who allow emotions to dictate the market they trade and influence the way they trade it will have a difficult time achieving financial success.

A symptom of the vengeful trader is a phenomenon known as *marrying a trade*. Traders often fall into this trap when they have done a great deal of research in a given market and feel overly confident in their speculation. As the market begins to move against the open position, the trader is susceptible to becoming attached to his opinion and dedicated to recovering lost capital, based on the premise that he is right and the market as a whole is clearly wrong. I have found that egotistical traders with the opinion that they are somehow smarter or are armed with more knowledge than all other market participants tend to be destined for failure.

In turn, I believe that the most effective means of combating feelings of ego and revenge in trading is humility. In my experience, successful traders are those who allow themselves to be humbled by the markets. We are all working with the same resources; unless you have a much faster Internet connection than everyone else on the planet or you have somehow figured out how to fast-forward your DVR, you and all market participants are equipped with the same fundamental news. Additionally, it is unrealistic to assume that you are capable of interpreting the news more accurately than everyone else. Although there is, without doubt, a pool of unsophisticated traders lurking in the futures markets, to achieve profits, you must compete with the well informed and even better trained. After all, each trader is in competition with the next. You might recall Gordon Gecko's view of market completion in the movie *Wall Street:* "It's a zero sum game. Somebody wins, somebody loses. Money itself isn't lost or made; it's simply transferred from one perception to another."

Capital Preservation, a.k.a. Risk Management

A majority of trading books and courses refer to the idea of capital preservation as risk management. The concepts are essentially the same, but my perception of the practice is slightly different. In my view, risk management is the practice of actively identifying and managing risk of loss in trading, whereas capital preservation takes it a step further.

In its simplest form, capital preservation is the acknowledgment that one bad day can end a trading career. Making money in the markets is impossible if you risk all your trading capital on one speculation. If you don't live to trade another day, you might as well hang up your trading hat; all speculative decisions should be made with this premise in mind. The bottom line is that markets can stay irrational, or what you believe to be irrational, far longer than most people can stay solvent. Therefore, trading them requires a certain amount of humility.

Accordingly, my belief is that traders are best off entering a market with the assumption that the position will likely lose money. Doing so could entice them to take profits and avoid running losses.

In Chapter 12, "Trading Is a Business—Have a Plan," I discuss the use of trading plans in capital preservation.

chapter 12

Trading Is a Business— Have a Plan

Trading it is not a passive investment. Trading is a business, and any activity engaged with the purpose of profits should be treated as such. Confirmation of this comparison can be seen in the odds of success. It has been said that approximately 80% of all traders fail to trade profitably, and some studies have suggested that the odds are even worse. For example, I have seen estimates that as many as 90% of all traders fail within the first six months. We can argue over the percentages, but it is clear that most traders are destined for an undesired outcome. Nevertheless, those who achieve success can be rewarded handsomely.

> "The average man desires to be told specifically which particular stock to buy or sell. He wants to get something for nothing. He does not wish to work."
> —William LeFevre

The probabilities of profitable operations are similarly stacked against small business owners; a large majority of new business ventures fail within the first year. Accordingly, whether your ambition is trading or starting your own business, you owe it to yourself to become familiar with the marketplace and organize a plan of attack. After all, those who can find a way to make money in business or trading often enjoy a considerable amount of success. The journey can be long, but if reached, the destination can be highly rewarding from both a financial and a psychological standpoint.

The Trading Game Plan

Contrary to what your perceptions might be, there are no right or wrong ways to trade in terms of strategy. However, I do believe that there is a right and

Trading isn't black and white, but making money is.

wrong outlook on the risks and opportunities the markets present, and this is ultimately judged by profits and losses.

Despite your strategy, risk tolerance, or trading capital, having a plan is one of the most important components of achieving success in these treacherous markets. Without a plan, traders are left to rely on their emotions and instincts. Let's face it; the average person isn't born with a knack for trading or for controlling feelings of fear and greed.

With that said, based on my observations, I have concluded that, along with the ability to keep emotions in check, one of the most important characteristics of a profitable trader is the ability to adapt to ever-changing market conditions. Being nimble is key; being stubborn is detrimental. Keeping this in mind, it seems logical to establish a game plan with the premise that rules are meant to be broken in *some,* but not all, circumstances. Thus, a trading plan should not be considered concrete, and in many circumstances, deviating from the original intentions of the trade is prudent.

Much of what you read about a trading plan involves specific entry and exit rules and risk-management tactics. Nevertheless, in my opinion, a trading plan must be flexible to accommodate altering environments and unforeseen events. For instance, I have witnessed too many traders fail to take a profit on a successful trade because a target price had not been reached. This type of mindset can often turn winning trades into losing trades and make constructive emotions into feelings of revenge that can be detrimental to trading decisions.

Simply put, I believe that a trading plan should, on occasion, have *some* human discretion for market entry, exit, and assumed risk. This is not to say that traders should make it a habit to completely disregard their trading rules or strategy, but they should have an open mind about making small adjustments. For instance, it is against the rule to speed, but if you are rushing a loved one to the hospital, being heavy-footed might be justified.

Automated Trading Systems

Throughout this chapter, I play devil's advocate when it comes to system trading. I'm not trying to brainwash you into believing that you should avoid system trading at all costs; this simply isn't the case. Instead, I want to open your eyes to the advantages and disadvantages of various trading approaches. Additionally, it is important to realize that even a proven system on autopilot should be monitored, and you might want to consider adjusting the parameters.

"What technology does is make people more productive. It doesn't replace them."
—Michael Bloomberg

Without involving some cognitive decision making, a trading plan becomes known as a *trading system*, which is the use of stringent and automated trading rules with little or no outside intervention. Assuming that the shorter the time frame of the system, the less vulnerable it is to changing market conditions might make sense. For instance, subtle price distortions might create arbitrage opportunities that the naked eye wouldn't identify, nor would a human be quick enough to react to them. If a programmer was capable of accurately creating something that could exploit such opportunities, a profitable system might have little intervention necessary, or even possible. On the other hand, system creation (or, at least, *profitable* system creation) takes a lot of time and dedication.

Although trading systems (as opposed to trading plans) that can be modified have grown in popularity due to technological advances and the availability of such system software to the general public, the odds of success facing retail traders haven't seemed to improve. This leads me to believe that, even in the absence of human emotion, significant challenges stand in the way of creating a profitable trading model. I am not implying that profitable trading systems don't exist, but I believe that, as is the case with any other type of market approach, developing such a system takes extensive time and trial and error.

A Trading System Alone Isn't a "Business Plan"

Opposing the views of many, I don't believe that a trading system is necessarily synonymous with a trading plan. Again, a futures trading system is a defined set of technical rules and parameters that ultimately determine entry and exit points for a given contract. If all the stipulated technical events occur, a buy or sell signal is created and a trade is automatically executed without human intervention. In essence, system traders are putting their trading profession on autopilot. I have yet to find a business owner willing to hand over operations to hired staff and, therefore, can't imagine a trader doing the same. That said, there is an undeniable amount of interest in system trading, and for those who are much more mechanically inclined than I am, it might be a positive venture. After all, some large hedge funds and proprietary trading desks rely solely on system trading, and I am sure they wouldn't allocate resources to such strategies if they didn't see potential for profit.

System developers spend an incredible amount of time optimizing the system to manage risk and increase the odds of profitable results in any environment. Each system consists of specific ingredients and circumstances, but they most commonly involve moving averages, stochastics, and other computer-generated oscillators. As you can imagine, the results are highly dependent on how well the rules perform in various market conditions; as a result, changing market conditions could prove to be a disaster. What worked for a purely technical system in one time frame might not work in another due to changing market characteristics. With little human intervention or discretion, the losses could be staggering. However, as we know, large profits and losses are the reality of any trading strategy.

Systems aren't all bad. They offer some distinct advantages, such as eliminated emotion, time saved by the freedom to leave the computer and the markets during the trading day, and the convenience of letting the system do all the work.

For some, system trading is the best fit for their personality, risk tolerance, and strategy; for others, the thought of being out of control can lead to high levels of anxiety and the tendency to detrimentally interfere with the system parameters. Going back to the small business analogy, you probably wouldn't trust your employees to handle and account for all the money, so why would you behave this way in your trading? Instead, I believe system traders should take a more proactive role; I discuss this idea in further detail later in the chapter.

Where System Trading Can Fail

Systems don't have common sense and, in the long run, might not have the capability to be profitable without some type of intervention. This is because technical systems are driven by specific parameters that were determined well in advance of trade execution. As a result, mechanical trading systems often generate signals that might be considered low-probability trades. For instance, a technically driven system might trigger a sell signal at or near the all-time low of a contract. Likewise, a system might look to buy a market at an exuberantly high price.

Although system trading is intended to eliminate the emotions involved in deciding whether to enter or exit a market, there might be unintended psychological consequences. For instance, enduring a trade that contradicts your opinion can be challenging. This could mean a system going long in a market in which you are highly bearish or short one in which your opinion is bullish. Either way, the turmoil that system trading is meant to avoid can easily be rekindled. Such emotions have been known to cause traders to interfere with the system and, in many cases, greatly impact the performance—often in a negative way.

> *Purchased trading systems should be viewed as a trading tool, not the "be all, end all" solution to making money in the markets.*

Another disadvantage to trading systems (as opposed to discretionary trading, which relies on some combination of technical, fundamental, and seasonal analyses paired with common sense) is that system traders rely on historical market activity to dictate their current and future trading.

Futures trading systems are often developed through a process referred to as *back testing*. In other words, they filter through historical price changes in search of system parameters that would have provided profitable results. However, doing so gives the system developer information on what the mechanical strategy would have done if the trader had implemented it in the past.

It isn't reasonable to assume that similar results would be obtained in real-time trading or, even more so, at any point in the future. After all, market conditions are dynamic, whereas the parameters of a trading system are constant. Even system developers dedicated to tweaking the elements of the trading system can sustain considerable losses before recognizing the need to adjust parameters. Also, temporary events or market behaviors can lead to an unnecessary alteration of the system. In such a case, proactive adjustments to the system ingredients can result in needless losses.

Despite what software and system vendors want you to believe, if making money in the markets were as easy as buying or leasing a trading system, there would be no need for you to be reading this book. In fact, I would have no incentive to write it. Instead, we would all quit our day jobs and let our money and our newly acquired trading system lead us to a life of luxury.

I am sorry to report that being a profitable market participant is much more complicated than purchasing a trading system. Although an unlimited number of sales representatives will do whatever it takes to convince you that their product can provide consistent returns, I have yet to find the Holy Grail of trading that many claim to be selling.

Two important factors are at play when it comes to system vendors. First, if their systems were "magical" and were successful in all types of market conditions and throughout all time frames, they likely wouldn't be selling them. There is much more money to be made in the markets than there is in selling products (although the hefty price tags of many suggest that it is possible for some to make a great living doing it). On that note, the higher the price of the system, the more you should be wary of claims.

Second, the Commodity Futures Trading Commission (CFTC) and the National Futures Association (NFA) regulate the futures industry. For the most part, the jurisdiction of these two agencies does not extend beyond those registered or required to register with the agencies. Those required to register are brokers, commodity trading advisors, and futures commission merchants. Many authors, software vendors, and system developers are not registered with the NFA and CFTC, nor are they required to be. Accordingly, they are not necessarily held to the same regulatory standards that those registered with the regulators must be. In some cases, no third party has verified the performance history disclosed by system vendors, and because they have not registered with industry regulators, they enjoy freedoms of speech that pave the way for possible deception.

I can't caution you enough about trading systems that promise spectacular returns. Just as anything else in investing and trading, if it sounds too good to be true, it probably is. You owe it to yourself to get the facts before putting your money on the line. As a consumer, it is imperative that you know who you are dealing with and what is realistic in terms of performance.

> "If there is something that you really want to do, make your plan and do it. Otherwise, you'll just regret it forever."
> —Richard Rocco

With that said, legitimate systems have proven to be productive over time and in the right circumstances. Additionally, some software and system vendors are honest and forthright with their products and what to expect from them. In all fairness to those who are not required to be registered with the regulatory bodies, certainly some *registered* members don't conduct business with the integrity that is expected of them, just as some who aren't registered do follow ethical practices.

Reading a book on trading without being exposed to the ideas set forth by Richard Dennis and Bill Eckhardt is difficult. They were the developers of the most renowned trading system of all time, the Turtle Trading System. The Turtle System was built around the concept of trend trading and is said to have enjoyed years of success. Based on the financial accomplishments of its developers, it isn't difficult to argue that the system was effective. Yet it is also important to note that these gentleman developed the trading system, which turned out to be one of the most successful of all time, and did not divulge the details of the system. In other words, they didn't attempt to buy success through the purchase of a system, nor did they opt to sell their success because they knew that the markets could potentially be more lucrative.

The accomplishment of such systems has led many hedge funds and institutional commodity traders to adopt trading systems as their primary method of speculation. Although this goes against my original argument that system trading might struggle as market conditions vary, their interest suggests that systems can be a viable market tool for those who can develop a sound set of trading rules and implement the plan efficiently.

Think Outside of the Box: Trading a Trading System

In my opinion, the success of any individual trading system cycles along with the market. Therefore, it seems as though trading systems might be best used as a trading vehicle rather than a long-term strategy.

Speculators can actively trade a futures system performance by implementing and ceasing trading of the system based on the peaks and valleys of returns. In essence, this is similar to buying or selling any financial instrument. As always, the goal is to buy low and sell high. For example, it might be an opportune time to begin trading a system that is experiencing a drawdown and call it quits after a good run. This is because market conditions often fluctuate in cycles in which the performance of technical futures trading systems also oscillates. In other words, when it comes to technical trading systems, traders might be better off avoiding a buy-and-hold mentality.

Constructing a Business Plan in Trading

The process of creating a trading plan should be based on the same premise as constructing a business plan. Just as a business develops a blueprint of its intended operations and the possibility of success, traders seek to make predictions on the likelihood of a particular event occurring and they use risk-management techniques to improve the odds of success and limit the chances of a devastating blunder.

The preparation of each individual trade should include a relatively detailed outline of the structure of the trading strategy and a contingency plan in case the market deviates from the original speculation. As I have previously mentioned, I don't believe that trading plans should necessarily be set in stone because of the evolving nature of the markets. From my perception, trading with overly strict trading rules could lead to financial peril. Nobody is perfect, and neither is any trading plan; therefore, being nimble but wise is ideal. Conversely, this is my viewpoint, and other books or courses might give you a completely opposite impression. The truth is that trading is an art, not a science; what is right for one might not be right for the next. I hope that the various opinions in this book give you the background you need to determine what types of trading styles work best for you.

A trading plan has two primary components: price prediction and risk management. Price prediction is simply the method used to signal the direction and timing of trade execution. This can involve fundamental or technical analyses or both. Risk management, on the other hand, specifies when to cut losses, when and how to adjust a position, or, better yet, when to take profits.

Price Speculation (Ideally, Prediction)

Regardless of the market or the instrument traded, the only possible way to make profitable trades is to buy low and sell high. Although this is a simple theory to grasp, implementing it can be challenging. For this to happen, whether trading futures, options, or baseball cards, the trader needs accurate speculation and timing. It isn't always enough to be right in the overall direction of the market; I can't emphasize enough that being right and making money are two completely separate events.

> Be honest to yourself about your risk tolerance. Failure to do so will result in incompatible indicators and a flawed business plan.

Many factors come into play to determine whether a trader can buy at a low price and sell at a higher price. Unfortunately, determining an opinion on where the market prices could or should go is only half the battle. In fact, I argue that timing and a properly capitalized account are more relevant than market direction, in some cases. After a trader has done his homework in fundamental and technical analyses (or a combination of both), he must construct a trade that will profit if the market moves as anticipated but will bring relatively little pain if it doesn't.

Timing Is Everything

In trading, timing is everything. Again, through my newsletters and conversations with clients and prospects, I constantly remind them that there is a big difference between being right in the direction of the market and actually making money. I have witnessed traders who were absolutely correct in their speculation of price movement but missed getting into the trade because they had unfilled limit orders (sometimes within ticks) or were too early, causing them to run out of money or patience before the anticipated price move actually occurred.

For example, as the stock market rallied in 2008 to reach a high in the Dow Jones Industrial Average near 14,000, an old friend of mine predicted that the Dow would soon be trading under 7,000. As many others did, I scoffed at the idea—and was later proven wrong by a vicious bear market. However, the man who had predicted the slide lost a substantial amount of money trying to sell into the rally too early; to my knowledge, he didn't reap much of the reward as the market fell precipitously. This is simply because, once the bear market finally became a reality, his trading capital had dwindled to the point at which he was largely unable to participate in a meaningful way.

Without a crystal ball, the timing of a trade can be uncertain. Unfortunately, knowing whether a trade was well timed is impossible until the results are known. That said, an unlimited number of tools and indicators is available to help traders find a timing methodology that works with their trading style and personality.

For instance, timing can be based on computer-generated oscillators such as stochastics, Williams %R, RSI, and so on. Some traders also use psychological barometers such as the amount of television coverage a particular market might be getting or market sentiment polls. Those trading the S&P 500 futures and options often look at the Chicago Board of Options Exchange's (CBOE) volatility index, known simply as the VIX. The VIX is often referred to as the fear index because it is said to be a rep-resentation of the market's expectation of volatility in the coming 30-day period. Some fundamental traders even look to supply-and-demand stats as a means of timing their entry and exit of a given trade.

> The difference between genius and stupidity is finding the balance between risk and reward.

I am a firm believer that there aren't right or wrong trading tools. The tool that works for one trader might not work for the next because of differences in personality and trading style. Therefore, traders must determine what they believe will help *them* achieve success, based on their needs and desires.

The indicator used to time entry and exit might not necessarily be important, but the tool chosen must be one that the trader is comfortable with and confident using. Clearly, indicators won't be accurate all the time. Therefore, it is necessary to use those that optimize the odds of any particular trading approach. In essence, a scalp trader likely wouldn't be wise to use a timing indicator that is relatively slow, such as the MACD. Similarly, a position trader wouldn't want a fast-paced indicator that might create many false and/or early signals, such as fast stochastics.

Based on my observation and experience, I have found that blindly taking all the buy-and-sell signals triggered by each of the computer-generated oscillators independently would yield similar results in terms of profit and loss before con-sidering transaction costs. Of course, transaction costs would weigh down the performance of quick triggered indicators. Simply put, a trader executing positions solely based on one oscillator would likely see similar results as a trader relying solely on another.

What does determine the success of a trader is the emotional constraint that prevents panic liquidation and the ability to properly place stop orders or exit adversely moving trades. In other words, good instincts and experience are likely more valuable than any technical indicator or supply-and-demand graph you will run across.

"You can't grow long term if you can't eat short term." —Jack Welch

You might have heard this motto: Guns don't kill people; people kill people. Trading indicators can be compared to guns, in this sense: The indicators themselves don't determine the outcome; the traders using them do. In trading, oscillators or charting tools don't siphon trading accounts; unfortunately, traders sometimes do it to themselves.

After you determine your speculative tool of choice and determine your conclusion on the direction (or lack thereof), it is time to construct a strategy that will benefit if your assessments are accurate and mitigate risk if you are wrong. This might include using options, futures, or a combination of both as the trading vehicle. The method you choose should be based on your risk tolerance, personality, and risk capital.

Choosing a Trading Vehicle

Futures and options exchanges list several products, and speculators bring enough liquidity to many of these instruments to create an abundance of "options" in terms of trading vehicles. Not only are there several contracts to choose from, but traders also have the ability to combine instruments to construct a strategy with a specific goal and risk/reward profile.

As with indicators, a strategy that works for one trader might not work for the next. The goal for every trader, aside from being profitable, should be to find a strategy that provides a manageable risk profile while still offering a profit potential that makes the risk worthwhile. In the world of finance, it is well known that increased risk is equivalent to increased potential reward. Conversely, excessive risk usually ends in a largely negative reward scenario. The appropriate balance between risk and reward is a fine line; the side of the line chosen determines the probability of a gain rather than an unfounded hope of one. Aside from a lucky few, traders who accept reckless amounts of risk will be prone to dismal trading results.

To illustrate the seemingly infinite possibilities of risk and reward, a Treasury bond bear might sell a futures contract, purchase a put option with various strike prices, sell a call option with various strike prices, or even use a combination of all of these. Each of these strategies can be constructed with various levels of possible risk and reward to conform to the personality of the trader.

The possible combination of instruments is extensive and, in some cases, complex. Therefore, covering the topic in detail isn't feasible; however, you should be aware of the alternatives available to you and know which fits your personal trading profile before you ever put money on the line.

> "Money often costs too much."
> —Ralph Waldo Emerson

Risk Management

All business plans must account for potential hardships and achievable recoveries. Similarly, a solid trading plan should include proper coverage of risk management and appropriate contingency plans in case the plan goes awry.

Because of the leveraged volatility and the inherent danger of being on the wrong side of a runaway market, the "meat" of a proper trading plan is risk management. As elementary as it sounds, the most important component to trading success is making sure your account lives to trade another day. As with any business, without sufficient capital, the outcome looks bleak. Traders must be ready and willing to pull the plug on any trade that endangers the ability of the "business" to continue, regardless of how much research they applied and how certain they are about their speculation.

To keep emotions at bay, it is critical that you establish thresholds of loss that you are willing to accept *before* you enter a market. Honesty is the best policy. If you are focused on the potential reward rather than the potential risk, the odds favor a dramatically unfavorable conclusion.

Establishing and following a risk threshold might simply mean placing an appropriate stop-loss order, along with determining a profit objective and placing a limit order accordingly. I can't emphasize enough that the trading plans are for guidance and shouldn't be followed blindly. Don't be the trader who misses taking a healthy profit because the price came within ticks of the limit order, yet he held out for the extra $20.

On the other hand, even if your trading strategy or plan doesn't involve a trailing stop, don't be a fool. Markets don't go up or down forever; if you have a large open profit, tighten your stop or place protective options or option spreads. Even better, lock in the profit and walk away.

The Art of Risk Management

Thanks to the plethora of tradable futures and options products made available by the various exchanges, traders have unlimited ways to adjust the risk and reward of a futures position. The idea of a trading plan is to aid your decision-making process, not bog you down and prevent you from ever entering the market. Therefore, a trading plan can't possibly cover all market scenarios—but writing down a few potential ideas can keep you from freezing in the heat of the moment.

For instance, imagine a trader who goes long a futures contract and finds himself with a nice profit yet believes there is room for the market to continue to move favorably. He might hedge his position by selling call option premium. Likewise, in line with this strategy, the trader might want to use the proceeds of the recently sold call option to purchase a put and protect himself from risk of an adverse price movement.

Risk and Reward: Give Yourself a Chance!

Contrary to your likely perceptions of trading, some of the best traders struggle to keep their win/loss ratios above 50%. Therefore, when assessing your risk tolerance on any given trade and your profit target, you must be realistic.

Knowing the average probability of success on each trade, even for the pros, it isn't practical to consistently risk more on a position than you plan to make if you are right; this is simply because you likely will have more (or just as many) losers as you will have winners. For instance, if your average risk on a trade is $600, you should have an average profit target of at least $600. Anything less than this is putting the odds greatly in favor of your competition and works against your long-term prospects of success.

Option Selling Provides Favorable Odds but Doesn't Guarantee Success

Although favorable odds are key to sustainable trading success, there are no guarantees. In this game, winning far more trades than you lose is only the beginning.

This concept is especially important for option sellers who face optimal odds of success on a per-trade basis but are subject to limited profit potential and possibly unlimited risk, if selling naked options. It has been said that as many as 80% of options expire worthless. Assuming these odds, a trader would win on nearly eight out of ten trades. However, the danger lies in the vulnerability of the two losing trades. An option seller must be savvy enough to prevent the small percentage of losing trades from wiping out months of profit and part (or all) of the original trading capital.

With that said, the perils of option selling shouldn't deter you from the strategy altogether. In fact, I prefer and recommend this approach to the markets. However, those who participate in this practice must be willing to face the consequences during drawdowns. They must also be humble enough to exit a poor trade before the consequences are too much for the trading account to bear.

A good rule of thumb is to risk the amount of premium collected for the option. Therefore, if a trader can collect $500, or 10 points, for a short e-mini S&P option, and the value of the option doubles to $1,000, or 20 points, it is likely a good point to admit that the speculation was incorrect and accept the loss of $500. At this point, it is fair to say that you were either wrong or really early, and liquidation should be strongly considered to move on to the next opportunity. As difficult as it is to admit fault and lock in a loss, it will be even more painful if the $500 loser doubles or triples in size.

Many options expire worthless, but odds alone are not enough to ensure success. Short-option trading requires ample skill and instinct to be profitable in the long term.

Keep in mind that placing stop-loss orders on most options or option spreads isn't feasible due to the nature of the bid/ask spread and the seemingly high probability of being stopped out prematurely. Instead, I believe in monitoring short options closely and having a mental stop loss in mind.

As mentioned, the double-out policy is simply a rule of thumb, and sometimes breaking it is prudent. Despite what you might have read in other literature, it shouldn't be looked at in black and white terms. In my opinion, trading is an art, not a science, and should be treated accordingly. For instance, if you are short a call in a rallying market and the option has reached the double-out point but you see significant resistance approaching, it might not be the best time to throw in the towel. Even if you decide that you are no longer comfortable with the trade, in many cases, the market will, at minimum, stall at the resistance area, allowing for a better exit price. Similarly, if you strongly believe that the futures price will hold resistance, exiting your position in panic and at top dollar doesn't make sense.

On the contrary, traders who begin to rely on hope instead of logic and research have let the trade go too far and have crossed the line between being a player and being a prayer. Unfortunately, seeing the line can be difficult until it has already been crossed; at that point, you will feel it.

Challenging decisions such as this make or break a trader. The difference between success and failure often comes down to a few decisions in crucial circumstances. The ability to properly manage such scenarios can be derived only from instinct and experience. Although reading books and attending trading seminars might be helpful, there is no substitution for hands-on trading.

The 10% Rule

Unless this truly is "the first book on commodities" you have read, you've likely run across the 10% rule of risk management. The argument suggests that traders shouldn't risk more than 10% of their trading account on any individual trade. This premise stipulates what the maximum risk should be, but it implicitly implies that the minimum risk should be similar. Although I can't argue with the logic of having a risk threshold, risking 10% of the trading account might not be feasible for everyone. After all, what if you were trading a $1,000,000 account? Risking $100,000 on a single speculation seems a bit excessive.

Additionally, a risk-averse or inexperienced trader might not be psychologically equipped to handle such a loss, and this can repeatedly lead to irrational trading behavior. It is easy to underestimate the consequences of trader psychology; nonetheless, after a trader loses his logical bearing, recovering can be difficult, leading to large losses.

Imagine the emotions felt by a trader who opens her first futures account with $10,000 and immediately loses 10%, or $1,000, on the first trade. Someone not in complete control of her psyche—and, therefore, her actions—might dedicate subsequent trades to recovering losses on the original. This type of destructive behavior often leads to overly aggressive trading, such as premature entry and a greedy refusal to exit profitable trades. It is feasible to imagine a trader reacting in this manner, and it supports my premise that some traders might not be capable of accepting a 10% loss without detrimentally impacting the trading plan.

It is also important to realize that restrictions come with the 10% rule that can work against the odds of success. In some markets and during volatile conditions, constructing a trade with realistic probabilities of success might not be possible without surpassing the 10% threshold. Whether this is the case depends greatly on the size of the account and whether options or futures are used, but it can be a drawback of the theory. Clearly, if you cannot derive a strategy in which the potential risk does not exceed 10% of available trading capital, the trade is better left untouched. Nonetheless, as humans, we are naturally drawn to that which we shouldn't be.

Don't Be Ashamed of One-Lot Orders

The thrill of calling a broker and placing an order for 10, 50, or 100 futures or options contracts at a time is unmatched. However, for those who don't have the experience and the trading capital to back the move, it is highly counterproductive and potentially devastating.

One of the most destructive behaviors I have witnessed is the execution of multiple contracts in a moderately funded account. Brokerage firms often extend to day traders lower margin requirements, relative to what the exchange requires, and this can lure traders into taking excessive risks. That said, just because higher leverage is granted doesn't mean traders should use it.

Raw traders assume that trading several contracts at a time will maximize their "return," but they are actually maximizing risk and minimizing the probability of a successful trade. If you are truly looking at trading as a business and as a means of making money as opposed to feeding an inner ego, you will be content with trading one contract at a time until you are comfortable enough to properly capitalize and manage multiple trading lots.

> *Take care of your money, and some day it may take care of you.*

Managing Risk with Stops

Using stop-loss orders is probably the most common form of risk management. As you have learned, a stop order is habitually used as a means of exiting an existing trade if the market moves adversely to the position. Depending on whether the stop order is trailed with the position, the stated price might result in a loss or might lock in a profit. Nonetheless, it is filled only after adverse price movement. As you should recall, a stop order becomes a market order when the named price is reached. Therefore, slippage from the intended price is possible.

Keep in mind that a stop order can also be used to enter a market. Such a stop order is often placed above areas of significant technical resistance or below support, in an attempt to capitalize on a potential price break-out. When used in this manner, stop orders don't fall into the category of risk management.

Stop orders are useful only if they are properly placed, and this is a task that is much easier said than done. Stop orders that are placed too close to the market regularly lead to premature liquidation of a trade that would have eventually gone in an anticipated direction. If stop orders are placed in a manner in which a fill is probable during the normal ebb and flow of the market, this is no longer a risk-management technique—it is a near-guarantee that you will lose money. On the other hand, stop orders that are placed too far from the market might create a scenario in which too much risk is accepted. This too, is highly counter-productive.

Although stop orders might be popular in the trading community, they are not necessarily the most effective. Remember, most retail traders lose money. As with many aspects in trading, placing stop orders is an art, not a science. In truth, many traders prefer to be without stops by trading "naked," or by using alternative risk-management tools such as options. I happen to share this view.

Deciding whether to use stop orders and where and when to use them isn't a black-and-white process. Many areas of gray involve market conditions and characteristics, as well as the personality, account funding, and risk tolerance of the trader. Understanding each of these aspects is critical; stop placement is a skill that comes only with experience and is shaped by personality.

Guidance on stop placement might be a good argument in favor of beginning traders using a full-service broker. Nonetheless, even an experienced broker cannot see into the future and faces the same challenges that you do. Still, you can't put a price tag on experience; in theory, using a seasoned and savvy broker might have a positive impact on performance, despite slightly higher transaction costs involved in doing so.

As you should already realize, stop orders aren't a guarantee of risk because of the potential slippage involved. In most cases, the difference between the intended stop price and the actual fill price is moderate. However, in some circumstances, the slippage can be substantial, such as in low-liquidity and high-volatility environments. I have witnessed rare cases in which slippage has equated to several hundred dollars.

In some cases, avoiding placing stops by using unconventional risk-management techniques might be possible—and wise. An experienced broker might help construct option spreads and buy or sell outright calls and puts as an alternative in risk aversion. For example, a short option or futures position might be hedged with a one-by-two ratio write if the volatility and premium allow. Likewise, futures traders can buy options that benefit from an adverse move in their futures position to limit risk of loss and avoid being subject to the risk of being stopped out prematurely. Doing so can be considered buying insurance against being wrong; it might be pricy, but sometimes it can be useful. That said, this type of protection is feasible only in markets and instances in which option premium is affordable.

I believe that using options in risk management instead of stop orders eliminates some of the stress and emotion involved in trading. Traders often have sleepless nights over concerns of being stopped out of a position, only to watch it recover without them. Traders who use options as a hedge or for absolute insurance can relax, knowing that the homework is done, the risk is mitigated, and the position isn't in danger of being prematurely offset.

It Is Your Money

In theory, we all participate in the markets with the same goal: to make money. (Believe it or not, though, some traders seem to be trading for the thrill as opposed to potential profits.) Despite our common goals, the road to success is much different for one trader relative to another. In fact, a strategy that one trader lucratively employs might not yield the same results when executed by another. The difference in performance from one trader to the next is typically not about the fundamental information available or the technical tools used; it involves the methodology and mentality in which the information is put to work. More important, it depends on the manner in which we react to stressful and timely situations. As I have attempted to make clear, trading is an ambiguous game; most aspects of speculation have no right or wrong answer.

We don't all wear the same shoe size or have the same hobbies, so why should we all use the same trading strategy and risk-management techniques? We shouldn't. By nature, we each have different boiling points and must be familiar enough with ourselves and the risks we take to avoid irrational and destructive trading behavior.

My personal perception of a reasonable trading strategy or approach and how much money should be risked on a particular trade is far different than that of many of my clients. I can honestly say that one mind-set isn't necessarily better or worse than the other—they're all just different. To specify, I tend to be a risk-averse trader (if there is such a thing in trading futures and options). Accordingly, I prefer some of the lower-margined and slower-moving markets, such as Eurodollars and the 5-year note. Some of my clients, on the other hand, are much more aggressive and prefer to trade markets that are capable of providing a magnified risk/reward profile. And that is okay, too.

Only you can determine what fits, and that requires patience, discipline, and an open mind. The most important feedback on your progress will be your account statements. That's not to say that you should hang up your trading jacket if you experience a drawdown or even a complete account blow-up, but you must be realistic. Some people tend to remember only the good trades; others remember only the bad. Each of these distorted perceptions of reality can have an adverse affect on your trading. Successful traders remember the good trades and the bad trades, but most important, they learn from all of them.

chapter 13

Why You Should Speculate in Futures

My aim has always been to provide readers with a candid account of the realities of trading rather than fill them with unrealistic expectations. I believe that doing so can better prepare traders for what lies ahead and, accordingly, might improve their odds of becoming a victorious trader. Throughout this book, I have outlined the difficulties of trading, but hopefully I haven't discouraged you from involving yourself in the commodity markets. After all, the futures and options markets can be potentially lucrative for those willing to accept and properly manage the corresponding risks. Furthermore, I am a broker who makes a living through commission. The last thing that I want to do is deter qualified parties from the futures markets. However, it is important that I encourage traders to come to futures and options for the right reasons and know what to expect when they get there.

Regardless of what your impression has been up to this point, let it be known that, along with the significant risk of loss involved in futures trading, there is potential for significant profits. That is why speculators flock to the markets and keeps them coming back, even if they didn't achieve what they were looking for the first time around.

There is a lot of money to be made, or lost, in all markets, but for those with the willingness and the capital to speculate, the futures and options on futures markets offer some glaring advantages over other vehicles.

Speculating in Futures Versus Speculating in Equities

Unfortunately, at times to their peril, humans tend to gravitate to what they are more familiar with. As we all know, in many cases, convenience and ease might not necessarily be the optimal choice. I believe that the same can be said of the option that speculators have in participating in either the equity markets or the commodity markets.

Horror stories circulating about large losses suffered by commodity traders and the forced delivery of 5,000 bushels of corn have kept the futures market a dark mystery for many retail traders. However, losses are possible in any trading environment, and well-organized traders don't have to worry about the hassles of the delivery process. I don't think it is fair to blame the trading venue; more accurately, it is often the fault of the market participants. As discussed in Chapter 1, "A Crash Course in Commodities," delivery of the underlying asset is rare; those who don't want to participate have several opportunities to avoid the process.

In this discussion, we focus on the most popular stock index futures contract, the e-mini S&P 500, in comparison to trading stock index ETFs (electronically traded funds), but similar principles apply to all commodities. For instance, for those speculating in the price of gold, ignoring cash market options, they have the choice to use a gold ETF, the stock of a gold mining company, or they can trade gold futures contracts. Similar stock and ETF opportunities exist for corn, soybeans, and most other commodities. Each choice can potentially enable traders to profit from correct predictions in the price of the underlying commodity—and lose if they are incorrect—but there are inherent advantages to trading futures over stocks that shouldn't be ignored. In addition, ETFs or stocks that are correlated to a commodity are likely not *perfectly* correlated, and this creates a less efficient means of speculating on the price of a given commodity. In fact, due to ETF fund rebalancing and the costs involved in rolling over futures contracts within the fund, it is possible for ETF buyers to miss out on profits despite correct speculation in the underlying asset itself. In other words, the ETF price doesn't always track the asset price it is intended to.

Leverage and Margin

Some people might say this is a reason you shouldn't trade futures, because it can work for you as well as against you. As you should realize by now, the use of leverage supercharges profits in accurate trades but has the potential to create dramatic losses for those on the wrong side of a market move. Naturally, the amount of leverage—and, thus, position volatility—is highly dependent on the market being traded and the strategy used. Moreover, traders can reduce leverage altogether by depositing the full value of the futures contract rather than the minimum margin the exchange charges. Specifically, although the exchange sets a minimum overnight margin requirement, the trader decides how much leverage to use through account funding and position size.

Throughout this book, I have noted that most futures brokers and brokerage firms offer relatively lenient day-trading margins, in addition to stringent yet generous overnight margins. At some firms, you can day-trade a single e-mini futures contract with as little as a $500 margin requirement. That said, just because it is possible to buy 20 mini S&P futures in a $10,000 account doesn't mean that it should be done. In fact, doing so would equate to the trader making or losing $1,000 per point of price movement in the futures market, or 10% of the trading account, on a small price move. On the other hand, futures margins are flexible; with the S&P valued at 1,300, an e-mini trader can eliminate the leverage provided in the futures markets by depositing $65,000 (1,300 × $50) and trading a single contract. Obviously, there's a big difference between day trading on a $500 margin and fully funding an account with $65,000 in margin per contract traded. This is a great depiction of how much control the trader has over leverage.

To put the leverage of trading commodities into perspective, consider an example. I have seen a long-option-only account go from a net liquidation value of $10,000 up to an intraday value of nearly $500,000 in a matter of weeks. Unfortunately, I witnessed the same account eventually give back all the profits, plus a lot more. The circumstances surrounding this incredible rise and fall are unique: It occurred during one of the biggest stock-market plummets of all time. I am sure the 2008 "crash" will be etched forever in the minds of those who let riches slip through their hands. However, the point is that aggressive traders can potentially make or lose life-changing amounts of money. Of course, not everybody is willing to lay so much on the line—nor should they be. Still, the potential is there for those who want to spin the roulette wheel.

On the other hand, I have worked with clients who, after years of familiarizing themselves with the markets, found a way to make a comfortable living trading futures and options on futures. It didn't happen overnight, and I can guarantee that they weren't quick to quit their day jobs. But after putting in adequate time and "paying their dues" in the form of expensive market experience, they are now living the dream. I can assure you that these types of traders are approaching the markets in a more conservative way than those looking for a get-rich-quick solution to their problems; nonetheless, easy access to leverage might have played a part in their triumph.

Conversely, stock traders are not allowed to use margin—well, at least not without paying for it. For a stock-market speculator to buy a greater number of shares than she has money for, she must first apply for a leverage account and then pay her brokerage firm a fee for the funds borrowed. The costs associated with using leverage can be substantial and simply make it more difficult for a speculator to trade profitably. Similarly, most stock brokerage firms require rather large trading account balances to qualify for margined trading. Many approve margin accounts only for clients holding more than $100,000 in their trading account. Others approve margin but charge higher rates of interest or margin for accounts of less than six figures. Conversely, all futures accounts are granted leverage, regardless of account balance. To give you an idea of how favorable trading on leverage in the futures markets relative to equities can be, a commodity trader with $1,000 is treated the same in regard to margin as a stock trader required to deposit $100,000 would be in the equity arena.

Liquidity and Efficient Execution

As I have pointed out throughout this text, it is important to speculate in liquid commodity markets. There are a handful of futures contracts that simply don't have enough market activity to enable seamless entry and exit; these contracts should be avoided. However, as is the case in the e-mini S&P, many futures contracts now trade electronically in high volumes and with narrow bid/ask spreads. Whereas many stocks and stock indices are also highly liquid, many of the commodity ETFs or leveraged stock index ETFs are not.

Of course, market liquidity provides speculators with an arena in which the bid/ask spreads are manageable. Accordingly, futures traders can easily enter and exit the market with minimal transaction costs and acceptable amounts of slippage in fill price nearly 24 hours per day. The price paid for executing a lightly traded ETF can be substantial and can only be done for about 7 hours per day.

As a trader, it is imperative that you fully understand the consequences of trading in markets that have few participants and, even more important, that you do your homework on each product that you are interested in trading. This is true regardless of the trading arena chosen.

Buy or Sell in Any Order

One of the most compelling arguments for futures trading relative to stocks or ETFs is the ability to quickly and efficiently sell a contract in anticipation of the market going lower. This is the case regardless of market circumstances or account size. The idea is to buy back the contract at a better (lower) price at some point in the future. Of course, things don't always work out as planned, and a short trader may be forced to buy back the contract at a loss (higher price).

An equity trader can also sell shares short, with the intention of buying them back at some point in the future. Nevertheless, to do this, he must first borrow the shares from his brokerage firm and pay interest charges accordingly. This is much less convenient, more costly, and more time consuming. Once again, stock brokers typically require an account with tens of thousands or hundreds of thousands of dollars to grant traders the same privileges; in addition, the broker must have shares on inventory to loan to traders who want to short them. Futures traders, on the other hand, enjoy the simplicity of buying or selling without any other hassles.

Low Account Minimums

Before equity traders can sell shares with the intention of buying them back at a lower price or trade with leverage by spending more money on shares than is on deposit, they must qualify for a margin account. The process of opening a margin account involves slightly more paperwork and a quick background and credit check by the brokerage firm. In futures, all accounts are opened on margin; additional paperwork and aggravations are not necessary. Nonetheless, a back ground and credit check are standard among futures brokerages, to prevent money laundering and ensure that futures traders are financially equipped to accept the risk of participating in such markets.

In addition to the supplementary barriers to entry for a margined *stock* account, most firms will not approve a margin account application for clients with less than $20,000—and they may require far more. On the other hand, some futures brokers allow clients to day-trade the e-mini S&P with initial funding balances as little as $1,000. In addition, long option traders face limited risk and are often free to open accounts with even smaller balances. Of course, an ultrasmall trading account might not provide an ample number of opportunities, but it is nice to know it is possible.

No Interest Charges or Borrowing Fees

As if the time delay and restrictions of borrowing shares and the obstacle of large account minimums weren't enough of an argument for futures market speculation relative to stocks, equity brokerage firms typically charge interest on margined positions. Such a trade might also incur additional transaction fees. Conversely, futures and options on futures traders are not expected to pay interest on leveraged trading activity. The exchanges and the corresponding brokerage firms provide the leverage free of charge. Simply put, for a stock trader to turn a profit on a short position, he must first be right enough in the direction to overcome the interest charges paid to the brokerage firm in return for borrowing shares.

I argue that, all else being equal, similarly skilled traders utilizing an identical strategy in similar products yet two alternative arenas, stocks and futures, might see superior results in the futures trading account due to a lack of interest payments. With that in mind, it is also important to point out that futures contracts do not pay dividends as some stocks and ETFs might.

Level Playing Field

Although this isn't the case in all futures contracts, the CMEs e-mini 500 futures are filled on a first-come, first-served basis, with little or no human intervention. The idea behind the exchange's electronic platform for trading e-mini contracts is to provide an arena in which a trader executing 1,000 contracts at a time and one that is trading a single lot will be treated the same in terms of execution. On the other hand, this might not be true in venues that involve market makers, such as equities, ETFs, illiquid futures, and options on futures contracts.

Favorable Tax Treatment

In general, profitable equity traders face a much larger tax burden than commodity traders do. In addition, the process of claiming trading profits and losses at the end of the year is much simpler for a futures trader than one who is actively trading equities.

The IRS requires equity traders to list each transaction and the net result of each trade. You can imagine the frustration involved for day traders. However, on a brighter note, it encourages a daily trading log and can make it easier for equity traders to look at their results realistically.

Futures traders, on the other hand, report a lump-sum profit or loss figure on a 1099 at the end of the year. The 1099 displays the performance of the trading account net of commissions and fees, accounting for deposits and withdrawals. In essence, your futures broker takes on the burden of figuring out the math; all you and your accountant need to do is input the final number on Form 6781 in your tax return.

However, the tax benefits of speculating in a futures account, compared to a stock account, don't end in convenience; there are substantial monetary advantages as well. All futures, and options on futures, market gains are taxed at a 40%/60% blend between long- and short-term capital gains, regardless of the time span of the trade. Because long-term capital gains are taxed at a more favorable rate than short-term gains, assuming that they are profitable, futures market speculators enjoy a considerable tax break relative to stock traders.

Excitement

Let's face it, commodity trading is exciting and unpredictable. Not only is it somewhat mysterious to the common investor, but at times it also can change the lives of market participants. I have seen call options in sugar bought for $200 grow to values in the several thousands. I have also witnessed a trader take an account from approximately $250,000 to more than $4 million and then back down. Of course, these examples are the exception rather than the rule, but the point is that nearly anything is possible.

I have come in contact with futures traders who have yet to find a way to consistently make the amount of money in their trading ventures needed to justify the time spent, but simply yearn for the adrenaline rush; that is enough to keep them coming back for more.

I could never recommend that traders come to commodities solely for entertainment because that type of attitude will likely lead to substantial losses resulting from unnecessary risks taken. Nonetheless, I cannot deny that this is one of the most compelling reasons traders venture into futures and options. In fact, from more than one avid commodity trader, I have heard stock trading compared to watching paint dry. Keep in mind, however, that I am referring specifically to speculation, not investing.

Commodities Won't Be Delisted and Reflect True Position

Most of the contracts of interest to speculators and listed by the futures and options markets have been traded for several years and have an ample amount of liquidity. On the other hand, many of the commodity ETFs that speculators use to wager on the direction of crude oil, soybeans, Treasuries, the VIX, or other commodities were brought to existence in recent years as a result of the commodity boom and financial market volatility. Unfortunately, with the financial collapse of the late 2000s, many of the newly listed ETFs have been forced to cease operations due to a lack of interest, and this trend might continue. Although investors in delisted ETFs do get their money back, this can be a significant speed bump in the progress of their speculative plays.

Another strike against trading ETFs are the so called "short" or "ultrashort" products that are designed to mimic the return of being short an asset or index. In many cases, due to the way the fund tracks the daily fluctuation of the asset it is intended to mock, the performance of the ETF will match underlying assets on a short-term basis, such as one day or two. Traders hoping to buy and hold the ETF might find themselves in a situation in which they were right about the market direction but incurred a loss because of the way the ETF rebalanced. Most agree that short or ultrashort (leveraged) ETFs are designed to be a day-trading vehicle and should not be considered an effective way of speculating in time frames beyond of a few days.

You Can Trade Futures in an IRA

I would never advocate allocating a major portion of any retirement account to commodity trading. However, so few traders even realize that this is an option that I felt obligated to mention it. As you can imagine, there are definite tax benefits to trading funds earmarked for futures speculation in a retirement account. Specifically, tax-deferred or tax-free growth depends on the type of qualified IRA (independent retirement account); rollover 401(k)s are also candidates for futures trading. In theory, trading accounts within the shelter of a tax-friendly IRA have the potential to grow at much more rapid speeds compared to those in a nonqualified account (outside the IRA umbrella).

Of course, only profitable traders enjoy the advantages of an IRA. For those less fortunate in the markets, trading within an IRA can become a burden: Losses are not tax deductible as they would be in a nonqualified account. Similarly, trading futures within an IRA typically involves incremental fees paid to an account custodian, which can slightly exaggerate trading losses.

Risk Capital Only

As this chapter has outlined, there are many reasons to trade futures, but there are also reasons not to. In a few cases, the same arguments for speculating in commodities are the reasons that attract speculators—and capital—that shouldn't be there.

Regardless of your intentions in speculation, one common rule persists: Never trade money that you can't afford to lose. If you are like me, it seems that there's no such thing as money that can be lost without some type of anguish. Nonetheless, risk capital is defined as an amount of money that, if lost, would not alter your current lifestyle. Even those who trade for a living will have bad days; it is important that they don't let a bad day, week, or month turn into ruin. A good way to ensure this is by limiting trading accounts to expendable funds.

Each trading account opened by a brokerage firm undergoes some scrutiny in terms of an applicant's net worth, income, and bankruptcy history, if any. Most commodity firms require that applicants have a net worth of at least $20,000 and a minimum annual income of $20,000. The reasoning behind the policy is twofold: First, it confirms that a trader could, or should, have some risk capital to allocate to the treacherous game of speculation. Also, as you should realize by now, futures traders can lose more money than they have on deposit in their trading accounts. Accordingly, brokerage firms must determine whether the risk posed by clients who might lose more money than they can pay back is worth the reward of accepting them as clients of the firm.

Yet despite attempts of brokerage firms to prevent traders from trading with money that, if lost, might cause significant changes in their financial well-being, such capital manages to find its way into the marketplace. Whether you are actively trading equities, futures, or options on futures, it is important that you realize that speculation is a risk, not an investment; only risk capital should be used.

Conclusion

The commodity markets provide speculative opportunities that other markets simply can't offer. In my opinion, the convenience of gaining leverage and the ability to quickly buy and sell trading instruments in any order creates an extremely efficient means of betting on anticipated price changes. Also, the tax benefits of profitable speculation in commodities, as compared to equities, are dramatic and can potentially have a profound impact on the overall results. For these reasons, those who fully understand speculation and are willing to accept the risks associated with it should strongly consider doing so in the futures and options markets.

As I have noted throughout this writing, speculation itself is a difficult task to master. In fact, some of the most successful traders in the world report account-draining losses on numerous occasions before gaining the experience needed to be among the estimated 20% of profitable traders. However, despite the challenge, achievement is possible, and under the right circumstances, life-changing profits can happen.

chapter 14

Futures Slang and Terminology

Outsiders might think that the futures industry has created its own language. Many of the terms brokers and traders use take a new meaning from their origin, and becoming familiar with the slang can prevent costly miscommunications. After all, even self-directed online traders will need to communicate with their brokerage firm from time to time regarding their account. Some of the terminology covered in this chapter has been covered already, but when it comes to building a foundation of trading knowledge, it is important to seal any cracks. I believe that these are worth a second look.

Bull Versus Bear

The terms *bull market* and *bear market* certainly aren't isolated to the world of commodities, and in recent years, we have seen record-breaking cases of each. Although you are most likely aware of the concept of bull and bear markets, and this might seem elementary, you might not be familiar with all the related terms and variations that you will likely be exposed to when speaking about the futures and options markets.

The origin of the bull and bear market comparison is bleak, at best, but one thing is for sure: It stuck. Theory suggests that the use of the bull to express a runaway market has to do with the herding action often seen in market moves that occur as the masses look to jump on the bandwagon. On the other hand, a bear depicts a dangerous and vicious beast that shares characteristics similar to a declining market. Moreover, it starts with a *B* and seems to ring well with *bull*.

Here's a recap of the seemingly obvious: A bull market is described as one in which prices are consistently moving upward or one that is forging higher highs and higher lows. You might hear the terms *bull* and *bear* attached to talk about the commodity or stock markets in general, but the terms also can refer to individual contracts. Industry insiders have dubbed a rallying market as a *bull run.* Conversely, consistent downward pressure is often described as a *bear market.*

Additionally, the expressions *bullish* and *bearish* are synonymous with *optimistic* and *pessimistic,* respectively. For example, a trader who believes that the price of gold will go higher is said to be bullish. If the same trader believes that the inverse relationship between gold and the U.S. dollar will remain intact, he will likely be bearish the greenback.

Bull and Bear Slang

Now for the slang. *Bullish* and *bearish* aren't always used to portray markets. They can sometimes be used to describe expectations of the economy, the potential impact of news events or data, or an option or futures spread.

We generally all agree that the economy isn't a market, and it isn't *directly* tradable. However, it is possible to speculate on the health of the economy indirectly through the commodity and financial markets. Nonetheless, you might hear your broker mention being bullish on the economy. Although this isn't correct in the strict definition of the term, the phrase is commonly used. Accordingly, in a broad sense of the statement, this might insinuate that your broker is bullish the stock market and bearish bonds. This assumption is based on the common premise that investors favor stocks during good economic times and avoid bonds.

As you should recall, we discussed futures spreads in Chapter 1, "A Crash Course in Commodities." *Bull* and *bear* are often attached to futures spreads as a way to identify the intended direction of the market. Ironically, for futures spreads, *bull* doesn't necessarily mean that the futures market must go up for the position to be profitable; instead, a spread trader simply needs the *spread* to move favorably. Nonetheless, futures spreads are labeled *bull* or *bear* according to the trader's market sentiment.

Option spreads, also covered in Chapter 1, are also labeled in terms of the desired direction of the futures price. For example, a bull call spread involves the purchase of a close-to-the-money call option and the sale of an out-of-the-money option. Those familiar with options can easily see that this is a trade that stands to makes money if the market goes higher. However, those who haven't learned the basics of option trading could easily identify the intention of the spread simply by picking up on the fact that it is labeled a bull. Likewise, if your broker mentions a bear put spread, he is referring to an option strategy in which it is possible to profit if the market drops. With that said, I don't recommend that you participate in any trades that you don't understand. Simply being privy to the fact that bear is equivalent to the market going down should not be enough to entice you to participate in a recommended bear put spread; there's much more to it than that. However, knowing this is step one, and being aware of the clues surrounding you might help lessen your learning curve.

Spread

The term *spread* is used loosely within the futures industry, and unless you are familiar with all the different uses of the word, you might be leaving yourself vulnerable to expensive miscommunications. Here are a few of the broadest contexts in which you will hear *spread* used.

Bid/Ask Spread

As covered in Chapter 1, the spread between the bid and the ask represents the difference in the highest price that a buyer is willing to pay (or the price you can sell it for) and the lowest price that the seller is willing to accept (or the price you can buy it for). In essence, at any given time and in any market, there will always be a price at which you can buy an asset for and a price that the asset can be sold for. The "spread" between the two prices is known as the bid/ask spread. Once again, the beneficiary of the spread is the floor broker who takes the other side of your trade.

In conversation, traders and brokers typically refer to the bid/ask spread simply as "the spread." Thus, any time you converse about the price of a commodity option or futures contract and someone mentions the spread, she is referring to the bid/ask spread.

Unfortunately, as a retail trader, you will always be forced to pay the ask when buying and sell the bid when going short. In other words, if you simultaneously bought and sold a futures or options contract, you would immediately lose the difference between the spread. Accordingly, you might hear your broker say that you need to *pay the spread* or *pay the ask* to get into a trade. This can come up if a limit order goes unfilled and it seems as though you need to increase your limit price to, or closer to, the ask to get filled. Similarly, if you *hit the bid,* you are agreeing to sell the contract at the bid price.

Option Spread

You rarely hear a broker or trader refer to an option spread as such; it is typically shortened to *spread*. When referring to the bid and ask of an option spread, a spread of a spread, the price quote is normally identified as the bid/ask, whereas the option spread is still referred to by a single word: *spread*. In reference to a spread between call options, it is common to hear *call spread* and, for those with puts, *put spread*. With that said, brokers have been creative in labeling specific types of option spreads with shortened terms. For example, a *put butterfly* is known as a *put-fly*.

Futures Spread

Based on my experience, option spreads are more common than futures spreads among retail traders. Perhaps this is why option spreads have become the default strategy identified by the single word *spread*. Futures spreads are normally referred to in conjunction with the contracts involved. For instance, a trader who is spreading July and December corn might refer to it as a Dec/July corn spread.

Contract Month Slang

Throughout the years, traders have been determined to eliminate confusion in communication and keep it short and sweet. It isn't uncommon for indications of contract months to be shortened or even nicknamed. In view of that, don't be thrown off if you hear *Deck corn*, short for December corn. Likewise, a less obvious example is *Christmas* or *Labor Day corn*, to identify expiration months in those of the corresponding holidays.

Red Months

Clearly, each of the 12 months occurs only once every year; therefore, it is necessary to distinguish futures contracts expiring in March (or any other month) of the current year from those that expire in March of the following year. If there is no reference to the year, it is assumed to be the closest to expiration. When a trader or broker refers to the following year, the term *red* identifies it as such. Thus, in January 2013, a trader looking to speculate on March 2014 futures would refer to the contract as *red March*.

Fill

A *fill* is simply a price at which an order was executed. You might often hear it referred to as a *fill price*. Explicitly, if a trader buys a T-bond 135 call option for 1 15/64, then 1 15/64 is said to be the fill price.

The term fill *is used to identify the execution price.*

It is a bit embarrassing to admit, but after several years of collegiate finance classes and months of rigorous studying for the Series 3 proficiency exam that is necessary to become a licensed commodity broker, I hadn't yet been introduced to the term *fill*. I distinctly remember the word showing up as I was taking the exam, and I was overtaken with a feeling of panic. Although I assumed the definition based on the context in which it was used, there was no way to know for sure whether my conclusions were correct.

Split Fill

A *split fill* occurs when a trader places an order to buy or sell a futures contract or option in a quantity in excess of one contract and receives a fill reported at more than one price. In other words, if a trader places an order to buy 10 December note futures at the market, the fills on each, or some, might be reported at different prices. For instance, a trader might buy four at 129'20, five at 129'20.5, and one at 129'21, and would be said to have gotten a split fill.

Partial Fill

A *partial fill* occurs when some, but not all, of the stated quantity of a limit order (an order to buy or sell an asset at a specific price) is filled. Going back to our note futures example, if the order were placed to buy 10 December note futures at 119'20, and that was the low print of the day, it is possible that only a handful of the ten contracts would be filled. Remember, in the case of a limit order, the market has to "go through it to do it." A trader isn't owed a fill unless the price ticks below the limit price. Had the low of the day been 119'19.5 (one tick below the limit price), the trader could have challenged any lack of fill on the trade.

"I'm not nearly so concerned about the return on my capital as I am the return of my capital."
—Will Rogers

Blow Out

For many, commodity trading is their first experience with leverage and margin. Beginners often underestimate the amount of control that a margin department rightfully has over their trading account in the case of an undercapitalized account.

A margin clerk, and even a broker responsible for a given account, is authorized to do whatever is in her power to prevent a trading account from going negative (losing more than the funds on deposit). For an account that is liquidated in this manner by someone other than the account owner, it is said to have been *blown out*. Similarly, an account on a persistent margin call might be liquidated to satisfy the exchange margin. This is also considered a blow-out.

Blow Up

A *blow up* is similar to a blow out, with the primary difference being who pulls the plug on a trade or an account. Thus, if a trader determines that he is undercapitalized and in danger of losing more money than was deposited in the account, he can liquidate the positions at his own hand. This is referred to as a blow up.

In the late 2000s and early 2010s, you likely heard of the many hedge fund blow ups resulting from commodity bubbles and their subsequent busts. These were funds that simply lost all or most of the money deposited in their fund and could no longer continue trading.

Keep in mind that, for all intents and purposes, *blow up* and *blow out* can be used interchangeably, but their most common interpretations are as previously noted.

Keypunch Error

If you notice a trade that you don't believe is yours or that is inaccurate in price, contact your broker immediately.

A *keypunch error* is just as it sounds. It occurs when a back-office brokerage employee or trading pit clerk mistypes a fill price, account number, quantity, or symbol on a reported fill. Given the massive volume and human involvement in open outcry trading, keypunch errors do happen. Fortunately, technology and electronic trade execution have dramatically reduced keypunch errors. If you notice what you believe to be a keypunch error in your account, contact your broker immediately instead of trying to trade out of it or offset the position.

As an account holder, if you attempt to exit a trade that was inadvertently placed in your account because of a broker or desk clerk miskeyed an account number, you are responsible for the order that you entered, even though it was done so as an attempt to eliminate a keypunch error. Unfortunately, I have witnessed the peril of such actions, and I urge you to keep proper trading records and know your positions to ensure that this does not happen to you.

Busted Trade or Moved Trade

A *busted trade* is most often the result of a keypunch error and is simply a position that is removed from a client account due to an error of some kind. When a trade is busted or moved from an account, the account in which it is moved from stands as if it never happened. The erroneous trade, along with any commission and fees attached to the position, is completely removed from the trading account.

To the surprise of many, it is possible for trades executed on behalf of one client to be inadvertently entered into the account of another client. With thousands of trades being executed on a daily basis, it isn't hard to imagine a clerk on the floor, a broker, or a desk order taker mistyping a digit of an account number. This is the most common need for a busted trade.

A busted trade can also occur when the original fill was reported at an erroneous price (keypunch error), making it necessary to remove the executed trade at the incorrect price (busting the trade) and replacing it with an accurate fill price.

It might also be necessary to bust a trade from a client's account if the floor broker accidentally reported a fill that should have never been triggered. For example, if a trader places a stop order to sell December gold at $1,560.00 and a fill is reported despite the fact that the market never reached the stated price, the trade will be busted (removed) from the account. Of course, few retail traders will use the pit for futures execution, making this an unlikely occurrence.

Some traders refer to this practice as a *moved trade* as if the terms are synonymous, but in reality, there is a small discrepancy between the two. *Moved trades* normally arise when a trade made it into the wrong client account; busted trades apply to the same circumstances but can also include inaccurate fill prices and erroneously elected orders.

If you notice that your statement shows a position that isn't yours, if you are missing a position that should be yours, or if you see what seems to be an inaccurate fill price, immediately contact your broker. Don't panic, and whatever you do, don't try to offset a trade that isn't yours or reestablish one that is missing. It is highly likely that the absent, mysterious, or incorrect trade, was the result of a keypunch error and can easily be corrected. Any client attempt to "correct" the situation could lead to substantial chaos and large monetary damage.

Remember, whether it is a winning or losing position, if you didn't place or authorize the order, it isn't yours—regardless of what might be showing in your account. Additionally, the person who did place the order and expected to see the position on her statement is likely looking for it.

Again, busted or moved trades are becoming less frequent due to electronically executed futures and options. During the heyday of open outcry trading pits, they were common.

Fat Finger Error

A *fat finger error* is a byproduct of technology. This term describes a situation in which a trader accidentally places an order for a much larger quantity than intended. For instance, a trader attempting to execute 10 contracts might add a zero, making it a 100-lot order. In extreme cases, this could mean thousands or tens of thousands of contracts inadvertently entered. The retail trading platforms most of you will have access to include risk-management parameters that prevent an overly excessive order from being placed, but professional traders might not have this safety net. If a fat finger error is large enough, it can cause a dramatic and temporary fluctuation in market pricing.

Net Liq

Futures and options brokers often use the term *net liq* to refer to the net liquidation value of an account. The net liquidation value is simply a snapshot of what the account would be worth if all open positions were closed at the prices displayed in the account. Note that assuming that the positions held in the account could be liquidated at the displayed prices is unrealistic, in that it doesn't reflect the impact of the bid/ask spread or any price change not accounted for in the snapshot. Additionally, in the case of intraday *net liq* values for accounts that are holding option positions, the most recent quote might not necessarily accurately reflect market value due to the amount of time that sometimes passes between fills of a given option contract. Nonetheless, despite its imperfections, this is the number that you should pay to the most attention on your brokerage statement and any intraday views of your account status.

It is important to realize that values displayed on account statements reflect the price at which all positions were assigned at the close of a given trading session. In a 24-hour marketplace, statement values often differ greatly from actual market values almost immediately after they are issued.

Equity

Equity is a word used in the world of finance in a ridiculous number of contexts. However, in futures trading, the term *equity* is most commonly used to describe the amount of cash held in a given account. Unlike the net liquidation value, which gives you a bottom-line figure, your account equity is the top-line figure. Plainly, it is the beginning cash balance in an account before accounting for any premium paid for long options, premium collected for short options, and profit or loss sustained on *open* futures positions (unrealized profits and losses).

On a futures statement, account equity is equivalent to cash, not a marked to market value of your account.

Before we look at details, you should know that option trades result in immediate cash in-flows (selling) or out-flows (buying). Futures trading, on the other hand, doesn't result in an actual cash transaction until the trade is offset. With that said, any commission and fees charged result in a cash transaction immediately.

In essence, if a trader put $5,000 into a new trading account and spends $300 on a March call option in the e-mini S&P, along with another $20 in transaction costs, his account equity would be $4,680 ($5,000 − $300 − $20) because $320 in cash was taken out of the account. The cash left in the account is the equity and is the cash available to use toward margin of a futures position, toward marginable option spread, or to purchase long options and option spreads. In other words, it is the tradable account balance.

If the same trader went short an April crude oil futures position and has an unrealized loss of $550 after paying $10 in transaction costs to enter the trade, his equity balance would be $4,670 ($4,680 − $10). The $550 unrealized loss in the futures position has not been accounted for because there has yet to be a cash inflow or outflow. Assuming that the same trader took the loss of exactly $550, the equity balance would be reduced to $4,120.

On the contrary, when a trader sells an option, there is an immediate cash transaction. Thus, the premium collected is added to the account equity. Using the preceding example, if the trader sold a March S&P put for $900 and paid a transaction fee of $20, the account equity would be back to $5,000 ($4,120 + $900 – $20). As you can see, the account equity gives you little information on the actual progress of the account. This particular trader has sustained a drawdown in net liquidation value in the account by approximately $900, yet his account equity is showing the original deposited amount. Given this example, it is clear that traders should focus on their net liquidation values instead of their account equity.

Customer Segregated Funds Account

These are accounts held at the bank in the name of the Futures Commission Merchant (FCM) that houses client funds. Simply put, when a commodity client funds his account, rules and regulations dictate that the money be held in an account separate from the brokerage firm's operational funds, or a customer segregated fund. The clear separation between firm and customer money is intended to protect customers in case of a brokerage firm bankruptcy. However, this safeguard exists only if firms follow the rules set in place and regulators enforce them.

Beans

This might seem obvious to many of you, but for others (including myself at one point), it isn't so obvious. As an accounting and finance major in college, I became accustomed to precise wording, and anything less than exact references added unnecessary confusion. I have since gotten accustomed to the lax language futures traders use, as you will, too. However, I felt it necessary to point this out and avoid some of you the embarrassment that I experienced.

If you hear a commodity trader refer to *beans,* he is speaking of soybeans, not coffee beans, pinto beans, and the like.

Commodity Currency

Commodity currencies are said to be correlated with the price of commodities. The two most common commodity currencies are the Australian dollar and the

Canadian dollar, but the New Zealand dollar often is lumped into this category. The correlation stems from the idea that the economies backed by the named currencies are tied to commodity valuations. You might recall the Canadian dollar reaching all-time highs along with crude oil and soybeans in 2007–2008.

The Aussie and the Loonie

The Australian and Canadian dollars have something else in common: They both have nicknames. The Australian dollar is often referred to as the *Aussie*, and you might hear industry insiders speak of the Canadian dollar using the term *Loonie*.

Pound, Pound Sterling, Sterling, the Cable

The British Pound is often shortened to *Pound*, but you can also hear it referred to as the *Pound Sterling* or the *Sterling*. Although they are interchangeable, most brokers and traders refer to the currency used in the United Kingdom as the Pound. Traders also sometimes refer to the relationship between the Pound and the Dollar as the *cable*.

Dead Cat Bounce

A *dead cat bounce* is a figure of speech industry insiders use to describe a scenario in which a substantial decline in a futures market is followed by a temporary bounce in prices. Use of the phrase *dead cat bounce* typically implies that the speaker is expecting the market to resume its downtrend. The speaker often assumes that the subsequent bounce in pricing is mostly the result of short covering in the midst of a technically oversold market. Remember, if short traders are taking profits, they are buying futures contracts to exit their position. This buying can be enough to artificially prop up prices in the near term.

Bottom Fishing

In general, *bottom fishing* is a method of catching fish that are lingering at the bottom of a body of water. In finance, bottom fishing is the art of speculating on a price recovery in a market that is trading at what is considered historically cheap prices.

For instance, as orange juice futures traded near 50 cents in the mid-2000s, several bottom fishers likely were hoping for an eventual rally, and they got it. Orange juice traded above $2.00 after an active hurricane season caused crop damage in Florida.

Expectations of higher prices typically stem from the cyclical nature of the market in regard to supply and demand. Bottom fishers know that, as commodity prices become excessively cheap, producers cut back, and consumers demand more. The subsequent decrease in supply will eventually have a positive impact on price.

Chasing the Market

A trader who enters a market well after a trend is established is said to be *chasing the market*. This scenario happens when a market has risen or fallen dramatically and traders try to enter in the direction of the move without regard to their entry price. Unfortunately, those chasing a market tend to regret it later when they discover the hard way that the trend is your friend only until it ends.

I have witnessed too many inexperienced traders anticipate a market move but talk themselves into waiting for confirmation. In the right context, confirmation might be a wise move. However, if the trader's idea of confirmation means several weeks or months of favorable market movement, the odds favor the miserable experience of getting into a trade just as the trend is ending. As a trader, you never want to be fashionably late to the party.

Limit Moves

The futures exchanges stipulate specified price limits on most listed contracts. The largest amount of change that the price of a commodity futures contract is allowed to move in a single trading session is known as the *price limit*. A limit move is one in which the market rallies or falls in the largest magnitude allowable and is measured from the previous session close, not from the current session open.

When the daily price limit is reached, it is said to be *locked limit*. When this occurs, trading a futures contract in the direction of the limit move is not possible. Therefore, if the set price limit in corn is 45 cents and the futures market rallies 45 cents, it wouldn't be possible to buy a corn futures (even if you are short and trying to get out). However, if you have nerves of steel, you could sell the contract. If there are enough sellers at the limit price, the market will eventually move off its limit and resume trading again.

While a market is locked limit, often large numbers of orders are waiting to be filled. These orders will be filled only if the market retreats from the limit price or in the following trading session.

Limit Up

This occurs when a market rallies to its daily limit and ceases executing buy orders.

Limit Down

This occurs when the market declines to its daily limit and ceases executing sell orders.

The Tape

The *tape,* also known as the *ticker tape,* is a term borrowed from stock traders that originally meant to describe the running record of scrolling paper depicting the trading activity in each individual stock. The advent of computer technology has replaced the ticker tape with electronic records of trading activity.

In commodities, it is often used to refer to the *time and sales* data, which records each trade price and the quantity of contracts traded at each price.

Trading Solution and Front-End Platform

The commodity industry is known for unnecessarily complicating otherwise simple terms. An order-entry platform that can be used to execute and monitor trades is often referred to as a *trading solution* or a *front-end platform.* Simply put, this is either a web-based (accessed via an Internet browser such as Microsoft Internet Explorer) or a downloadable software package that can be run directly from a trader's desktop that provides market access to retail traders. It might also be an application on a smartphone enabling traders to monitor their positions and place orders directly from their phone or iPad.

Proprietary Trading

The word *proprietary* indicates that a party holds exclusive rights of ownership, control, or use over an item of property, whether physical or intellectual. In reference to finance and trading, the term describes the practice in which a firm hires employees to actively trade in the financial markets with the firm's money as opposed to its customers' money. The goal is for the employees of the firm to profit from the speculative transactions executed by its employees. Of course, it also accepts the risk of losing trades executed on its behalf by authorized employees. Proprietary trading strategies are characteristically developed in-house and are considered trade secrets and are not released to the public.

Prop Desk

A *prop desk* is a trading desk where proprietary trading takes place.

Running Stops

When a market makes a quick and sometimes dramatic move through well-known support and resistance areas, it is often the result of *stop running*. In essence, this is a scenario in which market prices reach levels that contain substantial number of buy or sell stop orders, and prices move rapidly as stop orders are elected.

For example, if the S&P 500 futures are trading at 1,322 with obvious technical support at 1,320, a price drop below 1,320 could trigger sell stops placed by those long the market attempting to defend their positions against adverse price moves. If this is the case, there will be a temporary imbalance of sell orders executed, and market prices may drop quickly as the sell stops are filled. When all the sell stop orders placed at or near 1,320 are executed, it is not uncommon for market valuations to reverse higher. After all, the selling pressure is somewhat artificial, in that it isn't due to new bears entering the market, but is the result of bulls exiting positions as sell stops are executed.

Don't get frustrated with markets running stops; this will always be part of the trading landscape. Instead, be informed of the characteristics of the market you are trading and adjust accordingly.

Some speculation involves whether larger market participants actively "seek" stop orders by pushing the market prices to known areas of support and resistance in hopes of triggering stop orders and benefiting from the price moves. However, traders who speculate in markets with ample liquidity shouldn't believe this to be the case. Conversely, if a handful of manipulative traders can temporarily move the markets on the sheer size of their trading capital, it should be viewed as a market characteristic that can't be controlled but can be compensated for through trading strategy and decisions.

Short Squeeze

A *short squeeze* is a rapid increase in market price that occurs when there are large imbalances in buy orders over sell orders. A short squeeze scenario most often occurs when short sellers scramble to offset their open positions by buying back their contracts. As short traders continue to cover positions, a snowball effect in the quantity of buyers often takes place, and the resulting price increase can be surprisingly dramatic.

Short squeezes often begin as profit taking by the bears but are later fueled because a large quantity of buy stop orders are being executed or the market has rallied enough to force short traders out due to a lack of capital, margin, or faith. Specifically, traders are squeezed out of their positions.

Of course, long traders can also be squeezed out of positions in a sharp downturn. This is known as a *long squeeze*.

Babysitting

Babysitting a trade is the act of staring at a computer screen or a business news channel for an open speculative position. Although it is true that there is substantial risk in trading and all risk exposure should be responsibly monitored, obsession over market activity could do damage to the psychology involved in the trade.

Traders who are glued to their screens are more likely to give in to the pressures of fear and greed, or perhaps the opposite scenario of analysis paralysis. Too much information can sometimes lead to a deer-in-the-headlights reaction to adverse price moves, in which the trader marries an open position and refuses to exit before losses mount to devastating levels.

I believe that traders should diligently evaluate their position before entering the market; if this is done properly, they should be comfortable enough with the trade to avoid the pressures of living and dying by each market tick. Hopefully, doing so removes some of the emotion that can negatively dictate trading decisions.

Scalp

Scalping is a day-trading method in which trades are opened and closed in a very short time scale. A scalper typically leaves a position open for anywhere from a second or two to a few minutes. Naturally, the risk and reward per individual trade is relatively low due to the time in which the trader is exposed to price risk. However, wins and losses can quickly mount along with transaction costs.

Slippage

Slippage is the term used to describe the difference between the estimated fill price and the actual price. For example, if a trader places a buy stop order in January feeder cattle at 135.50 and was reported a fill price of 135.70, the trader would have suffered a fill that is 20 points worse than what was anticipated. Remember, a stop order is an order to execute the trade at the market when the named price is reached. Thus, in a fast-moving market, the price can quickly surpass the stop order price and create a scenario in which the fill is significantly unfavorable. Naturally, it goes both ways; it is possible for slippage to have a positive effect on traders and their accounts. However, slippage typically works *against* the retail trader.

> Slippage is an ordinary cost of business for traders. However, the amount of slippage suffered is highly dependent on the markets being traded. Just as in business, you want to keep your costs low; therefore, traders should choose markets accordingly.

Slippage can occur with every order type and varies greatly on the market traded. An electronically traded market with ample liquidity, such as the e-mini S&P, exposes the trader to much less risk of slippage than an illiquid and highly volatile market such as lumber.

With that said, although you often hear traders refer to slippage following what they believe to be an unfavorable fill on a market order, that usage is technically inaccurate. A market order is one in which the trader agrees to pay the best possible price. Because he is not specifying a price, he shouldn't refer to a deviation of his expected price as slippage—but he will. Instead it is simply an unfortunate fill and, quite probably, the result of wide bid/ask spreads or excessive market volatility.

Conversely, only positive slippage is possible in a limit order. When a trader places a limit order, she is requesting to be filled at her price or better; therefore, a worse fill is not feasible. For instance, an order to buy July soybeans at $15.45 on a limit might be filled at the stated price or lower; a fill at a price above

$15.45 isn't acceptable. Once again, you shouldn't expect to see positive slippage often.

Working Order

A *working order* is any order, other than a market order, that has been placed but not yet filled. A day order is working until it is either filled or canceled, or until it expires at the end of the trading session. It is possible for a GTC (Good Till Canceled) order to be working for several days, weeks, or months before being filled or canceled, or until it expires with the contract.

Unable

If the market price fails to reach a placed stop or limit order, the exchange is unable to fill an order; therefore, it is said to have *gone unable*. In other words, the order placed was not filled and is no longer working.

Handle

Many brokers and traders refer to a full point of price movement as a *handle*. The definition of a handle is different in each market but is typically identifiable as the largest manageable increment of price movement. Keep in mind that, as with any slang, there are various interpretations of the meaning and uses. Therefore, you might hear or read slight deviations of the examples that I discussed in this book. Nonetheless, you likely can decipher the user's meaning based on the context.

When it comes to the grains and energies, a *full handle* is a dollar in price. Thus, if corn rallies from $6.00 per bushel to $7.00 per bushel, it is said to have moved a full handle. S&P traders most often refer to every 100 points in price change as a handle. As a result, the difference between 1,200 and 1,300 is a handle. You can determine the remaining contracts from here; if not, you will find comfort in knowing that, when using slang, there is room for error.

Overbought/Oversold

Overbought and *oversold* are terms that describe a market that is believed to have moved too far, too fast. In the case of overbought market conditions, prices are deemed to have rallied sharply to what are believed to be unsustainable levels. Conversely, in an oversold market, prices are said to have dropped beyond realistic valuations. In either case, the market is often expected to digest the condition with a corrective, countertrend move, but that isn't always the case.

Overbought and oversold market conditions are normally identified by technical indicators such as computer-generated oscillators. Technical traders might look to sell markets that are technically overbought and buy those that are oversold.

Debit/Account Debit

Contrary to what you may have learned in Accounting 101, *debit* implies a negative balance. If a client is said to have *gone debit* or to have a *debit balance,* it simply means that the trader has lost more money than was on deposit in the trading account. For instance, if a trader starts with $10,000 and fails to properly manage risk, it might be possible for losses to exceed the original investment and result in a negative account balance of $1,000, $2,000, or more.

Keep in mind that brokers and brokerage firms do all that they can to prevent this from occurring because it poses a risk to their clearing relationships and their bottom lines if a trader cannot bring the account whole. Clearly, legal consequences for the trader will follow, but in the meantime, it can be a large inconvenience for brokerage firms.

Round-Turns

All transactions in commodity futures or options are referred to in terms of *round-turns,* which is a simplified way of describing the practice of getting in and getting out of a trade. For instance, if a trader buys a futures contract and later sells one of the same commodity and month, he is said to have completed one round-turn. If multiple lots are traded, the trader has completed the number of round-turns according to the number of contracts. Therefore, if a trader buys 20 contracts of the December e-mini S&P and then sells back 20, he is said to have done 20 round-turns. You might also hear this referred as 40 half-turns, or 40 trades.

Commodity brokerage firms traditionally quote commission rates on a round-turn basis. It is important to realize this before you begin shopping for a broker. If you are quoted $35 for a full-service brokerage account, be sure to confirm that this is a round-turn rate that covers the cost to enter and exit the trade. If not, you might be unknowingly agreeing to a per-side charge of $35, in which you will pay $35 to enter and $35 to offset a position. Firms that charge commission in this manner are said to be working on a per-side basis. Some firms try to mislead traders, or at least take advantage of the marketing illusion of lower rates, by advertising their half-turn rate. Be sure you are clear on what you're negotiating.

Trading Environment

Many firms have attempted to spice up their services with new and exciting terms. *Trading environment* is one of them. This expression is used synonymously with *trading platform*. I must admit that *environment* sounds much more welcoming than *platform*.

Index

FINANCIAL TIMES

In an increasingly competitive world, it is quality
of thinking that gives an edge—an idea that opens new
doors, a technique that solves a problem, or an insight
that simply helps make sense of it all.

We work with leading authors in the various arenas
of business and finance to bring cutting-edge thinking
and best-learning practices to a global market.

It is our goal to create world-class print publications
and electronic products that give readers
knowledge and understanding that can then be
applied, whether studying or at work.

To find out more about our business
products, you can visit us at www.ftpress.com.